Illustrated A-Z of Understanding
DREAMS

This is a Flame Tree Book
First published in 2002

04 05 03

3 5 7 9 10 8 6 4 2

Flame Tree is part of
The Foundry Creative Media Company Limited
Crabtree Hall, Crabtree Lane, Fulham, London, SW6 6TY

Visit the Foundry website: www.foundry.co.uk

ISBN 1 904041 74 4

A copy of the CIP data for this book is available from the British Library

Printed in China

Special thanks to:
Michelle Clare, Karen Fitzpatrick, Julia Rolf, Colin Rudderham, Tom Worsley

Illustrated A-Z of Understanding
DREAMS

GENERAL EDITOR: RASHID AHMAD
AUTHOR: ADAM FRONTERAS

FLAME TREE PUBLISHING

CONTENTS

THEMES

Each A–Z entry is tagged by themes which can be followed as threads throughout the book

 Animals Body, Clothes Houses Leisure Space Weather

 Birth, Death Fears Journey Relationships Vegetation

anma vansan nayan

INTRODUCTION

WHY DO WE DREAM?

The external world functions in a state of rapid, perpetual flux and involves many inter-relationships, which incorporate feelings and thoughts that originate from both yourself and other people; situations that may be ordinary or extraordinary, and all the subsequent information that arises from these relationships and situations.

The individual's journey through this cacophony is as varied and complex as it is important to the individual's development. It is not suprising, then, that in the midst of this confusion the human survival instinct surfaces and reinstates itself in the dream world, in an attempt to gain insight and understanding.

The profusion and confusion of information operating in any given moment requires sifting and sorting out in order to give it form and sensibility.

WHERE DO DREAMS COME FROM?

Firstly, there are the immediate sources: your home, family and friends. Add to these your own feelings and thoughts, in which you carry your hopes, fears and aspirations. This is your personal pool of information, that helps to shape your outlook and reactions to daily life. For example, an old house that you lived and played in as a child could be a comforting environment that you return to in your dreams, providing you with a sense of personal identity and security.

Then there is the body of information that comes from your social pool: people and situations that you encounter through work, business, education, dealings with the law and so on. Here you come into contact with the traditions, customs, ethics, values and principles by which society operates.

Finally, you have references that are common to all humans. These include the natural urges and instincts we experience through the different stages of life: childhood, puberty, youth, maturity and old age, and all that each phase of growing-up entails.

THE DREAM LANGUAGE

The dream world uses information collected by your senses from your waking life and reprocesses it, presenting it in a new way, so that you can understand yourselves and others, and the nature of the details relevant to a situation, with a lot more clarity and truth.

The language of dreams codes itself in two ways:

    Literal: presenting information directly parallel to everyday life.

    Symbolic: representing the information in a coded form, disguised from everyday life. The unconscious dream world uses signs, images, sensations and metaphors. The main form of information is presented in a visual way, although the unconscious will also use the other senses in order to draw the dreamer's attention to relevant details.

The main factor in understanding your dreams is crossing over the threshold of coding systems: from the logical conscious mind – which processes information in a sequential linear order – to the more free-floating realm of the unconscious.

In the unconscious, images and sensations float about as a minestrone of thoughts and feelings, which await selection and group together in order to give them coherence and meaning. These floating fragments of information remain non-associated or independent until enough components come together to form the basis of an answer to a question or puzzle, generated by the waking logical mind.

KEEPING A DREAM JOURNAL

Below is a method for keeping your dream journal. Naturally with practice you may find a better and more effective method but to start with this method is as good as any.

- Whilst still dreaming, make mental notes using key words. People are helping me/I am climbing alone etc.
- Record the details straight into a Dictaphone, as soon as you wake up.
- On waking, take a few minutes just to recall the salient feelings, and write down on a notepad what you remember. This is very useful particularly when there is a series or a recurring theme.
- And finally, bear in mind that they are your personal dialogues and so the most qualified person to interpret your dreams is yourself.

WHAT TO LOOK FOR IN YOUR DREAMS

- **The theme:** What was the general plot of the dream? Was it about a place, being chased, wearing clothes, a journey, drowning, falling, flying, snakes, and so on?

- **The action:** What is happening? Where is it happening? (Is it a place you know from the past? or perhaps somewhere unknown to you?)

- **Were you central in the dream or were you peripheral to the action?** This indicates your position and degree of significance in a situation in the real world.

- **The overall atmosphere/mood:** Was it bright and clear, or dark and murky? Was it a scary or an enjoyable dream? Or perhaps it was about a competition. (Did you win the race? Did you enjoy taking part in the race?)

- **The environment:** Was it on land, at sea, in the air, or underground? By taking note of the terrain we gain an insight into the root of the problem. Generally speaking, water represents emotions and land means money and aspects of self-worth, whilst air denotes the mind and thinking. To find yourself underground or deep in the bowels of the earth suggests reconnection with your true self.

- **Colours:** Sometimes colour might be the significant feature of a dream, and may be enough on its own to decipher the full meaning. On other occasions the colour might be incidental, but no less significant. You may find out that certain colours stand out in the dream, so try and remember if one colour predominated over the others.

- **Anagrams/numbers:** These could hold valuable information about schedules, games of chance, significant dates and perhaps significant times when events will happen.

- **Characters, objects and animals :** Different characters in dreams often symbolize different facets of the dreamer's psyche or character, such as their masculine and feminine side, and will often surface in dreams if a particular part of the psyche is being repressed or ignored. They can also often act as metaphorical stand-ins and represent a situation that needs clarifying, or a person under review. This removes any biases and prejudices that the dreamer may have, and allows the dream to present a clear picture of their true nature and character. When you see stand-ins in a dream, ask yourself this basic question: do they remind you of anybody?

ABANDONMENT

Trouble. If you have dreamt that you have been abandoned then you will find that over the next few weeks there will be a reconciliation with an old friend. If you dreamt that you abandoned someone else then you will find that this is a warning not to be ignored or you could lose contact with that person. If you abandoned something you did not like in your dream it signifies that you will be able to let go of it in real life.
➠ *Baby*

ABBEY

Tranquillity. If you dream of an abbey during daylight it indicates that you will experience peace

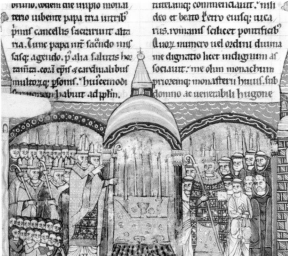

of mind and a sense of freedom. If the building is viewed in your dream under darkness, however, this presages a period of loss and sadness, albeit of a transient nature.

ABHORRENCE

Warning. To dream of general abhorrence indicates that you will be facing some difficulties soon. The rest of the dream should be able to give you a clue to where these difficulties will lie, but on the positive side you will be able to overcome these problems. To abhor a particular person in your dream is your subconscious saying that you will not be able to trust this person.
➠ *Childbirth*

ABORTION

Fear of failure. Very emotional dreams such as this have a different meaning depending which sex you are. If you a woman and are pregnant or contemplating pregnancy this is just an anxiety dream, although if you are healthy it indicates that you need to check your health. For men it means failure in a current relationship.
➠ *Bereavement*

ABSCESS

Sorrow. If you dream of developing an abscess it indicates that you feel overwhelmed at the moment by what is going on in your life. You feel out of control and the pressure on you is both financially and emotionally too much. At the same time you seem to be adding to the problem by taking on other people's misfortunes as well. You need help to sort this out.
➠ *Disease*

ABYSS

Tread carefully. Business dealings may be particularly difficult if you dream of stepping into an abyss. It may be a period during which you should tread very carefully. If you avoided falling into the abyss in your dream then you will overcome the impending difficulties that follow.
➠ *Unknown Places*

ACCIDENT

Warning. This can be a warning about a forthcoming accident and therefore it may be advisable to stay clear of long journeys for the next day or two. An accident at sea relates to emotional relationship issues; on land it signifies business issues. On the whole, this dream foretells dangers that should be avoided for the next two to three days.
➠ *Sea*

ACCORDION

Relief from sadness. If you dream that an accordion is playing, this means that although you are sad at the moment, things will get better, as there will be joy in your life shortly.

ACCOUNTS

Financial worries. Dreaming of accounts or accountants often means that you are troubled by financial issues, or that your accounts need to be sorted out. It is a warning not to overspend or invest in things that you cannot afford.

ACCUSATION

Warning. If you face an accusation in your dream then it is a warning that there are some people around you that may not be acting in your best interests. The warning is that if you take action now you can protect and defend yourself so that the situation does not affect your interests.

ACNE

Unhappiness. To dream of acne means that you are unhappy at the moment. In particular this dream relates to your emotional life: you wish to unwrap yourself from a difficult relationship. If you noticed the acne on yourself it means that you are self-conscious about your appearance and self image, particularly in respect of attracting a member of the opposite sex.
➠ *Doctors*

ACORN

Wealth. If you invest now, you will be able to reap your rewards in the future. Acorns in a dream signify wealth that will come to you and although it will take time your success is assured.

ACQUITTAL

Obstacles. Dreams of acquittal indicate that you are about to face an imminent problem that has

FAR LEFT: Consecration of the Abbey of Cluny by Pope Urban II in 1095.
LEFT: An accident at sea relates to the dreamer's emotions.
ABOVE RIGHT: Marc Chagall's Acrobats, *who may suggest inadequacy.*

some history attached to it. The obstacles that are ahead of you are surmountable, even though they seem impossible at the moment. Perseverance will lead to a successful resolution with an unexpected twist of good fortune in your favour.
➠ *Celebration*

ACROBAT

Overcoming problems. To dream of seeing acrobats is a sign that you feel that you are not able to balance your life at the moment. This dream also reveals feelings of inadequacy in comparison to someone else. If you are doing acrobatics in your dream, this is an indication that you are trying to regain control of your life.

ACTING

Assertiveness. To dream of being or meeting an actor or actress heralds a period of forcefulness and determination on your part to assert yourself if you want to achieve your ambitions. But be warned not to repeat anything placed in your confidence as you will lose more than just a friend.

ADAM AND EVE

A strong omen. If Adam and Eve play a part in your dream it is regarded as a good omen, indicating a new start and that your confidence levels are strengthened by your own truthful recognition of yourself.
➠ *Sermon Worship*

ADMIRATION

Vanity. If you dream of being admired then you have a need to take a closer look at your outward behaviour and examine yourself for signs of vanity that could mar and weaken the bonds of your friendships. To dream of admiring others means that help from your friends will soon spur you on the way.

ADOPTION

Fitting in. If you dream you are adopted (when you are not) it means that you feel that you are not quite fitting in with the people around you. You should find help from those family members who you feel understand you best. If you dream that you have adopted someone it signifies a good year for business speculation.
➠ *Twins*

ADULTERY

Setbacks. If you dream of committing adultery, it often means you have some secrets that you should keep carefully; trusting someone with these secrets will result in them becoming common knowledge. If you have the same dream on a regular basis it suggests there is something wrong with the relationship you are in at the moment; you need to sort this out before the relationship breaks down further. Dreaming of adultery can also herald a difficult time in a relationship, where there may be some miscommunication.

AEROPLANE

News from afar. If you see an aeroplane or travel in one in your dream, it is a general indication of news and business opportunities from another country. If you fall out of the plane, or it experiences difficulties in the air, you should take it as a warning to watch overseas investments.
➠ *Airport, Flying*

AFRAID

Bravery. If you dream of being afraid of a particular situation this means that when the situation arises you will find that you have the ability to overcome and tackle your fears. If you are afraid of a particular person then this is a warning that they may let you down.

AGATE

Communication. Agate in dreams represents the need to communicate with others. If there are a lot of hectic things going on in your life you must try to communicate properly with others, then you will be able to reach your objectives, particularly in business. This

ABOVE LEFT: Good omens Adam and Eve, from a Catalan altar painting.
ABOVE RIGHT: An albatross being shot down can indicate trouble.
RIGHT: Alligators in your dreams warn that caution is necessary.

dream is an indication that you should make sure all plans are put into the right order.

AGE

Worry. To dream that you have aged indicates worry; it may also mean that you are feeling a bit down and perhaps should see a doctor. To see old people in your dream is a good omen; to see someone younger, or even a younger version of yourself, indicates that there is a need to take a fresh approach in the way you live your life.
➥ *Teeth, Time*

AIRPORT

Business investments. If you dream of being at an airport then it means that you will receive news from someone abroad. This dream often brings news of investments in business ideas.
➥ *Flying*

AISLE

Decisions. If you dream of walking up an aisle it means that you have some important decisions to make; it suggests, though, that you should take extra care over these decisions as they will have long-term influence on your life.
➥ *Church*

ALBATROSS

A long distance journey. While all birds indicate a quest for a higher spiritual level, dreaming of an albatross is said to indicate a wish to see the world, or the possibility of an overseas journey. Take heed of the sailors warning: an albatross shot down indicates a stormy passage in your life.

ALIENS

New acquaintances. If you dream of an alien encounter it means that you are about to meet someone new who will have a strong influence in your life and will bring about a change of direction for you. If *you* were the alien in your dream, this suggests that part of your personality is trying to emerge which could surprise or shock you and those around you.

ALLIGATOR

Caution required. An alligator in our dreams is a symbol of the mind's ability to move between the subconscious and conscious areas, represented by the water and the land. An alligator in a dream indicates caution regarding a new project and other people. The project or the people could affect your life dramatically, so be on your guard at all times, constantly weighing up your thoughts and feelings.

AMETHYST

The mind. To see amethysts in your dreams means that you need to take your time over decisions that need to be made shortly. It is a warning not to allow yourself to be rushed into things you might later regret. Amethysts in dreams signify understanding your needs.

AMPUTATION

Unexpected help. If you dream that you have a limb amputated then it means that someone else will help you out of a situation. If your dream shows another person with one of their limbs amputated then it indicates that you will help that person overcome their difficulty. The loss of a limb is more often associated with property rather than health.

➡ *Arm, Hands, Leg*

ALMOND

Temporary domestic issues. Almonds in a dream bring sorrow and this dream is about teaching you to snap out of feeling disillusioned. There will be some temporary setbacks for your family, but they are only fleeting and you will be able to move forward again shortly.

ALTAR

News. To dream of standing at an altar signifies some unexpected news and a celebration. This might mean that a marriage is about to be announced or occur, or it could simply bring some welcome changes to your life.

AMBULANCE

An ambulance in a dream is essentially a warning to be careful, usually of sexual indiscretion rather than anything else. The flashing lights and warning sirens are telling you to hold back, as infidelity may be exciting but it may have repercussions for you.

➡ *Hospital*

AMUSEMENT ARCADE

Beware of gambling. This dream is a warning that you are about to take unnecessary risks. Be careful with business ventures at this time as more will go into a non-productive market than will yield profit for you. Oddly though, if the winnings in the dream were small then you will reap satisfactory rewards, whilst large payouts will yield only tiny, if any, rewards.

ANAGRAM

Find a solution. If you are struggling with an anagram in your dream, it means that you are desperately seeking an answer to your problems. Pay attention to the anagram, as being able to rearrange the letters later often gives the name of the person involved or a possible solution to the problem.

➡ *Unknown Places*

ANCESTORS

Help from the past. Ancestors play an important part in many ancient and indigenous religions. Dreaming of your ancestors perhaps reflects your desire to

communicate with them to seek advice on an issue that is causing you concern.

➠ *Adam and Eve*

ANGER

 Compromise. If you dream of being angry with someone then it indicates that they may have caused you a problem but you may be overreacting. Your assistance and input would significantly aid the situation and help resolve and finalize a difficult decision. Equally if you dream that someone is angry with you then they are asking for your help.

➠ *Colour (red)*

ANGLING

Keeping your integrity. Angling indicates that you would be wise to hold true to your values, ethics and principles, especially where financial concerns are tied up with emotional issues and partnerships. The type of fish you are angling for will clarify in which area of your life you must hold fast to your vision. The type of fish may give further enlightenment to this dream (look up the name of the fish in this book for assistance).

➠ *Fish, Rowing*

ANNOYANCE

Speedy fulfilment. If you dream of being annoyed about something or with someone you will actually find that the next day you will no longer be annoyed. In fact, this dream bodes well for a pleasant, breezy day.

ABOVE: The type of fish caught in an angling dream may be significant.
ABOVE LEFT: A piece of amethyst crystal, which advises you to take your time.
ABOVE FAR LEFT: Ash and Almond trees, from a children's ABC book.

ANT

Little worries make lots of work. To dream of ants indicates that you have lots of little problems; none of them are major in their own right, but together they are threatening to overwhelm you.

ANTELOPE

Good prospects. Seeing antelope in your dreams represents a successful and prosperous future. If you have dreamt of an antelope which is ill, however, financial problems or lean times are on their way. If the antelope is shot by someone in your dream, you have a business acquaintance that you cannot trust.

ANVIL OR COBBLER

Increase in wealth. If the anvil is working or the cobbler is mending shoes then it indicates all is well and financially things will improve. However, if the anvil is broken then this is a sign that there are financial problems to be sorted out.

ANXIETY

No need to worry. Dreams are often a way of playing out fears and teaching you ways to overcome the situation. The outcome of these situations is always in the positive. Anxiety in a dream is actually presenting a contrary message; that you have the confidence and ability to go out and tackle a dilemma.
➡ *Breathing*

APATHY

Step up a gear. If you dream of being apathetic towards something or someone then your dream is telling you to stop being a defeatist, and to take up the challenge and continue with your objectives. To experience the apathy of others in a dream signifies that you may need to review your aims and not to allow the despondency of others to discourage you.

APE *SEE* MONKEY

APPARITION

Message. Seeing a ghost or apparition in your dreams may mean that someone is trying to communicate with you. You become more psychically in tune when you are asleep, and it is therefore possible that you are being visited by a lost loved one who dearly wishes to relay a message to you. This is usually good news, but in order to understand the dream completely you will need to work out what the message might be.

APPLE

Temptation. Apples are considered a good omen, particularly if you are eating one in your dream. It can also be a sign of new love, and if you are not sure yet then you may be led into temptation earlier in the relationship than perhaps you had planned. Apples are

considered to be magical in a dream because if you chop them in half you can see the five pointed stars or pentacles used by witches and believed to have magical properties.

➧ *Cider*

APPRENTICE

Hard work. To dream that you are an apprentice signifies that you will need to work hard to gain the respect of others. Such a dream can also suggest that there are new, practical methods that you need to learn, and that you would benefit from honing your observations for maximum success.

➧ *Learning*

APRICOTS

Luck – but not in love. To dream of apricots on a tree is a sign of good luck, but to eat apricots indicates that you will have problems in a relationship and that a friend is being deceitful to you. To dream that you are eating dried apricots indicates that you are wasting your time on small issues.

APRON

Material gain. Seeing an apron is generally good news as it indicates your finances will improve. However, if the apron is torn this can indicate family problems. If a female dreams of a torn apron difficulties in educational pursuits will arise, while for a male, apron strings indicate a need to grow up and to become more independent.

➧ *Kitchen*

ARCH

Heading in the right direction. If you dream of walking through an arch then it indicates that you are going the right way. This dream also signifies that you will receive recognition by others as a result of your efforts.

BELOW: Walking through an arch indicates that you are going the right way.
LEFT: Matthew Smith's Apples, symbols of magic and temptation.
BELOW LEFT: An apparition of a priest photograhed in Arundel church.

ARCHITECT

Planning. An architect uses plans and this indicates that you will be using your skills at planning a way forward. It is a dream of success, providing that you pay attention to detail and ensure that everything is planned meticulously. Take note of whether the architect in the dream is a traditionalist or a modernist – this will help you to focus on the type of details that will construct the success for you.

ARGUMENTS

Problem resolution. This type of dream allows your mind to look at your subconscious to enable you to analyze both sides of the problem. If you argue about a problem that you are experiencing in your life then you will be able to resolve it when the morning comes. However, if you lose your temper in the dream it indicates that you are trying to rush a decision.

ARK

Prioritize and Prepare. To see an ark signifies the need to prioritize and prepare to seek help against an unexpected deluge of problems, particularly those connected with emotional disputes tied up with financial matters. To be on board an ark warns against rising waters, especially if you reside in an area of low water.

➠ *Rain, Religious Icons, Sea,*

ARM

Good feelings. If you feel an injury in a particular area of your arm in your dream then it may mean that you should get it checked out. Arms in dreams generally relate to friends and supportive colleagues, hence the phrase 'shoulder to shoulder'; however, if an arm should be chopped off in a dream it means that a friendship will end through a lack of candour and trust in those around you.

ARREST

Obstacle. Being arrested shows that there is something that you need to sort out. The positive aspect is that the obstacle is a temporary block to your progress and once it is overcome you will achieve the desired results. To see others arrested means that you will gain promotion in your work situation.

ART

To develop your creativity. Learning art in a dream should be taken as encouragement to indulge your creative side. If you are involved in a discussion about art, however, this means that promotion could be on the way as a reward for your creativity.

ARTIST

Disagreements. An artist in a dream signifies a disagreement with your partner. You may also be going through a time when you are reconsidering your options. For those involved in creative endeavours, the direction of your research and indeed commentary may well come from the artist or type of artwork that you see in your dream.

➠ *Colours, Statue (sculpture)*

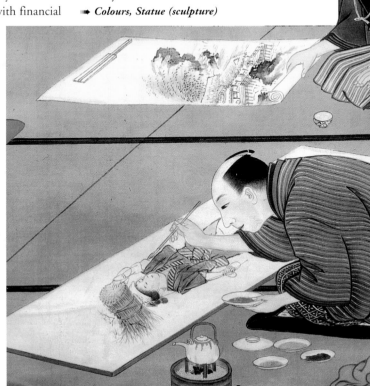

ASPARAGUS

 Rewards for effort. If you dream of eating or growing asparagus it shows that, although you will have to undertake hard work, you will be rewarded for your efforts in the long run. To sell asparagus means that you are able to delegate responsibilities and bring wealth to others.

ASTROLOGY AND HOROSCOPES

To dream of having your horoscope read or your astrological birth chart drawn up suggests that you need to sit down and plan your future. Important changes will shortly take place and you need to work out how to make the best of the opportunities that present themselves. If you take this advice on board you will achieve success in all that you do.

ATTIC

Aspirations. The meaning of this type of dream is dictated by your age. In the young it can represent the hidden mysteries of sex and therefore it can be a warning against rushing into things. In older people it can represent the aspirations of comfort and security.

AUCTION

Successful outcome. To dream of auctions indicates success and you will find that financially there is a bonus for you. In any business dealing you will find that you get a fair price and negotiations will be pleasant.

AUNT

Help. Much of the meaning of such a dream will depend on how close the relation is to you, but in general dreaming of

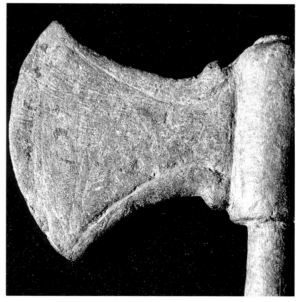

an aunt means that you will receive help in sorting out an issue that involves a third party. It is possible that this issue is one relating to your family.

AURA

The real cause of the problems. If you dream of seeing an aura around someone then this will help you to gain insight into the cause of a problem being experienced by that person. They may not be telling you everything or what you see may not be the whole story, but the dream will help you to understand and therefore help this person more fully.

➡ *Colours*

AXE

Cut through the confusion. Dreaming of an axe means that you will have to force your way through the confusion that surrounds you at the moment. However you have the determination and will do well. In order to achieve this success, though, you must be clear in your goals.

ABOVE: An axe in your dream urges you to clear your way forward.
LEFT: Artists, such as in Kawahara's watercolour, could signify a falling out.
ABOVE LEFT: Noah made preparations, as must those who dream of an ark.

BABY

Contentment. At its basic level, dreaming of babies is a sign of contentment and happiness in a relationship. It can indicate a wish to settle down and have children, particularly if you have dreamt of many babies. The baby's temperament also has an influence; for instance, if the baby is happy, you will have many friends. If you dream of a crying or ill baby, this can indicate disappointments that are to come and troubles ahead.

➠ *Abandonment, Celebration*

BACK

Trust. If you dream of a bare back, whether it is yours or someone else's, then it indicates that you need to be aware of financial risks, as you could lose out, particularly if you are planning to lend someone money. Ill health should also be considered.

BACON

Eating bacon indicates that you will enjoy ongoing contentment with your lot in life. Rancid bacon signifies that a visit to the doctor's may soon be needed and to cook bacon heralds the arrival of a surprise gift, either as a token of affection or of recognition for work done.

➠ *Pig*

BADGER

The badger indicates good news. To dream of seeing a badger, which is in itself rare, means that you should receive news from someone that you have not seen or heard from in a long time. The tranquillity of the woodland setting, which the badger inhabits, indicates that the news will be good and will stir strong emotions. However, if you dream of an aggressive badger, this relates to pent-up anger over a friendship.

BAGGAGE

Forget the past. If you dream that you have a lot of baggage it means that you have not been able to forget someone from the past, and before you go on you need to consign that person to history. Maintaining an emotional attachment to them is preventing your development and stopping you making a new attachment, because you are looking backwards instead of forwards.

BAKING

Domestic happiness. To dream of baking indicates that you are satisfied with your domestic situation. It can also signifies that there is going to be a big family reunion and a happy celebration for you to plan.

BALCONY

News. Dreaming of being on a balcony is an indication that you are looking out for information from friends. As long as the balcony does not collapse the news will be favourable.

BALLET

Jealousy and quarrels. Dreaming of dancing in or watching a ballet is a sign that you are about to enter some arguments, which tend to be of a personal nature. Watch out for the jealousy of others.

➠ *Theatre*

attraction but little else. This is also a forewarning that the relationship is unlikely to stand the test of time.

BANJO

Misunderstanding. To dream of playing a banjo heralds a time of joy and celebration. However, to see someone playing a banjo means that there will be a misunderstanding with someone.

BANQUET

Abundance and celebration. If you dream of a banquet then there is going to be a big celebration for family and friends soon. If in the dream the banquet goes well, so will the event. In the dream, however, if the banquet fails then it means that there are issues that need to be sorted out in the family.

BAR

Nosiness. If you dream that you are at a bar by yourself then it is an indication that you wish to eavesdrop on someone else's conversation. If your dream shows you at a bar with a friend or partner, it suggests that you want to spend a quiet time with these people to discuss personal issues.

BAREFOOT

Financial problems. If you dream of being barefoot when the rest of you is fully clothed it indicates that financial problems may come your way. People around you are not helping either and so you will have to sort these problems out yourself.

BALLOONING

Calculated ambition. To dream of flying represents your ambition to fly in a balloon and implies a calculated rise and focus towards your ambition. To pilot the balloon safely means success will come but only if you adopt a leisurely approach. A sudden descent may mean that you feel your career is going nowhere and you need to take control.
➡ *Storm, Wind*

BANANA

A relationship based only on sexual attraction. To dream of a banana indicates that you are about to enter a relationship where there is strong initial sexual

ABOVE: A balcony can indicate good news, as long as it doesn't collapse.
LEFT: Dreaming of a Degas dancer could be a sign of impending disagreements.
FAR LEFT: Baking brings domestic happiness to the dreamer.

BASEBALL *SEE* CRICKET

BASEMENT

If the basement is dry or well-stocked with wine this can mean a firm foundation to the other details in your dream. To find relics or treasures in the basement suggests that you have ancient wisdom and that you would benefit from digging it up and using it. To see rot or vermin in the basement indicates petty vexations that will destroy the foundation of your work if you do not attend to them very soon.

BASKET

Opportunities. If the basket is full then you have opportunities; if the basket is empty then you have to be careful that you do not lose anything over the next few days as a result of your own carelessness.

BASTING

Extravagance. If you dream that you are basting your meat then it is an indication that you have been frivolous and selfish with output lately and others may view you in less than a favourable light than usual unless you quickly curb your excesses. Only by doing this can you ensure a secure future and regain a sense of dignity and credibility for your efforts.

BAT

Bats mean that business dealings should be avoided. Bats in dreams generally indicate bad news; business deals should be avoided on the day that you have dreamt of them, particularly deals of a financial nature. The bat can represent someone that is deceitful and who is trying to close in on you. To see many bats indicates many people closing in on you.
➡ *Vampire*

BATHING

Renewal. Bathing in a dream symbolizes cleanliness and purification, and means that we are in need of relaxation. If the bath is empty, the dream is telling you not to make hasty decisions. If the temperature of the

bath is not quite right, then this is a signal to adjust your plans. If you dream that you are shaving, whether in the bath or not, it means that you should not make important financial decisions for some months to come. Soaping yourself, or another person in the bath, indicates that you should relax about a relationship that has started to develop: do not rush things and the relationship will begin to develop at its own pace.

BATHROOM

Inner emotions. Dreaming of being in a bath or a bathroom indicates that you are trying to unravel your emotional thoughts at the moment and you are probably in need of the time to contemplate. If the temperature of the bath is too cold then it suggests that you are not sure of your feelings, too hot and you are not ready to plunge into the relationship, which may be too hot to handle.
➡ *Water*

BATTERY

Recharge required. It can be common for people to dream that they go to switch on the lights and they do not work or that they try to start their car and the battery is flat. If you get this sort of dream chances are it is your own battery that is flat and you have been overdoing it lately. This is a message to take stock and recharge your life.

BATTLE

An internal battle. To see a battle in your dream represents an internal struggle. It can represent a battle that you are having with a friend or loved one and is a warning to sort things out before they get worse. The more you see the other person's point of view, the more likely it is that the argument will be settled amicably.

BEAN

Worries and illness. Growing beans hints that there will be sickness for youngsters around you. Eating them foretells that a close loved one will suffer a bout of illness. Beans on toast implies that you will lose valuable friendships through lack of consideration and not helping in their hour of need.

➡ *Eating*

BEAR

The bear indicates dealing with a friend. The meaning of the bear in your dream depends on whether the bear is aggressive or friendly. If the bear is chasing you in an aggressive manner, this means that a friend is trying to cause you a problem. On the other hand, if the bear appears friendly, and you are able to stroke it, then a friend needs your help and support.

BEAUTY

New confidence. Dreaming of seeing beauty indicates that your heart is opening again and preparing for a new relationship; if you dream of someone dabbing perfume on beautiful skin, you will be happy. This is particularly true for women. The stronger the smell, the more passionate and fiery the relationship will be. If your nails suddenly grow longer or shine in your dream, you will receive news of a loved one from a distance. For a man to be aware of beauty in a dream, reveals complicated business deals, brought about by a display of vanity that could upset things. For both sexes the greater the joy at sensing beauty in the dream, the greater and deeper the passion will be in a new relationship, be it business or love.

ABOVE: A bear is fond of honey and attacks a beehive, only to regret it.
ABOVE LEFT: The Bayeux Tapestry, showing the Battle of Hastings
ABOVE FAR LEFT: Dreaming of bathing symbolizes renewal.

BEAVER

Indicates hard work. The beaver, of course, is known for building dams and working hard to protect itself from the elements. Like the beaver, this dream indicates the need to get down to work. Whether you need to start work on your own or with others will often depend on whether you have dreamt of seeing a couple of beavers working together or one by itself.

BED

New undertakings. If you dream that you are making a bed it indicates that you will shortly have some visitors. If you dream of being in your bed then it is an indication that you have been overdoing it lately and need some time to yourself.

BED MITES

Unwelcome people. Bed mites or house mites in a dream bring unwanted news – normally from relatives or friends for whom you care little. There can be family disagreements and petty nuances that turn into serious squabbles unless you rid the mites from your dream, in which case you will not be drawn into the disputes but will be able to amicably solve them for the others.

BEE

Wealth and prosperity. To dream of bees is a sign that you are going to come into wealth and status, and Honey-bees in particular indicate wealth and prosperity. The bee is often used on a coat of arms, and therefore, dreaming of bees also represents prestige. Bees are also responsible for pollination, and so bees also represent fertility. For lovers to dream of eating honey indicates a wish for children. A vicar or priest on the other hand dreaming of bees will see an increase in his congregation.

➡ *Bite, Sugar*

BEEF

Tragedy. If the beef in your dream has gone off it indicates physical harm to the body. To witness either eating or cooking rotten beef means that there is likely to be much suffering followed by a period of instability. To see quality beef served and cooked is a harbinger of joy in business and love situations.

BEER

Good fortune. If the beer in your dream was tasty and had a good head, then it indicates good news in business dealings. However, if the beer was flat, then

not only is this a sign of a dubious landlord, but also you are warned not to trust your friends, as they are about to let you down.

BEETROOT

Watch out. If you dream of eating beetroot then it suggests that someone is trying to undermine you at work. However, if you dream of cooking beetroot then your career will prosper.

➠ *Root*

BELLOWS

Wasted effort. If your dream contains bellows then you are putting too much effort into an area that is not going to yield worthwhile results. If bellows are used to start a fire in your dream, it may suggest that you are about to cause a stir with some information that you have come across recently.

➠ *Fire*

BELT

Financial issues. To dream of your belt is an indication that you need to watch your finances. Chances are that you will have to tighten your belt, as they say. To dream that you have a brand new belt indicates that you are about to enter into negotiations with the bank.

➠ *Clothes*

BEREAVEMENT

Frustration and sadness. This dream often indicates that you are worried about someone close to you. However, this dream also suggests that there will be news of a wedding or birth. If you do not receive this good news then you are frustrated by business plans.

➠ *Death, Morgue, Widow(er), Wreath*

BETRAYAL

Be aware. If you dream that you have been betrayed by friends then it is a warning to look at the situation closely. They may not be trying to betray you intentionally but maybe things are not as clear as they should be. If you betray others in a dream then this heralds that you may be contemplating deception as a means to an end. Think it through, for the repercussions will be dire in the end.

BETTING

You are about to take a gamble. It has been recorded that certain people who have dreamt of placing a bet, on a racing horse for example, have gambled the following day and have indeed won some

money. You have to be careful, however, as this type of dream is not always necessarily a premonition: the outcome of the dream will decide the events that follow. More often than not this type of dream refers to a gamble that you are taking in your business life.

➠ *Numbers*

BIBLE

Rewards and help from others. If you dream of the Bible then it indicates that you will receive kindness in return for compassion you have recently shown towards others. The psalm that is seen in the dream can give an indication of the identity of the person who will show you this kindness.

BICYCLE

Steady progress. If you dream of riding a bicycle then it indicates that you are making slow but steady progress towards your goal, although you may need to make a great effort to get there in the end.

ABOVE: Betting on a racehorse may mean you should gamble the next day.
LEFT: Cornelius Caton's ale has a good head and thus indicates good news.
FAR LEFT: To dream of a honey bee may indicate wealth or fertility.

BIER

Losses. To see a bier (coffin stand) indicates a loss and could be a way of your intuition telling you of unfortunate news regarding a friend or relative. To see a bier with flowers in a church indicates the breakdown of a marriage.

BIGAMY

Loss. If a man dreams of committing bigamy it indicates that he may be not be performing well sexually and perhaps a medical check-up is in order. For a woman to dream of bigamy means that she has chosen some unwise friends.

BIGOTRY

Watch the actions not the words. If someone accuses you of being a bigot in a dream then it is a warning to watch their actions. Likewise if you accuse someone else of bigotry in a dream then you will need to have to re-examine your motives.

BIRDS

Spiritual growth. All birds indicate the growth of our spiritual being in addition to the individual meanings of the birds themselves. They are said to relate to our wish for more spiritual heights in life, and are therefore significant in relation to where we are going in life and in pointing the way to our higher life. Birds often bring with them a message: but one that you have to listen out for.

➡ *Flying, Magic and the Occult*

BIRD'S NEST

Time to leave the roost. A bird's nest in dreams implies that it is time for someone to leave the home environment. This dream is often dreamt by mothers when their children are due to move out of the family home. A young person dreaming of a bird's nest indicates that it is time he or she moved.

BIRTHDAY

Good luck. To dream of a birthday indicates celebrations and enjoyment. To receive presents or to give them indicates progress in your life. If you

had difficulty blowing out the candles it heralds poverty and false friends, with gossip or rumours, about you, circulating.

➡ *Cake, Celebration*

BISCUITS

Disputes. If you dream of eating biscuits then petty arguments could break out in your family. These are shown to be easily resolved if you can get the family to sit down and work things out together.

BITE

Discovering the truth. If you were bitten then something difficult lies ahead, due to false friends and misplaced trust. You are likely to discover the truth about a matter that has been kept a secret from you. If you saw someone else get bitten, the dream is telling you to avoid prying into other people's affairs for you will be seen as interfering.

➠ *Mosquito*

BLACKBERRY

Illness and financial bad luck. Blackberries in dreams are not good news as they symbolize loss. Finances could be in trouble and you may need to reorganize them carefully in order to prevent any losses. Eating blackberries is a sign you could be ill – or about to fall ill if the blackberries are unripe.

➠ *Bramble*

BLACKBIRD

A dark omen. This can be quite an evil omen, as it is often indicative of magic used wrongly. The blackbird represents the shadow, and it could be your

BELOW: A blacksmith, signifying long-term advantages, works at his forge.
BELOW LEFT: The Dionne quins with their birthday cakes, July 17 1935.
BELOW FAR LEFT: A first century Roman mosaic of water birds.

shadow or someone else's. Blackbirds bring with them a message and it is important to listen to that message.

BLACKBOARD

The writing is on the wall. To see a blackboard in a dream means that something has already been decided; the wording on the blackboard will reveal more about what this might be. If you are erasing words from a blackboard it suggests that you are trying to begin again, or 'wipe the slate clean'.

➠ *Chalk, Colours*

BLACK PEPPER

Watch your reaction. To dream of pepper is a warning against acting irrationally or without thinking things through. Arguments are too easy for you to get involved in. If you dream of your tongue being affected by pepper then it is a warning not to react to gossip.

BLACKSMITH

Long-term advantages. If you see a blacksmith in your dreams it is a hint that the hard work you are undertaking now will be rewarded in the long term. If the smith shapes and fashions his metal with ease it indicates that your success will astound others as well as yourself.

➠ *Apprentice, Anvil, Bellows, Fire*

BLADDER

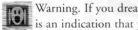 Business problems. The first thing to note is that more often than not dreaming of your bladder in the night actually is a signal that you need to go to the toilet. If this is not the case then dreaming of a bladder indicates business problems and that you should be careful not to waste energies in fruitless tasks.

➡ *Urine*

BLANKET

State of marriage. Bedclothes represent how stable you feel in your emotional situation. Care should be taken to look at the colours of the blankets and sheets, as this is significant. If you feel that the bedclothes are falling off you or are frayed and tattered it means that the relationship with your partner is also suffering at this time.

➡ *Colours*

BLASPHEMY

Warning. If you dream that you are blasphemous it is an indication that you need to be careful over the next few days in your choice of words, otherwise you could lose some good and trusted friends.

BLINDFOLD

Excitement and fear. The meaning of this dream is different according to the circumstances: if you were blindfolded it is a way of testing yourself and your level of faith in others when there is nothing visible to latch onto but only words and promises. If you blindfolded others it suggests a wish for anonymous affairs.

➡ *Fear*

BLINDNESS

 Deceit. If you or someone else is blind in your dream then someone is being deceitful to the other. You are entering a decision without seeing the truth and this will cause a major problem for you if you are not careful.

BLOSSOM

A pleasurable time. Seeing blossom on trees in your dreams indicates a pleasurable time. Joy and

romance will be entering your life and you will feel elated during the weeks ahead.
➠ *Flower, Fruit, Tree*

BLOUSE

New options. A clean blouse is a good omen of new opportunities, while a dirty blouse indicates lost opportunities. If a man dreams of a woman's blouse this indicates that he is making a song and dance about nothing.

BOARDING HOUSE

Temporary entanglements. If you dream that you are in a boarding house it suggests that sometime in the next few weeks you will have temporary residential arrangements and you will quickly move on to somewhere else.

BOAR SEE PIG

BOAT

Relationship issues. If you are in a boat or a canoe then details of the river or sea must also be taken into account as these represent your emotions. If you are alone in the boat or canoe then it means that you feel that you are alone in love. Where the boat is heading will indicate the place where you will find love.
➠ *Water*

ABOVE: Blossom in your dreams means there are pleasurable times ahead.
LEFT: Perhaps the boiling of these covetous people will aid their self control.
RIGHT: Brueghel's Parable of the Blind; an omen of deceit in a dream.

BOBBIN

Negligence. To dream of a bobbin indicates that you are not paying enough attention to your business at the moment. As a result of this you are likely to lose out. For those in business this is a warning to check if your company is threatened by the risk of a takeover by unwelcome predators.

BODY ODOUR

Self-esteem. The way that you see your body in a dream represents the way that you view yourself in life. Therefore, if you dream that you are perspiring or that you smell badly, it indicates that you have low self-esteem. If you see yourself or someone else sweating from hard work in your dream it indicates that assertive action and positive self-image will require hard work but the rewards will be beneficial for all concerned.

BOILING

Self-control. If you dream of boiling water or other liquid, then it indicates that you are in danger of losing your temper and self-control over an issue at the moment. You need to try and keep calm over the situation and the problem will dissipate.

woman dreams of a new bonnet then it indicates a new romance. A great deal depends on the colour of the bonnet in your dream: a blue one brings a loyal relationship, a pink or red one a passionate but short lived relationship and a green one indicates that you are likely to be deceived.

BOOKKEEPER

Encountering a bookkeeper in your dream is a warning to get your accounts in order. It may mean that you have one or two financial worries, but the purpose of the dream is to force you to address these sooner rather than later.

BOOKS

A record of your actions. Books represent the details of the things you have done and the things you have yet to do; they are a record of your life. Dreaming of books, therefore, represents the drawing up of plans. To see others reading in a dream indicates that you could learn from someone else's knowledge, thus enhancing your life plans.

➡ *Reading*

BONES

Bones represent structure. The saying the 'bare bones of the facts' indicates that this is a dream about stripping down problems to the basics. It is a time of looking at the structure of your life. Skeletons in a dream represent a need to sweep and start again. This can be a time of positive change and also often brings new friends and acquaintances. A skull, on the other hand, means that the changes will be swift and perhaps not as easy as you would have liked. In the end, though, the change will have been for the better. If you dream of pains in your bones it would indicate a need to have a health check-up.

➡ *Rheumatism*

BONNET

Engagement opportunities. If a man dreams about a bonnet it indicates that his thoughts are of marriage and he will not be single for much longer. If a

BOOTS

Promotion. Boots that are well polished indicate that there will be promotion opportunities at work. This is particularly so if you dream that you are buying them, which represents an interview. However, if the boots are dirty then there is a need to pay attention to yourself as you are creating the wrong impression with people. To dream that your boots are on someone else means that you have a rival in a love affair.

BOTTLE

Celebration. Dreaming of full bottles is a portent of celebrations and a party with much merriment for all concerned. Broken bottles means problems from which you need to disengage before serious quarrels break out.

BOUQUET

A happy time. If you dream of receiving a bouquet it indicates a happy time and a romantic opportunity. However, if you see a wilted bouquet then it indicates that you should consider having a medical check-up.
➠ *Lily*

BOW

A reminder. A bow or bow tie is like a knot in a piece of string and in a dream represents something that you should not forget to do. A flamboyant bow tie in your dream means that you want to show off your individuality.

BOW AND ARROW

Travel in the right direction. Arrows in dreams represent movement and our way forward: arrows act as a signpost, signifying the need for action. A broken arrow, however, is a warning that there could be difficulties in your relationship that need to be looked at.
➠ *Death, Killing*

BOWLING

This is generally a fortunate dream as it means that you will have a healthy retirement and will be content. To see others playing suggests that there will be frivolity and enforced loss of

BELOW: Diana with her bow and arrow, omens of movement and travel.
BELOW LEFT: If you dream of books, you may need to draw up plans.
LEFT: Tree of animal bones shown at the Burning Man festival, Nevada desert.

employment. For a woman to play a good game implies light ephemeral pleasures but with a finality of sorrow.
➠ *Games*

BOXING

Over-confidence. Whether you win, lose or are just watching a boxing match in your dreams the same meaning applies: your levels of confidence are too high. You need to be careful of this, otherwise events could turn against you if you don't weigh up the situation and the opposition carefully in advance.

BOY

Positive image. A boy in a dream, regardless of what sex you are, is a positive image and represents a force that can help you along your path. It sometimes represents a wish for a child, but more often than not stands for activity and action.

BRAGGING

Warning. If you dream that someone has been bragging to you then it may mean that you have to look closely at any business dealings that you are involved in with this person. If you are bragging in your dream then it is important that in the morning you think carefully about what you have said to others: you may need to make some changes.

BRAIN

Consider others. If a brain appears in a dream it indicates that you are not emotionally considering the needs of others. If you dream of eating brains, however, it means that you are about to gain knowledge. Basically you need to think of everyone's needs, not just your own.

➡ *Head*

BRAMBLE

Obstacles. Brambles as a dream omen represent obstacles that you have to fight your way through. If you get through them then you will be successful but you need to show a lot of perseverance and effort. To be pricked by the thorns means that you have some legal issues to deal with as well. If you escape without infection in your dream, you will survive the problems raised.

➡ *Blackberry*

BRANCH

Family ties. If you dream about the branches of a tree you are actually dreaming about your family tree. Getting caught in the branches of a tree means that you feel that you are being held back by your family. Seeing branches sway is an indication that family members are not happy with the way things are going.

➡ *Blossom, Forest, Tree*

BRANDY

If you dream of drinking brandy take is as a warning that, although you seem to have many friends, they are only there because of what you can do for them financially. If your financial generosity slackens, your friends will drop away. Perhaps you are attracting friendships that are too materialistic.

BREAD

Family state. If the bread is fresh – and particularly if you have dreamt of baking the bread yourself – then this indicates contentment in the family. However, if the bread is stale then there is a problem in the family and perhaps the feeling is that the relationship has gone stale and may require some changes to improve circumstances.

➡ *Wheat*

BREAST

Nurturing. For both male and females a breast in a dream represents the need for emotional nurturing and comfort. It is a dream we face when we feel in need of support and indicates that we are feeling vulnerable. If you lay your head on someone's breast in your dream it indicates that the person you are lying on will be very supportive in the future. If you dream of yourself or someone else having more then two breasts or nipples this indicates that you are being unfaithful. A dream where someone's nipples are pierced suggests that you want to win an argument with that person. If a woman dreams that her breasts are getting larger this indicates the wish for a child.

➡ *Baby, Mother*

BREASTFEEDING

Nurturing. For both male and females breastfeeding in a dream represents the need for emotional nurturing and comfort. It is a dream we face when we are in need of support and indicates that we are feeling vulnerable at the time.

BREATHING

The life force. Breathing in a dream represents your own abilities and direction, and as long as it is pleasant then there are no problems. However, if breathing is difficult then it is a warning that your chest could be playing up. If you are a smoker then it indicates that you want to give up.

➤ *Smoking*

BREWING

Long-term satisfaction. If you dream you are brewing then expect a visit from customs and excise or the income tax man. You will find that someone is about to investigate your income and expenditure, but although it will cause a few worries and headaches to start with, you will eventually prove to them that your figures had been correct all along and no further action needs to be taken.

BRIDE

Luck. Dreaming of being a bride or seeing a bride is an indication of luck and future happiness. Be aware, though, that you should take other factors in the dream into consideration as a sign of things to come. For example, if the bride looks unhappy then someone is displeased with you.

BRIDGE

Change. Crossing a bridge in a dream is a sign of making a change for the better; it means that you are starting on a new venture and indicates positive action. The only issue that needs to be addressed is the state of the bridge; if this appears unstable then you should take it as a warning that you are not yet ready to make that change.

➤ *Water*

BELOW: Seeing a bride in your dream indicates good fortune.
BOTTOM: The Rialto bridge in a dream could predict changes for the better.
BELOW LEFT: An 1823 sign for an Italian shop selling bread and milk.

BROOM

A clean sweep. A broom in a dream represents sweeping away the past and ushering in the new. This often relates to home and relationships, where a new broom symbolizes the throwing out of the old. The exception is that of a witch broom, which suggests that others will mock your old-fashioned ideals.

BROTH

To make broth in a dream signifies that you are indeed the master of your own destiny. To share or feed broth to others implies sincerity of friendships and companions. For a woman to dream she is drinking broth suggests that a love situation has a strong and lasting relationship potential.

BROTHEL

Fantasy. Women are unlikely to dream of a brothel, but in men this fantasy as a dream is not that uncommon. It can simply be a way of bringing some excitement in to your life and the dream may imply an improvement in your domestic sexual life soon.

➤ *Prostitute*

BROTHER

Support. For a man, dreaming of your brother indicates quarrels, while for a woman it suggests long-term support and security. A dream involving solidarity between brothers indicates financial stability.

➤ *Sister*

BRUSH

Out of sight, out of mind. If you dream of a small brush, such as a dustpan brush, then it indicates that you want to get rid of something. Generally, brushes in dreams indicate that you are putting off facing an issue, pretending that it does not exist.

BUFFALO

 A warning not to gorge. The buffalo was of great importance to the Native Americans; its appearance in their dreams signified that it was important to store up for what might be a harsh winter, although good times were near. The warning is to make sure that you save for the future.

BUG

Sickness will follow. If you dream of bugs then it is normally a message that illness is about to descend upon you. Dreaming of bugs will often be your subconscious mind telling you that you are about to come down with a bug.

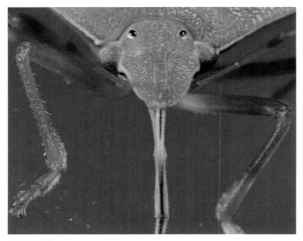

BUGLE

Celebration. To hear a bugle is to hear good news. It is a signal that someone you have not spoken to for some time will soon be with you. Strange forces are working in your favour, making synchronistic events the order of the day. Many unexpected but good things will line up after hearing this solitary instrument being played.

BUILDING

Structure. Buildings represent foundations stones of your life, and so if the building is well-kept and strong then you have a suitably stable structure in place in your life. If the building is falling apart then the structure to your life is in decay and this can indicate personal or financial issues that need to be addressed.

BULL

Competition Awaits. To dream of a bull, particularly if you are male, indicates that a competitor is waiting in the wings for the affection of another. If you are female this dream indicates a competitor for your affections. If you dream of a white bull, you will be successful in your relationship.

BULLET *SEE* GUN

BUS

Steady but slow progress. If you are on a bus in your dream then it indicates that you will reach your goal, but there could be many stops and starts before you finish your journey. To be the driver of this passenger carrier suggests that you know what the journey ahead entails and that you know the route – so relax and enjoy the scenic ride.

➠ *Road*

BUTCHER

Legal problems. If you dream of seeing the butcher, this is a warning that you should not sign any important documents as the agreement may go wrong. You need to delay decisions for a week and perhaps look at alternatives. To see a butcher slicing meats signifies that you will need a medical check-up soon.

BUTTER

Good health. Butter in a dream represents health and energy as well as being an indication that you will succeed in small projects. This dream can herald some small financial benefits.

ABOVE: Dreaming of a bull could signify a rival in love.
ABOVE LEFT: Adult Southern Green Stink bug, feeding on a ripe tomato.
RIGHT: A butcher slicing meats indicates the need for a medical check-up.

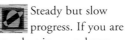

BUTTERFLY

A positive change. Generally this is a good dream as you are going to hear from friends and people that you have not heard from in a while. However, there is a negative aspect to this dream, as these same people will leave your life just as quickly. It is also a dream of transformation, and just as the caterpillar changes into a butterfly, so your life may change soon, ushering in a new era.

BUTTERMILK

Decisions. If you dream of buttermilk then it means that you have some small decisions to make. None of these decisions will be easy, regardless of whether you dream you of drinking the buttermilk or giving it to someone else. You may not want to make these decisions but they should be faced.

BUTTONS

Buttons represent money in dreams. To have bright new ones, particularly gold buttons, indicates that you are going to come into some money. Losing buttons means that you are going to have financial difficulties. Cloth-covered buttons denote sadness.

BUYING OR SELLING ANIMALS

Represents a financial transaction. If your dream involves the buying or selling of an animal it is most probable that you need to pay heed to your instincts in a financial transaction. The type of animal will indicate the area of concern (look at the entry in this book of the animal that appears in your dream for more information). If you feel uneasy about a financial or legal issue then perhaps you should pull out.

➡ *Shop*

BUYING OR SELLING A HOME

This is a dream which reflects your desire to move house. It can also occur, of course, when you are due to move, and can represent an anxiety situation. Often this type of dream will occur when you are looking for commitment in a relationship or thinking of starting a family.

To see an estate agent in your dream indicates that concerns about false promises and lack of commitment from a partner need to be addressed before hard cash is invested into joint ventures that have no longevity or solid foundations.

CABBAGE

Calamity. Dreaming of eating or cooking cabbages is an indicator of all sorts of problems about to descend on you. Relationship issues and financial problems are highlighted by this dream and they will be difficult to resolve, possibly even leading to total collapse.

➡ *Eating*

CABIN

Issues to resolve. If you dream of a wooden cabin then it indicates that you feel that you need some peace and quiet with a loved one. However, if you dream of a ship's cabin, then it indicates emotional turmoil in a relationship.

CAGE

Cages represent restraints. If you dream about being stuck in a cage, this means that you are having difficulty getting your ideas across to others and are feeling trapped. Learn to use your dream as a way to find the solution to your problem, to help you find the key to free you from the cage, and allow you to escape from the situation which is causing you anxiety.

➠ *Zoo*

CAKE

A joyous time. Cakes indicate happy times, although the type of cake will reveal more about this time. If you see a wedding cake, then this can obviously suggest a wedding is in the air. A thickly iced cake denotes a party; it could be a birthday or the news of a birth of a child. Cream cakes indicate promotion and celebration at work while a plain sponge cake can indicate a family gathering.

CALF

Successful plans. To dream of seeing a young calf indicates that you will be successful in any projects you are about to start. To see a calf carcass indicates disillusionment and even abandonment of potentially successful projects.

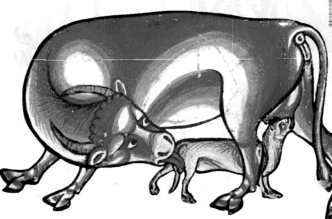

CALMNESS

Change of pace. If the weather is calm in your dream then it indicates that change is about to take place and that you will find that the next few weeks generate a very hectic time. If you are experiencing bad weather at sea, but then the sea becomes calm during your dream, this indicates that your relationship will be placed under scrutiny.

CAMEL

Endurance required. It is very positive to see a camel in your dream. However, just as the camel is able to go without food and water for days, you will also need to pace yourself. If you dream of camels coming towards you, which are laden with cloths and goods, expect some money or inheritance to come your way.

➠ *Desert*

CAMERA

A warning of an insincere person. To dream of a camera means that you could be dealing with an untrustworthy person, so caution is needed. The person taking the photo is likely to be the person that you should be careful of. Depending on whether the photos are instant or require sending off for processing tells you if the insincerity is immediate or will emerge once the details are processed and the truth is revealed.

CANARY

A message to listen out for. The canary has a lovely, sweet voice and you must try and listen to its voice in your dream, as it has a message that will make everything much happier for you.

CANDY *SEE* SWEETS

CANNIBAL

Avoid risky action. If you are the cannibal, or the one on the menu in your dream, you should be careful if you are planning any illegal activities: you will be caught out and in the work situation you could lose your job. To see the cannibalism of others, oddly enough, implies that you are contemplating becoming an accomplice in dangerous activities, through persuasive threats and pressure, the

BELOW: Van Gogh's Les Roulottes Campements de Bohemiens, *which in a dream could indicate a need for change.*
LEFT: If you are on the menu in your dream, take care in any illegal activites.
FAR LEFT: Dreaming of a young calf predicts success in upcoming projects.

is a wish for change and control in your life. Sharing a caravan site means that you are finding it difficult to decide what you want to keep in your life; you may be considering the lives of those around you as guidance for your new emerging tastes.

CARDS

 Your destiny awaits. Your destiny is laid out – if you can remember the cards that you saw, it is important to write them down once you have awoken. The Ace often represents the start of a new project; to see Hearts represents love, while Diamonds represent financial issues. Clubs represent strength and perseverance, and Spades represent obstacles.

The court cards also have meanings: the Queen represents a stable woman, the King represents a man between 35 and over, and the Jack represents a young person. As for the numerical cards, the higher the pip the more established along the path of that suit you are and completion with its finality of success draws close.

consequences of which are indicated in the dream. If you were seen by another in your dream, you will be found out; if not then you will escape.

➠ *Corpse, Killing*

CANOE *SEE* BOAT

CAP

Positive news. Wearing a cap in your dream indicates that the problems that you have been having lately are about to be resolved. If the cap is dirty then the problems may get worse for a while before they get better. A military cap bodes well for triumphing over difficulties.

CARAVAN

This is a dream about taking time out to work out what is important to you and what can be consigned to the past. To dream that you are in a caravan

CARNIVAL

A celebration. Generally dreaming of a carnival indicates that you will receive good news in the form of a celebration. The exception is if the people at the carnival in your dream are masked, as this could mean that you are open to deception but cannot see it.
➠ *Harlequin*

CARPENTER

Enjoyable time ahead. A carpenter in your dream is considered to be a very lucky symbol: it shows that your endeavours will reap rewards. The nails will indicate

how hard you have to work to achieve your aims – the larger the nails the harder it will be. The strength with which the carpenter is sawing is also an indication of how hard you will have to work. It is also an indication that you will be able to saw your way through your problems. The carpenter's plane will indicate how smooth the trip will be.

CARPET

Good luck. Providing they are new or are in good condition, dreaming of carpets is a good sign in relation to your income. If the carpets are threadbare, then it indicates that financial problems may become an issue. Oriental rugs or carpets suggest visitors from overseas.

CARROT

Financial luck. Dreaming of carrots means that your income is going to increase shortly, through extending your relations. If you are still single then it may suggest that your future husband is about to enter your life and together you will have a large family.
➠ *Root*

CART

Hard work. Reaching your goal in a cart is achievable, but it is going to take a lot of hard work and effort. You need to be sure that you are willing to put the energy in before starting on new projects. You will also have to make sure that you put the finances in place as well.
➠ *Road*

CARVING

Business negotiations. If you dream of carving for someone else then it indicates that someone will do better then you out of a business venture. If, however, you are receiving the carved meat then you will do well in business. This dream indicates the obstacle of business negotiations and how difficult the carving is will also reflect how tough the negotiations will be.

CASK

Parties. Seeing a cask indicates a party or celebration, and an empty cask will mean the party is over and it is time to face reality.

CASTLE

An Englishman's home is his castle. Castles in dreams are reflections of the home and the protection it affords. If the castle is solid, then it indicates

a domestically stable and enjoyable time. However, if there are problems with the castle or it looks in a state of ruin then it is a warning to sort out the domestic situation before the family crumbles.

CAT

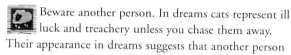 Beware another person. In dreams cats represent ill luck and treachery unless you chase them away. Their appearance in dreams suggests that another person

could be trying to steal your affections, while kittens indicate toying with affections in a playful manner. But be warned – for kittens grow up into cats and if the toying goes on for too long then treachery looms on the horizon.

CATERPILLAR SEE BUTTERFLY

CATTLE

A forecast for the year. Cattle in dreams have always been a good sign regarding the impending year. The origins of this dream's meaning can be traced back to the bible and before. Basically if you see healthy cattle everything is going to be fine; however, if the cattle are thin and starving, take this as a warning of problems to come.

➠ *Hide, Hunting, Killing*

CAULIFLOWER

Work issues. If you dream of eating cauliflower then it indicates that your heart is not in your current job and that you are not putting as much work into it as you should; it's time to re-evaluate this area of your life. To see this vegetable growing in a garden portends a marriage of convenience or arrangement.

➠ *Eating*

CAVALRY

Rescue. Just like the old Western films, if you see the cavalry charging into your dream it indicates that metaphorically a rescue party will arrive to save you from a problem that you are facing at the moment.

CELEBRATION

Upcoming event. Dreaming of a celebration is a sign that you will shortly be invited to one; perhaps there will be a surprise party for you. A celebration also brings a potential romantic involvement.

➠ *Childbirth, Judgement, Marriage, Party*

CELEBRITY

An ideal. Celebrities in dreams are quite common and unveil a fantasy that you have of meeting a rock start or actor. This dream also represents a wish to take on some of their star qualities and perhaps their lifestyle. This dream can give you inspiration to achieve a level of celebrity confidence, allowing you to be more productive in your life.

➠ *Feelings*

CELERY

To dream of celery is a good omen, and indicates that you will be wealthy and healthy. For a young woman to dream of eating celery indicates a passionate romantic week ahead. If the celery is rotting then it signifies that a family loss is soon to occur.

➠ *Eating, Garden*

ABOVE LEFT: A rather disgruntled cat sitting on a highly polished car bonnet.
LEFT: The decidedly solid Bodiam Castle in Sussex, England, which could indicate domestic stability and happiness if seen in your dreams.
ABOVE FAR LEFT: A carpenter's plane indicates the smoothness of your future.

CELLAR *SEE* BASEMENT

CEMETERY

 Prospects. Cemeteries in dreams have different meanings depending on how well the grounds are kept. If the grounds are in a tidy condition then there will

be happiness and financial rewards in the future. If the grounds look dreary, there may be trouble ahead, though news from friends will bring prosperity, resolving your problems.

CEREMONY

Friendships. To dream of a ceremony indicates that you have lots of friends around you who are willing to support you when needed. It also symbolizes the anticipation of a social event which will prove a significant event for you.
➡ *Celebration, Marriage*

CERTIFICATE

Reward and honour. To receive a certificate suggests that you may be in line for an award. Such a dream also indicates that the effort you put in now will be repaid in the end. To simply see a certificate in your dream should be taken as a warning to nurture the acorns if you want to see oak trees grow.
➡ *Power, Tree*

CHAINING

Being chained means being restrained. If you see yourself as a person, or an animal chained up, then you may be having restraints placed upon you by other people. If you visualize someone else chained, this

indicates that you feel that this person is being restrained. Your dream will indicate whether it is you chaining that person or someone else.

CHAIR

News. To see an empty chair in a dream indicates that you will receive unexpected news soon of someone who would normally occupy that chair. To sit in a chair yourself means that you have to prepare something. A rocking chair means that you will benefit from the labours of others.

CHALK

A message for you. If the chalk in your dream is simply lying around, with no writing nearby, it suggests that someone is having difficulty in getting a message through to you; possibly because you are putting up some form of block. If the chalk has already written the message, read it carefully to get your answer.
➡ *Blackboard*

CHAMELEON

Change with the circumstances. Just as a chameleon is able to blend into new surroundings and camouflage itself, this dream is a message suggesting that you will need to do the same. It is a warning that you may have to protect your true nature and blend into your surroundings.

CHANDELIER

Status. Seeing a chandelier in your dreams indicates that you will be given an important role. A chandelier brings status and honour and indicates a successful time in both social and career circles. If the light was shining through it then you can expect to become the centre of attention in a forthcoming social event.

CHAPEL

Political turmoil. To dream that you are in a chapel indicates that you could find some difficulties dealing with others. You will find that there is a lot of political manoeuvring amongst your social group that could spoil the harmony you are currently enjoying.

CHARITY

Dreaming of donating to charity means that you need to be careful, as financial problems loom. If you dream of giving a house away then this is a warning that there is going to be expenditure connected with the house. If you dream of being given charity then something beneficial will happen to you very soon.

CHEATING

Your luck will change. If you dream of being cheated, then it means that there is some good news on its way to you soon, as something you thought you were not going to achieve will work out in your favour. However, if you dream of cheating someone else then this is a warning that it is best for you to act above board otherwise your deception will be discovered.

CHEESE

A warning. It is said that eating cheese before you retire to bed will give you nightmares. Cheese in a dream will have its meaning modified by the type of cheese you see. Gorgonzola and other strong-smelling cheeses can herald career problems, while Cheddar and Edam relate to love. Dreaming of grating cheese suggests that you have to sort out one or two financial issues.

CHERRY

Troubles brewing. Cherries on a tree in a dream predict business problems that will have to be carefully controlled. If you see cherries in a bowl,

however, or are eating them in your dream then this is a sign of sexual adventure. If the cherries are green or spoilt then the relationship will not progress.

CHESS

Strategy and political movements. Chess is one of the oldest games, originating from China. Just as chess can be a complicated game, you will need all your powers to manipulate events around you: there are political matters that need to be sorted out at work. If you win in your dream, then you should win in the real

situation that faces you. Even if you lose, you can still win in real life, but you will have to change your strategy. You may also have to adjust your social life, manoeuvring your position and playing the game.

CHESTNUT

To dream of chestnuts indicates that there can be some temporary delays to your plans, but they will not cause a problem in the long run. The significance of this dream is that you must ignore delays for they will be temporary and the more you press ahead the greater your success.

ABOVE: A game of chess in a dream can reflect a situation in real life.
LEFT: Cherries on a tree: a possible indication of business trouble.
ABOVE LEFT: The old cemetery in Prague's Jewish ghetto quarter.

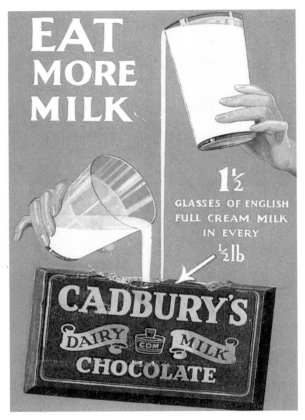

EAT MORE MILK

1½ GLASSES OF ENGLISH FULL CREAM MILK IN EVERY ½ lb

CADBURY'S DAIRY MILK CHOCOLATE

CHICKEN

A warning message. Dreaming of chickens is said to be a bad omen, as it brings trouble. In particular, the trouble is associated with partners, in both business and relationships, indicating that there is a need to tread carefully in these areas of your life. Traditionally, this dream meant that your partner was being unfaithful.

➡ *Egg*

CHILDBIRTH

Fertility. Childbirth often indicates that fertility is on your mind and could bring news about a forthcoming pregnancy. If you are not pregnant and are not planning to get pregnant, then this dream indicates accomplishments in work that you are about to undertake: they will be successful but a lot of hard work will be required.

➡ *Abhorrence, Celebration, Deformed Birth*

CHILDREN

Support. Parents never stop worrying about children and so it is important to realize that most dreams involving your children are simply reflections of waking anxieties. If you hear your child calling you in a dream, however, it may be that they need your help in some matter.

CHIMNEY

Accomplishment. The taller the chimney in your dream the more successful your accomplishments will be, just like the smoke signals of the north American Indians; smoke at the top of a chimney means a message is on its way to you.

CHOCOLATE

Pleasure seeker. Regardless of whether you dream of eating chocolate or drinking chocolate it is an indication that you are trying to seek pleasure: this could suggest that relationships are not going well and that you are in the mood for finding someone new to light up your life.

CHRISTMAS

Family celebrations. To dream of Christmas implies that you are looking forward to celebrations and family reunions. It indicates social gatherings in the near future and domestic happiness.

CHRYSANTHEMUM

Parties and gatherings. If you dream of this flower then you will find that your social life improves significantly over the coming weeks. If in your dream you are given them as a gift, it indicates that you will receive a promotion or an honour of some kind.

CHURCH

To see a church from the outside in a dream is a positive sign, to be inside a church can be interpreted as a bad omen. Outside a church indicates celebrations on the way. Being inside a church in your dream suggests that you are in a difficult situation with another person.

➡ *Mass*

CIDER

Good luck in exams. Dreams of cider bring good luck, particularly if you are a student and about to undertake exams shortly. On the negative side, though, you will need to keep yourself from being involved in some gossip.

CITY

Change of location. To dream that you are in a different city indicates a possible change of location; much of the dream will depend on your own attitude to the cities, but it is normally connected with work decisions regarding the movement of businesses.

CHURCHYARD

Prospects. A churchyard with graves has the same meaning as the cemetery entry. However, if there are no graves in the churchyard, it indicates that you will live away from where you were born. A churchyard in spring or summer bodes well but in winter financial difficulties are set to cause problems for you.

CLAIRVOYANT

To dream of seeing a clairvoyant indicates that you need help with planning your future. You are considering a lot of options at the moment and you need to give everything proper consideration. Occupational changes are due soon and you need to have a clear idea of what lies ahead down the different paths you could

choose. If you happen to be a clairvoyant, this dream is a confirmation of your attributes and abilities.
➡ *Vision*

CLAM

Successful negotiations. Shellfish in general relate to negotiations in dreams; this may be because they are often found together in groups. To dream of clams indicates that you will have to negotiate with an obstinate person, but you will win them over with your ideas. Traditionally, if women dreamt of clams it meant they would win the key to their partner's heart and generosity, both emotionally and financially.

CLARET

Drinking claret leads to success. Drinking claret signifies that extra money will become available to you. This will be through patrons and higher-authority sources which will also grant you recognition and nobility. To see broken claret bottles indicates that you will find that persuasive people are trying to lure you into directions that lack virtue and will bring you disgrace.
➡ *Wine*

ABOVE: Dreaming of a clairvoyant suggests you need help planning your future.
LEFT: Seeing the outside of a church in your dreams is a good omen.
ABOVE LEFT: Chocolate tends to appear in the dreams of pleasure-seekers.

CLARINET

 Frivolity. To hear someone play a clarinet in your dreams indicates that you are not taking a particular issue seriously enough. If the clarinet does not play properly, or is broken in some way, causing it to play badly then the augury is one of displeasure from a close friend or associate of influence in your life.

➠ *Orchestra, Theatre*

CLIMBING

General success. If you see yourself climbing, it indicates progress towards a certain goal and you will almost certainly reach your target. How arduous the task will be depends on how difficult you find the climb, although perseverance will pay off in the end.

➠ *Hill, Tree*

CLOISTER

Warning. This is a dream that warns you about impending changes. Although you welcome change,

this time it may not be as easy as you would like to accept it. This can be a difficult and emotional time, but it will improve once the initial period of change has passed.

CLOTHES

Prepare for the future. In a dream the more clothes you wear the more you will have to prepare financially. The less clothes you wear the easier things will be financially. The colour of the clothes also represents how you feel about the situations around you. If the colours are bright, whites, yellows and reds you will be full of optimism. However, this may mean that you are full of adventure but lacking in knowledge and not taking a situation seriously enough. If all the colours are dark, deep shades then it shows that you are aware of the responsibilities you face and have a strong knowledge.

➠ *Colours*

CLOUDY

 Approaching conditions. Clouds in dreams represent the conditions that you face over the next few weeks. If the clouds are white and the sky is bright then you can expect positive results, particularly with romance. If clouds are obscuring the Sun then it indicates obstacles to overcome. Storm clouds suggest that there will be problems to face, but that if you persevere you will succeed in your endeavours.

CLOVER

Happiness. To dream of clover indicates wealth, health and happiness. You will want for nothing and if you are single you will soon meet the person of your dreams for a long-lasting relationship.

COACH *SEE* BUS

COAL

Security. Dreaming of a warm glowing fireplace indicates that you are content with your domestic situation. Coal represents comfort and contentment. The brighter the coals glow the more comfortable you feel.

COAT

Financial opportunities. If the coat is new then it represents new business opportunities; however, if the coat is the latest in fashion and is flamboyant then your business is not going to succeed. Wearing someone else's coat indicates that you are going to ask that person for a financial loan. A torn coat indicates that your children will rebel against you.

COBWEB

 A veil. Cobwebs in a dream tend to symbolize veils over areas that need to be addressed; this is particularly true if the cobwebs are in unusual places. If the cobwebs are in a cellar or attic then it shows good news can be found by a little hunting. If the cobwebs are in the bedroom then emotional issues are being hidden from view and tears will eventually follow.

COCKEREL

Dawn of a new event. Just as the cockerel greets each new dawn, the image in your dream signifies

a new dawn in your life and suggests that it is time to start new projects. It is an uplifting dream that indicates a time of prosperity.

➡ *Egg*

COCKTAILS

Immoral life. If you dream of cocktails then it indicates that you have been giving an impression to some that you are home-loving or, if single, a serious student, when in reality you have been spending every night at clubs and pubs.

COCOA

 Pleasure seeker. If you dream of drinking hot cocoa or chocolate it is an indication that you are seeking

new sexual pleasures; it may be that your relationship is not going well, and this dream means that you are in the mood for finding someone new to light up your life.

COCONUT

To dream of coconuts indicates that there are some difficult times ahead, but if you persevere then you will succeed and may reap unexpected gifts from unknown sources.

COFFEE

News. If you dream of drinking coffee then it indicates that you are shortly to receive some important news, which you should act upon as soon as possible. If you spill coffee, though, take it as a warning not to act on the news you receive.

ABOVE: Cocoa in your dream could indicate a need for new sexual pleasures.
ABOVE LEFT: A dream involving Chagall's Le Coq signifies new beginnings.
LEFT: The gothic cloisters of a monastery warn of impending change.

H MATISSE 52

COFFIN

Sadness if occupied, joy if not. To dream of a coffin with someone inside represents financial problems. It also means quarrels with someone close to you and therefore represents the death of a friendship. If the coffin is empty you will make amends with someone over a dispute.

COLLAR

Love affairs. There is the old saying that lipstick on the collar is the first thing a wife will look for if she feels her husband is having an affair. In dreams a dirty collar indicates an affair. To put on a vicar's dog collar in your dream is a wish to do something more spiritual with your life.

COLLEGE

To dream you are at college can be an indication that your academic ambitions may be unfulfilled. Often this dream encourages someone to learn something new. It may also suggest that you are about to be sent on a training course.

➡ *Building Certificate*

COLLISION

Stalled. You have halted at something that you were going to do, and you need to move forwards. It is time to make decisions and not let others hold you back as you have been letting them do lately.

COLONEL

Loss of position. To see a colonel in your dreams means that you will lose out in a job opportunity and fail to reach a position of any real significance. If your were the colonel then it implies that you are seeking and trying to control and wield power as a show of influence and stature over your friends.

COLOURS

Colours in dreams are very significant as they give an indication of your mood with regard to how you and others react. The dreams will be modified by what actions and objects are taking place but the basics are:

Blue gives calmness and a sense of spirituality; it promotes spiritual well-being and understanding; it is also a good dream for friendship and help from others. It means that people are around to help you with your ideas, offering emotional support and advice.

Green brings luck and help in finances. It also brings love issues and fertility to the meaning of dreams. It is a good colour as far as financial negotiations are concerned and it means luck is on your side. Green is also ideal when looking at issues to do with the family as it greatly enhances fertility and growth of the family.

Orange is a vibrant colour that promotes health and energy; it is a fast colour which means that when orange is seen changes will take place quickly. It is a colour of optimism and therefore the energy that you deliver at the moment will be rewarded in success.

Pink brings romance and affection but also honour and the honour of being looked up to by others. Pink is often shown at the start of a new relationship.

Purple represents career success and achievement. It also represents royalty and the church and therefore is often associated in dreams with forthcoming news of promotion or being honoured. It can mean meetings with important people may be able to promote you in some way.

Red is for passion, love and also strength and anger. It is common in dreams when emotions are high. If you are wearing red in your dream then you want to attract attention from another person, and if another person is wearing red then they want you to notice them. Red faces can show anger and so caution should be applied with this sort of dream.

White is for purity and clearness. White means that everything will go well, and that the choices you have taken are correct. It is also the colour of protection so that you will be protected and you will be protecting others.

Yellow brings strength of mind and determination; it is a colour of communication so is very good in business dealings and negotiations. Yellow is a good colour when connected with messages and the start of new ventures.

Magenta brings hope of new projects, as well as enthusiasm and motivation from others.

Cyan brings reflection and thought; it means negotiations will go well, as you will be able to sit down and discuss your options in a constructive way.

Indigo in a dream means that you will have the authority of others to help

you with your decisions; they will support you while keeping a tight hold on the reigns.

Brown represents hesitancy and uncertainty and therefore in a dream can indicate events that need to be looked at carefully. You should be cautious, but brown is also a colour that represents hard work to get the rewards that you want.

Grey is a neutral colour and can represent reaching stalemate. It is a message that things will take their time to sort out.

Black is an unfavourable omen, as it brings difficulties and obstacles to overcome.

If the colour is a fluorescent, it brightly reflects whatever light source there is and in dreams this indicates that the effort you put in will swiftly be rewarded. If the colour is a glow in the dark then it indicates that changes are already on the way.

If you see colours in your dreams that you would not normally see when you are awake – such as ultraviolet and infrared – this indicates that your perception is being opened and that you are able to perceive people's invisible issues rather than just the surface impressions. You will find that this will often give more insight into a situation when you are awake.

ABOVE: Matisse's Harmony In Red – *a strong, passionate colour in dreams.*
LEFT: Seeing purple in your dreams can represent a successful career.
ABOVE LEFT: Matisse's Nu Bleu IV *in a dream would signify calmness.*

COMEDY

Temporary escapism. If you dream of a comedy, then it indicates a little light relief is on its way to you.

➠ *Television, Theatre*

COMET

Sudden changes. A comet in your dream heralds rapid changes for you. These could be unexpected and quite profound; they might be emotional break-throughs concerning a new viewpoint in relationships, whilst for those involved in inventions and intellectual inspirations, new insights and discoveries will lead to the creation of new professions. Your life is about to undergo a boon of sudden changes – so be prepared.

COMMANDMENTS

Rules and regulations. To dream about the Ten Commandments indicates that you have not been true to yourself or to others and that some people will feel let down by your attitude. The Commandment you have broken in the dream will give an indication of the lesson you need to address.

COMPASS

Finding a direction. Using a compass in a dream means that you need to set a new direction. It can indicate a difficult time, as you may have strayed off course. If your compass is pointing north this can suggest that you have strayed but have found your way back to the right path. To see south implies your goals lie in the opposite direction to the areas in which you are currently engaged. West indicates your goals will be realized by looking back in time at an old pursuit. East denotes that you must face a future with changes that are modifications of your existing circumstances.

➠ *Map*

CONCERT

Good news. This dream is often a sign that you want to be involved with the person or group performing in the concert, indicating that you want to be part of their creativity. If you dream that you were taking part in the performance it signifies that you would do well to put your talents on display as they will be received with applause.

➠ *Orchestra*

CONDUCTOR

Guiding people. If you dream you are a conductor on a bus then it indicates that you will be soon be helping someone find their way in life.

If you dream you are conducting an orchestra then you will be helping someone develop their creativity, although this will not be without some difficulty.

CONFETTI

Significant success. To dream of confetti hints at a social celebration that will be significant for you, regardless of whether it is a wedding or not. If you cannot see others through the swirling mists of confetti then it indicates that you will be tidying up after the event.

CONTEMPT

Warning. If you dream that you are held in contempt by others then this is a warning that you should change your attitude; with positive change you will be able to gain their respect and admiration. If you dream that you are in contempt of court then it indicates that you have made an indiscretion in your social life that you need to apologize for.

CONVENT

Reflection and solitude. To dream that you are in a convent represents a wish to have some time to yourself for thought and reflection. It is an indication that perhaps events have been too hectic recently and you feel tired and drained.

CONVICTS

Escape. To dream of being a convict means that you are feeling tied down in a particular situation. The good news though is that this won't last for very long and soon you will be able to break free. If you dream that your partner is a convict then you are worried that they have not been as open as you would like regarding their past.

COOKING

Social state. Cooking in a dream represents how you feel about the current family situation. It indicates the growing and nurturing of a family and your satisfaction in that role.

COPYING

Repetition. If you dream you are standing by a photocopying machine then there is an aspect of your life that you feel is repetitive. The quality of the image on the photocopier will help you see how you clarify your responses to the nature of the repetition. A high-resolution colour copy denotes that the friendly environment more than compensates for the mundane nature of your work, but a poor black-and-white copy implies that everything about the environment is monotonous.

➠ *Photography*

CORKSCREW

Dissatisfaction with love life. If you dream about a corkscrew your dream is suggesting that you need to re-evaluate your relationship if you are in one, and if you are not then re-evaluate your attitude towards relationships. A broken corkscrew means that habits will lead to disastrous consequences. If the corkscrew breaks into the bottle it indicates that you should take aggressive action now to overcome your cravings, or the habit will break you.

CORN

Prosperity. To see a corn field in a dream indicates prosperity as long as the corn looks good. If you are a gardener or work in agriculture then this dream indicates a bumper harvest. For others it simply foretells that they will succeed in present undertakings. However, to see corn ready for baking indicates that you will have problems with people, but you should persevere because you will succeed in the end.

ABOVE: If you are conducting in your dream, you could soon display similar leadership qualities in your daily life.
FAR LEFT: Moses receives tablets of the ten commandments on Mount Sinai.
ABOVE LEFT: Compasses in dreams represent a need for new directions.

CORPSE

Sadness. Corpses in dreams bring disappointment. To see the corpse of your partner indicates that all is not well with the relationship. If you see the corpse of someone you know in a shop or your workplace in a dream this indicates a major problem at work.

CORSET

Confusion. If you dream of a corset it indicates that you are confused at the moment, particularly over the way that someone has been following your every move. If you are having difficulty removing or putting on

the corset then this is an indication that there will be quarrels with friends that will make you feel as though you are too tightly bound.

COT

Changes for the better. To dream of being in a cot signifies that events are going to changed for the better. Many cots in your dream indicate that you will have friends around to support you. However, if you dream of a rocking cradle, it indicates that someone is gossiping about you.

COUGH

Take care. If you are dreaming that you have a cough it can of course indicate that you have a sore throat. Often a cough in a dream is a warning to take care of your home possessions. There is a need to check your house insurance is up to date, as you could lose something through fire, water, wind, damage or burglary.

COUNTER

Financial issues. If you are not counter staff or a bank teller then dreaming of such things is an indication that you need to sort out financial issues. This may mean arranging a meeting with your bank manager. If you are in this line of work, however, your dream is merely a reflection of everyday anxieties.
➡ *Money*

COUNTRY

New opportunities. Visiting other countries in your dream represents new opportunities in both business and pleasure. Foreign people in dreams are seen as a good omen, suggesting that you will do well with overseas connections. You may not actually visit the country featured in your dream, but you will have an encounter with that country and its culture in some way. This dream implies the broadening of horizons and experiences.
➡ *Foreign Lands, Unknown Places*

COURTROOM

Optimism. Courts in dreams often relate to financial matters. There is a need to ensure that you are looking at long-term answers with regard to your life and not just short-term solutions. Courts indicate time and structure and that is what you have to focus on.

COUSIN

 Arguments. Cousins can indicate arguments, often over the matter of an inheritance. Dreaming that you are romantically involved with a cousin means that family arguments of a different nature are about to erupt.

COW

 Abundance. Dreaming of cows generally brings good news and success in abundance. The only

warning is if the cows are chasing you, or they are shown as lean and hungry, as that can indicate problems.
➠ *Horns*

COWSLIP

 Unlucky in love. Cowslips are an ill omen in love. Friendships seem to collapse at this time. This is not due to anything in particular you are doing; it is merely an indication that you are growing apart and need space from each other.

BELOW: Rousseau's Landscape With Cattle. *Cows in dreams are considered to be symbols of abundance.*
BOTTOM: A Sally Lightfoot Crab from the Galapagos Islands.
BELOW LEFT: Dreaming of a corset means that you are in a state of confusion.

CRAB

 Sideways negotiations. Crabs indicate that you have got to side-step someone before they overtake you. You will have to employ some tricky tactics to ensure that you come out the winner in the negotiations.

CRADLE *SEE* COT

CRANE

Focus on your ideals. Cranes are very faithful birds, so if a crane appears in your dream it means you are thinking about long-term commitments. Cranes are also able to balance on one leg, indicating that this is a time for you to focus on your future and bring balance into your life.

CREAM

Good fortune. Regardless of your occupation, dreaming of cream indicates that business is about to enter a prosperous period. It is especially good for businesses involving share-dealing or the stock market – here you will do exceptionally well.

CREMATION

 Trust in others. If you see your own cremation in your dream then you will be let down by another person – the augury being one of self-reliance as the only way to your success. To dream of another person's cremation indicates that you will receive some good news inheritance-wise. If you didn't know the person you will receive a windfall of an unexpected nature.

➡ *Fire, Priest*

CRICKET (*Insect*)

Listen to the inner voice. In Chinese mythology the crickets' sound is one of cheering you along on

a journey. It is, however, also a sign to listen to your inner voice and trust your instincts to guide you, as your journey will be a hard one, fraught with pitfalls and surprises.

CRICKET (*Game*)

A long wait. To a certain extent dreaming of cricket will be influenced by how you feel about the game. If you are in a cricket team, and you win the match, you will feel that you have achieved something; the dream indicates a gathering of friends. If you lose, you are scared of letting your friends down. If you are watching the game, you need to relax at work, to avoid things getting on top of you.

CRIME

Change of circumstances. If you dream that you are a victim of a crime then it means a change for the better: you should receive something soon to boost your spirits. However, if you dream that you are committing the crime then it is a warning to hold your tongue or you could do a disservice to a friend by speaking out of turn.

CRIPPLED

Help where required. If you dream that someone is crippled then it indicates that you will be called upon to help someone out. If you are crippled in your dream then you will receive the help that you need shortly.

CROCODILE

Caution required. If the crocodile does not move but just looks at you, it indicates that you have an untrustworthy friend. It is a message to stand your ground. If the crocodile chases or injures you, then you will lose out, but if you escaped, or killed the crocodile, then you will win through the efforts of your own tenacity and diligence.

CROCKERY

Domestic happiness. China indicates happiness in domestic circles. If it is broken, though, then it can indicate problems in the home that need to be sorted out, particularly issues relating to paternity and family trees.

CROSSROADS

Decisions to be made. If you dream of a crossroads it literally means that you have reached a crossroads in your life. It is time to think carefully about decisions that you need to make and what direction you go in next. This can be a time of major change and turning points so you need to think and reflect deeply on any decisions before you race off in any one direction.

⮕ *Compass, Mercury, Signpost*

CROW

Time to turn ambitions into physical reality. To hear crows cawing indicates that you need to attend to your aspirations and begin to act upon them now. In dreams a crow gives you magical insight and ability to see into future realities. Be warned though, as a crow flying or circling represents being stuck in a situation through fear of the future changes.

CROWD

Energy. A crowd – providing it is not unruly – brings energy and hope in a dream. The crowd supports you and allows you to take friends to task. It indicates new outdoor opportunities for you.

CRUST

Hard work. If you dream of eating the crust off the bread it implies that you will have your work cut out over a particular issue, and much of the problem will

BELOW: Picasso's Weeping Woman *in your dreams could signify good news.*
BELOW LEFT: Did this Medici family plate bring domestic happiness?
LEFT: A Great Green Bush Cricket, urging you to listen to your inner voice.

be because you may have been careless in the past, causing you to work much harder to make up for this mistake.

⮕ *Bread*

CRYING

Good news. Crying in a dream indicates that things will get better; if a baby is crying then good news is on its way. If the person crying in your dream is an adult, you will be called upon shortly to give help and advice.

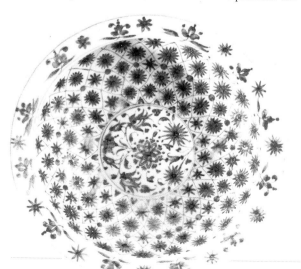

CUCKOO

A time of change. The cuckoo is known for laying its eggs in another bird's nest and therefore indicates that you have a problem that someone else has given you. Traditionally, a woman on hearing a cuckoo in her dream was able to tell when she would get married, depending on how many times the cuckoo called: each 'cuckoo' call represented one year. For a man to see cuckoos means that a love affair or marriage is in urgent need of repair or reform if it is to be salvaged. To hear a cuckoo clock indicates a time to spruce up the house.

➦ *Egg*

CUCUMBERS

Illness and financial issues. To dream of eating cucumbers is a sign that you have been ill recently but that you are now on the mend. If you dream of serving cucumbers then you need to watch out for financial mistakes otherwise you could find yourself running over your budget.

➦ *Eating*

CUFFLINKS

Opportunities to impress. If you are a man and you dream of wearing cufflinks then it indicates a job opportunity for you, where you will have the chance to impress. If the cufflinks are decorated – the decoration may add more insight to your dream – you will do well in an interview and will have plenty of confidence.

CUNNING

Friendship. If you are behaving in a very cunning manner in your dream it indicates that you will do well in a social get-together that is being arranged. However, if someone else is being cunning then you need to watch out because a friend or business acquaintance is trying to deceive you.

CUPBOARD

Money issues. An empty cupboard is a warning to be careful of extravagance otherwise you could find yourself in serious financial trouble. A full cupboard indicates a family get-together and an enjoyable time.

CURTAINS

Obstacles. Curtains in dreams represent obstacles and dealings hidden from view. If you are able to open the curtains then it indicates that you will solve the problem. Closed curtains imply that it may be best to leave things alone for the time being; do not indulge any confidence to anyone until the unseen dangers have passed.

CUSHIONS

Selfish. To dream of lying on cushions indicates that you could be acting against others' interests. To dream of making cushions suggests a forthcoming marriage. Damaged or ripped cushions imply small returns from a great effort in a long-term project.

CUSTARD

Guests. If you dream of making or eating custard then it is an indication that you will have to get the spare bedroom ready as you will be entertaining unexpected guests in a few days' time.

CUTLERY

Domestic arguments. Dreaming of cutlery is a warning not to be impulsive and not react to quickly to what others might say. A dream such as this indicates arguments around the home.

CYCLONE

Warning. If a cyclone or hurricane appears in your dream it is a warning to sit tight and not do anything for the time being. To rush into things now would jeopardize plans, while waiting will remove the present dangers causing the impasse. If you follow this advice your patience will be rewarded by the presentation of the right opportunity for rapid success.

DAHLIA

Good fortune. To see dahlias in your dream brings the promise of good fortune and success. Romance

will blossom and you will gain new friends at this time. Financial matters are also improved and you may well find your salary is increased.

DAISY

If you dream of daisies out in the fields then this indicates a happy time, but if they are in a vase indoors or in a bunch, then it signifies a sadness connected to a relationship that is not going according to plan.

DAMSON

Richness. To dream of damsons is an indication that you are about to come into money. If you see birds eating damsons on the trees, it indicates that a romantic connection will usurp your resources. If you dream of making damson jam then it indicates that you will have a family gathering.

ABOVE: A cyclone provides a rude awakening for two Alabama women.
LEFT: If he dreams of the daisy he sits upon, this spider can expect happy times.
FAR LEFT: A dream involving cutlery can warn of domestic disagreements.

DEATH

Regeneration. Death in a dream does not literally mean 'death', but refers to the closing of one activity and the start of a new one. Often it means that there will be a complete change in your life, indicating the death of the past. You are going to give up all that you have now and go down a different avenue in life. So it's off with the old and on with the new.

➡ *Bereavement*

DANCE

Dancing symbolizes transformation. People nowadays still use dance as a way of communicating with the higher spirits, such as the Dervishes of Islam, or the Native Americans in their rain dances. To dance is our body's way of trying to get in touch with our inner spirit. Dancing indicates joy and excitement at new prospects; it also represents a sexual awakening, indicating that romance is in the air.

DATE

Commerce. Dates in dreams can indicate financial transactions. It is better to see them on a tree as the transactions will continue to flourish and sprout new business. If you dream of eating dates, it indicates that a marriage proposal could result from a business-related transaction.

DAUGHTER

Support required. A mother dreaming of her daughter indicates a forthcoming argument, whereas a father dreaming of his daughter is more likely to find himself sorting out an emotional entanglement from which the daughter wishes to extricate herself.

➡ *Father, Mother*

ABOVE: These dancing Ballet Russes costume designs indicate transformation.
ABOVE RIGHT: Death in a dream is positive and represent new beginnings.
RIGHT: A picturesque desert, symbolizing a successful outcome to a problem.

DECORATING

Fertility. If you dream of decorating a house it is a symptom of nest-building and indicates that you are content in your relationship and could be planning on having children. To decorate the outside of your home means that celebrations are around the corner, of which you will be the focal point.

DEER

Relationship issues. Deer in dreams can signify relationships. If the deer appear in their natural surroundings in your dream, all is going well for you. If the deer are in a zoo or an unusual environment, this dream acts as a warning that someone around you should not be trusted; their intentions are loaded with conditions.

DEFORMED BIRTH

Sort yourself out. If you have dreamt of a deformed birth, it indicates that all will be well in the future, but there are issues at home that need to be sorted out: someone is undermining your position and this needs to be sorted out.

➡ *Childbirth*

DEMAND

Embarrassment. If you receive a demand, it indicates that you are embarrassed by circumstances around you, usually financial. If the demand is from a partner then it indicates that you have been treating them unfairly lately.

➡ *Money*

DESERT

If picturesque, dreaming of a desert can indicate a successful outcome to a problem. If a sand storm is brewing then it indicates many small obstacles that will cloud your judgement, hinting that by facing these you will ultimately succeed through sheer perseverance.

➡ *Camel*

DESK

Effort required. To see a desk means that you have your work cut out to achieve your goals on time. If the desk is small and the pile of work on it large then it implies that you need to cut to the chase before time runs out. If the desk is large and the pile comfortably organized, then you have time to mull over the finer details.

DESTRUCTION (OF HOME)

Dissatisfaction. If you feel that your home is under threat then it indicates that you are not happy with the home life. If you fear violence in your dream then it is an indication that your family life needs to be looked into fast and seriously. It is important that you do not act impulsively but that you do act quickly.

➡ *Mouse, Bug*

DETECTIVE

Resolution. If you dream that you are a detective then it indicates that you are trying to resolve a situation. If you dream that you have a detective on your tail but you are innocent then it means that someone is trying to get in touch with you in order to give you welcome news. However, if you have just committed the crime of the century and dream of a detective chasing you then your guilt is showing through and you will be discovered regarding the crime that you have committed.

DEVASTATION

 Control your temper. To dream of devastation and the ruin of others means that you need to curb your temper. If you do so you will settle any arguments and all will be well. Otherwise you could lose your friends and your liberty. To see the devastation of a building suggests that you need to urgently re-evaluate your skills and abilities, as your foundations may not be as solid as you believe they are.

DEW

Expectation. To dream of dew on the ground indicates that you have good foundations in your

current relationship, and this will lead to a more secure and long-term footing. Engagements and marriage could well be in the offing at some point.

DIAMOND

A girl's best friend. Giving or receiving diamonds in a dream is a sign of commitment to a relationship and symbolizes your desire to settle down with that person.

DICE

A gamble in life. For a woman this implies a romantic gamble but there are many risks and dangers attached. Think again is the message of this dream, especially if the pips show very low numbers. For a man it implies gambles in large business ventures. But, unless you threw sixes, this a dream of great loss to you personally. To throw winning streaks in a dream indicates a large windfall but not significant enough in size to change your lifestyle.

DICTIONARY

Say what you mean. If you see a dictionary in your dream it means that you are not explaining yourself properly to others; the consequent confusion could result in the loss of an important friend. You may also need to tone down what you are saying to avoid arguments.

DILIGENCE

Fear of failure. To dream of working hard reflects a fear of failure. You are about to be tested and you need to make sure you have all the resources available to put in the time and effort required.
➡ *College, Examination, School, University*

DIRT

Forewarning. If you dream of walking on dirt then it is an indication that you may need to change location soon. If dirt is thrown at you then someone is using gossip or information from the past to get at you and cause problems for you.

DISEASE

Good health. Although it does depend on the type of disease, generally disease in dreams signifies good news, as it indicates that things will work out for you or the person with the disease. This dream may mean that you are going to fall ill, but if this is the case the illness tends to be mild. The exception are dreams about venereal diseases, which are a warning that your lifestyle needs to be considered.

DISGRACE

Love issues. Fearing disgrace in a dream is more often than not related to love affairs. It is a fear that you will do something that will upset others or someone in the family. Treat it as an issue that can be looked at when you are awake to see how much of a worry it actually is. Most of the time you will find that you have worried over nothing.

➠ *Failure*

DIVING

Establishing your feelings. Diving into water in a dream is a way of diving into your emotions. The clearer the water, the clearer your feelings. If the waters seem murky, and you are unsure of yourself, this indicates emotional distress at the moment. If the water is clear, then you are diving into a situation that will bring you

ABOVE: Unsurprisingly, dice in your dreams indicate gambling.
LEFT: The giving and receiving of diamonds represents commitment.
ABOVE LEFT: Dew on the ground refers to the dreamer's relationship.

happiness and an enjoyable sense of stillness as you ponder and rediscover yourself.

➠ *Swimming, Water*

DIVORCE

If you are single or have just embarked upon a relationship when you dream of divorce, this indicates that you are not ready for this relationship and it will break up before it has even got off the ground. If you are married, this dream suggests that the marriage is stable and you have nothing to fear.

➠ *Lawsuit*

DOCTORS

Improvement. Generally seeing a doctor in your dreams is good news, as it means that your health is improving. The part of you that the doctor is examining will lead to further clues in your dreams. The only proviso here is if the doctor is taking blood from you which could be an indication that you are about to lose some money.

➠ *Hospital*

DOG

A man's best friend. Just like the saying, a dog in your dream can indicate a best friend, as dogs are loyal and do not question your judgement, sticking by

you at all times. You do have to watch out for the tone of the dream however; if the dog snarls or is otherwise unfriendly in the dream, a problem exists between you and a friend.

If the dog barks at you, this is a warning that you are about to do something foolish. If you see two dogs fighting together then you will interrupt an argument between two friends. If you are being protected by the dog, then you will be protected by a friend; if you are left unprotected then a friend will let you down.

The type of dog in your dream indicates the nature of the friend; a sleek sporty person will be seen perhaps as a greyhound. It is often said that dogs look like their owners and this is also true regarding your dreams, where the dog may take on the characteristics and bear a facial resemblance to your friend.

DOME

Recognition. Seeing a dome in a dream means that someone is about to honour you because of your commitment to an event. It may have taken a long time to come about but it will be worth it in the end.

DOMINOES

Caution advised. If you dream of seeing dominoes but do not actually play the game in your dream, you should be cautious; any purchases that you wanted to make should be delayed. If you are actually playing with the dominoes, it indicates that you have already taken a risky gamble, in which case it is time to retreat, as you are not going to win.

DONKEY

Attitude in relationships. The donkey in a dream tends to be closely related to any sexual relationship you may be having. If you are riding the donkey, or if the donkey seems peaceful, then there is no problem in the relationship. If it is refusing to move then something is

not quite right and one of you may be uncomfortable with the relationship. If the donkey is braying then beware that a secret will be let out into the open.

DOOR

Regrets and opportunities. Closed doors in dreams represent lost opportunities. Open doors suggest new opportunities which may be worth investigating as they have the potential to yield the highest rewards for you. Going through multiple doors in your dream indicates that you will experience a series of opportunities. Strangely, though, a door that creaks implies that an old opportunity simply needs to be reworked and soon you will be able to head successfully on into the future.

DOORBELL

News. Someone ringing your doorbell is bringing you news of an opportunity. If you dream of ringing someone else's bell then it indicates that you are about to take them some important news.

DOVE

A symbol of peace. In the bible a dove brought back an olive branch to Noah, and that symbol today is used as a sign of peace. Therefore, a dove in a dream represents peaceful times ahead. Also white doves mean an end to quarrels – whilst a flock of doves suggests reunion with a very old friend, perhaps involving reconciliation.

DRAGON

Energy. Dragons in dreams are a potent symbol of what lies ahead. They frequently indicate help in career choices and situations, as they can give rewards for effort. A dragon can also represent an influential person who will be instrumental in your success.

DRAMA

Boredom. If you dream of watching your favourite drama or soap opera then it means that you are unhappy with your current situation, suggesting possibly that you feel bored. This dream also warns that you could be about to take unnecessary risks to try and make your love life as spicy as (and with all the consequences of) the dramas that you watch.

➠ *Theatre*

ABOVE: Dreaming of a dragon could signify a reward for your efforts.
LEFT: This Joan Miro donkey seen in your dream would represent relationships.
FAR LEFT: A greyhound, which could represent a sporty friend.

DRAWING

Creative inspiration. To dream that you are drawing indicates that you are about to go through a period of creative inspiration. For further information, look at the object or the person that you are drawing and then look up the specific entry in this book. This dream also heralds a new phase in your imaginative prowess which will heighten and may even usher in an invention or creative idea of notable value. To see other drawings means you long to express your creativity but seek outlets of your imagination through others.

➡ *Architect, Artist, Carpenter*

DRESS

Putting on a new dress is indicative of an increase in social opportunities and may represent some upcoming parties. If the dress is very flamboyant it means that you are looking for a romantic involvement; however, you should be careful as you may attract the wrong sort of Romeo.

DRINK

Drinking cool water is considered a good omen, particularly if you are due to face exams, as it symbolizes refreshing the mind. If the water is dirty, though, it can mean illness is to follow. Drinking fizzy drinks such as cola indicates that events in your life will be moving fast. Milk gives energy and success to plans. Certain drinks are said to indicate romantic liaisons, but if you are drinking from the bottle in your dreams, this is unromantic and you will lose out in the relationship.

If you dream that you are drunk after having alcohol then that is good news, heralding financial gains, but if you dream that you are drunk after not drinking any alcoholic beverages, then you may wake up to some unexpected bills. Oddly enough though, if you dream that you are drunk in front of others it indicates that you will be honoured shortly.

DRIVING

Take your time. Roads mean journeys and suggest life decisions. However, if you are driving in your dream then you could be trying to push things too fast; it is also a warning against gambling. On the other hand if you are a passenger and someone is driving you then that is good news, bringing financial benefits and career advancement.

DROUGHT

Difficulties to overcome. To dream of a drought suggests that some difficult times lie ahead, but that the situation can be overcome with some careful preparation. This might mean putting some money aside for added security in the future.

➡ *Fire*

DROWNING

Emotional pain. If you dream of drowning it is because you have a fear of your emotions at the moment. This is a time when you have to look at relationships very closely. This dream also indicates that

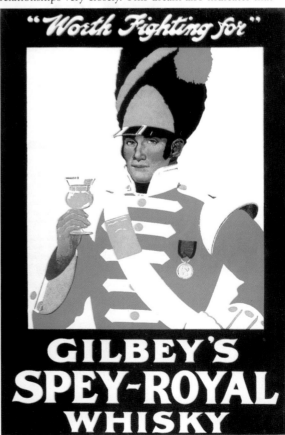

BELOW LEFT: Drinking alcohol in a dream can signify good news.
LEFT: An ancient terracotta musician playing a drum, from Equador.
BELOW: A sixth-century pavement mosaic of a duck.

DRUNKENNESS

Slow down. If you dream that you are drunk then it is an indication that you might be abusing your own body, not just with drink. This is a warning dream for you to get back on course and to prevent straying into overindulgence, for you will be found out – perhaps even prosecuted.

DUCK

A message is on its way. If you dream of seeing ducks in flight or walking towards you, a message is on its way to you by post or email. To see ducks swimming is good news regarding health, or if you have had health problems recently then you will see an improvement.

you feel emotionally vulnerable in business dealings. If you managed to save yourself or someone saves you then it is an indication that you will get the help you need to overcome the problems.
➠ *Water*

DRUGS

Stop drifting. To dream of taking recreational drugs indicates that you do not have a clear direction to go in and that you are trying to escape reality. It is also a warning that you are about to be led astray. If you are taking narcotics, this dream is simply reminding you of your situation.

DRUM

Success. To hear drums in your dreams indicates that successful news is on its way. Just as drums were used in Africa to carry messages before the advent of telephones, the drums now signify a message on its way to you.

DUNGEON

Trapped. You need to try and find a way to escape the situation, because at the moment you feel trapped by circumstances around you. If in your dream you managed to escape then the indications are that you will be able to resolve the problem.

DUNG

Dung represents problems. Problems need to be resolved quickly, before the dung hits the fan, as they say, and things could get worse if you do not resolve these problems. However, if you are already having problems and you dream about climbing to the top of a dung heap, then it means that there is a change for the better in store for you.

DWARF

Magical changes. A dwarf is generally lucky in a dream, as it means that the problems that you thought you had are not as large as they seemed and therefore will disappear. The only proviso here is if the dwarf is ugly, as this represents a false friend and distressing problems that could occur.

DYE

Change. Just as we are able to change the appearance of a cloth by dyeing it, in our dreams it means that we are about to change the appearance of our life. Changing a cloth to bright colours indicates a change for the better. Dyeing it golden indicates a financial benefit and dyeing it black means sorrow.

EAGLE

A spiritual vision. Eagles, particularly in Native American mythology, have a very important spiritual meaning, which may hark back to the Aztec god, Quetzalcoatl, who was half-eagle, half-serpent. The eagle is a sign of spiritual vision and the rebirth of ideas. If you have dreamt of an eagle it indicates that you will achieve your goals. The higher the eagle is in the sky, the higher your prosperity and position.

EAR

Listen. An ear in a dream indicates the need for listening. If an ear plays a prominent part in a dream it means that you are not listening to someone and this is likely to cause you problems. If you dream of many ears then it can indicate that you are fearful of others overhearing you and finding out about your problems. If you get earache in a dream then the dream is a warning to get your ears checked out.

➟ *Jewellery, Pain*

EARTHQUAKE

Change. If you live in an area subject to earthquakes then such a dream can act as a warning to prepare you for minor difficulties. However, if you do not live in an earthquake area then the indication is far more cataclysmic, as it suggests profound changes in your life and the need for major adjustments. These changes will be brought about by circumstances beyond your control. If your response to the earthquake in the dream is fear then you will prosper. Neighbourhood losses will reunite the community if you feel the presence of God in this dream.

EATING

Contentment. Generally, eating with a group of people is a dream of family contentment. However, if you dream that you are eating alone then it indicates that you have upset people around you. If you dream that your plate is taken away before you have finished what you were eating then it indicates that you have been thoughtless about those who work for you.

ECLIPSE

Worry. If you dream of an eclipse it can indicate that you are feeling unsure of yourself. An eclipse of the Moon is believed to refer to health issues which may need to be checked out. A solar eclipse tends to bring business problems that need to be sorted.
➠ *Moon, Sun*

EASTER

Fertility. To dream of Easter brings thoughts of fertility and spring. There will shortly be news of a pregnancy in your family or some other change.

ECSTASY

Unfulfilled. To dream of ecstasy can indicate that your sex life is suffering at the moment and you feel that your routine is boring. This is perhaps a time to talk things over with your partner and consider what can be resolved. If you are single this dream indicates a need to make the effort to socialize and get out and meet new people.

EGG

A symbol of fertility. Dreaming of eggs is often linked with fertility issues and can indicate gain and prosperity. Broken eggs, however, are a warning that your dreams may be shattered. If you dream of eating eggs, it can mean your body is telling you that you may need to consider your diet and nutritional intake. Eating raw eggs suggests that you should allow further incubation and contemplation of your ideas before you try them out.
➠ *Kitchen*

ELBOW SEE ARM

ELECTRICITY

 Energy in your life. Electricity in a dream represents the energy that is coming into your life. The brightness of the spark will dictate how quickly things will take off. If you dream of switching electricity on then it indicates the start of a new project. Equally, if you switch something off then it indicates the end of a project or relationship.

If you suffer a power failure then it means your task has stalled and you need to regroup before going forward. Depending on the severity of the situation this dream may well be asking you to consider whether you should cut your losses and move on to something else.

If you see bare wires or broken electrics of any sort then it is a warning to tread carefully – you need to re-evaluate the situation around you before going on. It may be that you will have to wait a while until the situation is resolved.

Getting an electric shock means that you are just about to get some unexpected news. In this sort of a dream the greater the shock, the more surprising and exciting the news.

ELEPHANT

A wise omen of the past. Elephants have always been associated with having long memories. An elephant is considered to be a wise and powerful omen

and when it appears in a dream it often signifies something or someone coming from the past that will be able to help you on your way.

ELIXIR

New pleasures. To dream of being given elixir or a tonic to pep you up means that you will have new energy soon. You also have the support of others and you will be able to get back on your feet soon.

ELOPEMENT

 Disappointment. If you dream that you have eloped with your partner then it signifies that your relationship will not stand the test of time. Likewise, to dream of encouraging another couple to elope will result in bitter recriminations.

EMBALMING

Status loss. To see yourself being embalmed in a dream indicates that there is going to be a sudden status change for the worse. There is a need to prepare for this and make sure that you have adjusted your lifestyle appropriately. To see yourself being embalmed indicates that your own involvements with those lacking in ethics and values equal to those that you are used to will result in disgrace through false friendships.

EMBRACE

Resolution. If you dream of embracing someone in your family it indicates that a recent quarrel will soon be resolved. Suddenly embracing someone at work or a stranger in your dream should be taken as a warning against being impulsive.

EMERALD

To see emeralds in a dream indicates that you will come into property and is a sign of good fortune. Emeralds also indicate honesty in friendship and promote growth in all relationship matters. Investment in Asian-based industries and commercial enterprises should do well for you over the next few months.

EMPLOYER

If your employer appears in your dream then he or she is trying to tell you something at work. The mood in the dream will reveal what they have to say to you, but it is important to ensure that all work is up to date.
➠ *Anxiety, Learning, Work,*

EMPLOYMENT

Unemployment. To dream you are happily employed could mean that things are about to change and unemployment looms for you. To dream of giving employment to others means that you could find that someone else gets the job that you were after.
➠ *Work*

BELOW: A brooch made with emeralds, a symbol of good fortune.
BELOW LEFT: Raja Sarup Singh on a boar-shooting expedition (detail).
BELOW FAR LEFT: Electricity in a dream signifies the dreamer's energy.

ENCHANTMENT

Time-wasting. If you dream that you have been enchanted by someone then this is a warning that someone is exerting too great an influence over you. This can mean that you have been detracted from the things you should be doing and suggests that it is time to get back on track and move on.

ENCYCLOPEDIA

New things to do. When you see an encyclopaedia in your dream it indicates a desire to break free from your current routine and do something new. This may perhaps mean giving up your job and embarking on a less lucrative but more rewarding career.
➠ *Blackboard, Books, Chalk*

ENEMY

Friends. To dream of enemies means that you are about to discover your true friends who will rally round and support you in your endeavours. If you are perpetrating hostility towards another then this dream is a warning to hold back as there is a great deal of missing information that will later reveal itself, showing that your friends are indeed loyal.

➥ *Destruction, individual feelings: Anger, Fear, etc.*

ENGAGEMENT

Problems. To dream of engagement often brings problems. If a young couple dream of an engagement then it can indicate a belief in the relationship that is too idealistic and that it cannot live up to. A mother dreaming of a son or daughter's engagement fears the loss of her children from the home and her control. If you dream of an engagement ring then it can indicate a wedding plan.

➥ *Diamond, Gold*

ENGINE

Friends to aid you. To dream of an engine – regardless of the type of vehicle it drives – signifies that there are many friends around you who will help in times of trouble. A disabled engine may bring misfortune and illness for someone close to you, or it may be simply your subconscious telling you that you have left the car lights on and are in danger of draining the battery.

ENGINEER

A person to aid you. To dream of an engineer means that you will need and receive the help of someone soon.

➥ *Engine*

ENTERTAINMENT

Good news is on its way, as watching entertainment is seen as a time of pleasure. If you are the one providing the entertainment it may mean that you have the responsibility of organizing all the elements that will host pleasurable activities for others.

➥ *Acting, Television, Theatre*

ENVELOPE

Concealed message. Receiving a letter is a direct message from your subconscious or from someone trying to communicate with you, but if you just see an envelope, it signifies that there are obstacles to be overcome before a situation can be resolved. An open envelope indicates that the problems will be easier to deal with than you think.

ERRANDS

An obstacle. If you run an errand in a dream it means that you have an obstacle to face. How successful you are in the errand will influence the actual obstacles you face in real life and your success in negotiating them.

ESCAPE

Obstacles. A common dream indicating that you will encounter obstacles that you must try to overcome. If you escape from prison then it indicates

BELOW: Watching entertainment, such as in this theatre, is a sign of good news.
BOTTOM: An exploding shell in 1916, a questionable symbol of improvement.
LEFT: An engine in your dream indicates that you have many good friends.

encapsulates your anxiety about them. If you do not have an exam coming up, however, it suggests that you are about to be tested: whether you pass or fail will indicate how successful you will be in dealing with this trial. Failing can simply be a warning that you are overstretching yourself, while success means you will face the obstacle without difficulty.

➡ *Diligence, Fear*

EXCHANGE

Negotiations. If you dream that you are exchanging money, this can mean an unexpected trip abroad. However, if you are dreaming of exchanging documents or other objects then this can represent business meetings and difficult negotiations.

EXCREMENT

Material gain. Although this dream is not the most pleasant one in the world, it does in fact represent material and commercial success. This is particularly true if a new venture is based on something from the past: you are now in a position to reap the rewards.

that you are feeling confined and trying to get out of a situation. Escaping from disasters like fires etc. indicates an anxious transformation with a successful outcome. Escaping from water means escaping from an emotional involvement. Escaping from animals represents escaping from people who are holding you down.

EXAMINATION

Fear of failure. To dream that you are taking an exam symbolizes a fear of failure. If you have exams coming up this is a common dream and simply

EXPLOSION

Improvements. Explosions in your dreams indicate that you are about to go through an explosive time, although changes for the better will be made. It is also a time to pay attention to business decisions that need to be made: make sure that you get the best possible deal.

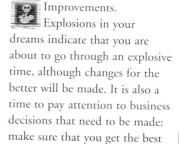

EYES

Look around you. Eyes in dreams mean that you may not be looking at things in the right way. The eyes also represent our soul. If you just see eyes in your dream and nothing else it represents a change for the better. To get something stuck in your eye is a warning that someone is out to injure your business interests. The colour of eyes is also said to be indicative of meaning. Brown eyes mean a new passionate affair but also that someone could deceive you. Blue eyes indicate a new friendship but they may also let you down. If someone has very bushy eyebrows then it indicates surprise, while thin eyebrows mean that there is someone that you should be careful of trusting. A fear of going blind means that you are unwilling to change your mind over something, even though you know you should, but feel that you cannot give in. Long beautiful eyelashes mean a new and exciting love affair, but do not trust someone with no eyelashes, otherwise scandal is sure to follow. Someone who keeps twitching indicates that they are hiding the truth from you.

➡ *Beauty*

FACE

Faces in dreams have a message and if the face is smiling then things are going to be good. However, if grotesque then a business loss is possible. Looking in the mirror at your face denotes that you are not entirely happy with the way you have acted recently. A luxuriant beard on a man represents new business opportunities. On a woman it brings unfortunate business dealings. A person wearing a grey beard, however, indicates that you will lose out in a quarrel with someone. To see a beard being shaven off indicates that you may lose out on a property deal. If a woman dreams of a beard on a man it is a very good omen and indicates that she will meet someone soon: if he is young she should be wary of his intentions.

Moustaches indicate that you must not let a small problem get the better of you. To shave off a moustache indicates a one-night-stand relationship that has not worked out.

To see your own nose in a dream indicates that you are feeling happy. To touch another person's nose or to have your nose touched indicates a romantic opportunity; however, a blocked nose indicates financial problems. Though dreaming of a cold nose may mean that you are preparing for a bout of flu or a cold. Lips in dreams represent relationships and the fuller and sweeter-looking the lips the better. If they are thin and cruel it means that there are miserly tendencies.

➡ *Beauty*

FAILURE

Work hard. Dreaming of failure is your mind's way of telling you to keep on working at a project. If you stick at it then you will succeed; you just need to put more energy into the situation. Regardless of whether this situation is to do with love or business, change your attitude, put the effort in and you will be rewarded.

➡ *Examination*

FAIRIES

Granted wishes. To see a fairy in a dream means that you are about to be successful in something that you have planned. You will find that others are favourable to your ideas and will help you out as much as possible.

FALCON

A symbol of honour. The falcon indicates that you will receive a message which will bring you prestige and honour; perhaps you will be honoured with an award or medal, or perhaps honoured publicly and gain an increase in your stature through recognition, possibly involving a promotion.

FALLING

Fear of failure. Falling in a dream is very common and represents a multitude of different fears, including fear of failing at business and sex, and also having to endure a lack of respect. The type of fall you experience in your dream determines the outcome. If you fall a long distance then the changes you make in your life will take a lot of effort to go forward. On the other hand, if you fall a short distance then you will be able to get over the setback quickly. If you are walking and you fall over in the company of others, then their friendship is not to be trusted. To fall into water can represent financial stress, but to see others fall means that you will win the day.

FAME

Be realistic. To dream of fame is quite common and represents a fantasy rather anything based in reality. This dream is therefore reminding you to make sure that you are setting realistic aims. If you dream of meeting someone that is famous this means that you should persevere in your endeavours, for you will get help from an unexpected source very soon.
➡ *Celebrity*

FAMILY

Unity. Dreaming of the family as a whole can mean many things, and interpretations of the dream depend upon the expressions on the faces of its individual's members. If they are largely happy and smiling, it suggests that all is harmonious in the family at the time.

FAMINE

Troubled times are expected. If you dream of a famine then it suggests that tough times are ahead financially. This is a warning dream, hinting that the time is right for cutting back on your expenses and trying to save some money.

FAMISHED

Hungry for something new. It is possible that in this dream your body is telling you that you are hungry – particularly if you went to sleep without having eaten for a while. As an omen, this dream is informing you that you are not entirely happy with the way things are going in life at the moment.

BELOW: The Fall of Icarus – his fear of failure would have been well-founded.
BELOW LEFT: Louis Coulon's 3.3m beard: a good omen to a lady dreamer.
LEFT: The lapis lazuli eyes of this funerary mask could symbolize new friends.

FARM

 Farms represent the Earth. If you dream that you are on a farm, or are a farmer, this indicates that you have an understanding of nature and the Earth. Also, a project that you are working on will bear fruit if you are patient and give the time needed for your plans to grow.

FARMHOUSE

Prosperity. Dreaming of a farmhouse is an indication that you will be prosperous in your work. The image of the farmhouse shows that hard work will bring its rewards and though it may take a while, and you will continue to have to work at it, you will be successful and comfortable in the end.

FATHER

Support. A son dreaming of his father is in need of advice in business and finance, as his work may be experiencing financial difficulties. A daughter dreaming of her father is in need of help in an emotional matter and wants her father to either approve of her current relationship or help her sort it out.

➡ *Daughter, Son*

work out a resolution so that when you experience the situation in real life you will be able to face it without fear. To dream of sorting out your fears means that you will overcome the obstacles.

FEATHER

A gift from someone. In dreams a feather is considered to be a gift and it represents the quality of the person or bird giving it to you. The feather is given as a gift to help you on your way.

FENCE

Obstacles. Fences to climb over represent obstacles. They can also symbolize the barriers we put up to prevent other people getting to know us. Just as we fence our home off from others, this dream suggests that you may be putting up obstacles to others to avoid having to get to know them on a deeper level.

FATIGUE

Relax. If you feel fatigued in a dream it actually means that you will be able to relax a bit more in the coming weeks. Financial issues will dissipate a bit and you will find that you are able to recoup and enjoy life a little more.

FEAR

Conquering problems. Fear in a dream is a way of playing out a scenario; in this way you are able to

FERN

Ferns in their natural surroundings are seen as a positive influence in a dream, but if they are all dried up, or indoors in a flowerpot, then a misunderstanding with another person could lead to major problems at both work and home.

ABOVE: Lattice fence and peacock from a Roman fresco of a garden scene.
LEFT: Feathers, symbols of support, make up this headress which is said to have belonged to Montezuma (1466-1520), the last king of the Aztecs.

FIDDLE

Harmony. This barnyard instrument lights up the atmosphere with merriment, warming up the hearts of those who hear its musical treats. To dream of playing a fiddle indicates a happy and joyous gathering of close friends and family. This dream particularly favours events abroad involving the reunion of family members and long lost friends.

FIELD

The way ahead. If you see a field in your dreams it means that the world is your oyster. Even if you feel lost now you are certain to succeed; you have just got to set yourself a target and go for it.

➠ *Harvest*

FIG

Embarrassment. If you dream of figs it may mean that you need to pay attention to what you say or do, as you may be in a situation where something you say could backfire leading to a public apology for your words or actions.

FERRET

Ferrets represent ideals. If you dream of ferrets then it indicates that you would like to escape from the situation you are in. Perhaps you feel that you are destined for greater things in life. You will need to focus your mind on your work to find where you want to be in the future.

➠ *Hide, Hunting, Killing*

FIGHT

A decision. A fight in a dream means you are struggling with a decision that needs to be made. The outcome in your dream will have a bearing on the success of this decision. To lose the fight means loss of home; to emerge triumphant implies that you will overcome the opposition and win any legal matters pending. To see fighting among others means that you have squandered money, leaving you with a bad business reputation.

➠ *Gun*

FEVER

Anxiety. To dream of a fever indicates that you are worrying too much: what you are worrying about may never happen. In fact, in all probability you are entering a very exciting period of your life, full of action and activity.

ABOVE: A fight in your dream represents a decision to be made.
ABOVE RIGHT: Fireplaces can signify contentment both in dreams and in life.
RIGHT: Engraving of a firework display, along with the Orders of Architecture.

FILE

Put your life in order. If you dream of files it means that you may have some filing of your own to sort out. Finances and business can be difficult around this time. Such dreams can also signify unexpected interruptions in business which can leave you feeling out of control.

FIRE

Impending trouble. If you see fire in a dream it indicates trouble ahead. Problems will pursue you particularly if you are burnt by the fire in your dream. If you manage to put out the fire then you will be able to deal with the obstacles you face, even if they appear insurmountable to begin with. A fire also signifies strength and determination and so if the fire seems to be under control then it indicates that you have strength of purpose and will be able to deal with the problems that are facing you. Flames in a fire can provide a message of where the trouble will come from and you might be able to see pictures in the flames.

➠ *Tree, Cremation*

FIREPLACE

Contentment. A fire or fireplace in the home in normal circumstances can represent domestic bliss and happiness. However, if the home itself is on fire then this is a warning of brewing family trouble. Prepare for some domestic truths to be exposed. You will be acting the role of arbitrator, so consider only the facts and you will burn away the discontent.

FINGER

Indicates a direction. A finger pointing in a dream indicates where you are going, while a broken finger may indicate a need to retreat. If the finger is missing then legal problems are likely to appear very soon. A cut finger indicates that you have done something wrong.

Long fingernails in dreams mean that you have a problem communicating with the opposite sex, though it will also indicate that you are endowed with scholarly attributes. Dreaming of damaged or chewed nails is a warning that perhaps a health check is in order.

Sore thumbs in a dream indicate problems in business and; the larger the thumb is, the greater the difficulty will be to gain control of the business environment.

➠ *Jewellery*

FIREWORKS

Fireworks in your life. Fireworks can represent a celebration or passion in a new relationship. Also, this type of dream can mean that you will be involved in heated arguments with others. Much depends on the other issues within the dream.

FISH

Our subconscious mind. Water, and in particular the sea, represents our subconscious mind, therefore fish have a very important influence in our dreams and indicate our feelings, particularly with regard to new projects. If the fish are swimming in clear, open water then this is a strong indication of new prosperity. If the water is cloudy and polluted, then the project heralds emotional confusion. If you are fishing and you catch the fish, it means that you will have success in your current undertakings.

Like the fisherman who patiently waits to catch a fish, dreaming of fishing means that you may have to wait for success. However, your wait will be worth it. If you snare yourself on a fish hook in your dream, you are being warned against employing unscrupulous or deceptive tactics for the only person who will get ensnared with trouble is yourself.

If you dream frequently of being a fish, then it indicates that you prefer to use the subconscious part of your mind. You prefer to stay away from others; this dream suggests that you are trying to escape reality.

The species of fish that you see in your dream will have an influence on its meaning, for example; dolphins or porpoises mean you have fun exploring your inner subconscious mind, suggesting that you should do this more often to awaken your psychic and imaginative gifts.

Eels represent a problem that needs to be looked at, otherwise your 'dreams' will slip away from you. They also relate to aspects of love and may indicate the slipping away of a partner.

Goldfish on the other hand, whether swimming in a pond or a bowl, are seen as a lucky omen in finances, while herring are the opposite. Salmon and trout indicate that your social life will be elevated, while sardines indicate involvement with social circles that will undermine your stature and position.

Tropical fish indicate ephemeral pleasures, and that you can be scared of commitment.

Sharks denote other enemies: you had better watch out, as they are after you. Be particularly careful with sharks; they represent a strong financial adversary. If you are having difficulties with finances and mortgages etc then it will not be a surprise dreaming of (loan) sharks pursuing you through the seas.

If you see the fins from above the water in your dream, you should sort your finances out now, before the debts become too big to handle.

➥ *Angling, Colours, Sea, Water, Whale*

FISH MARKET

Prosperity in sales. Seeing a thriving fish market in your dreams indicates prosperity and reward. However, if the fish market smells, and looks decayed, with poor specimens of rotting fish, then it indicates lost opportunities through unscrupulous negotiations leading to financial losses.

FISH POND

Good times. As long as the pond is clean and well-stocked with fish, this dream indicates pleasurable times, even if you fall in. A muddy pond, on the other hand, can indicate problems and that you need to be wary of others.

FLEA

To be irritated by the actions of others. To dream of fleas in the night would indicate that you are annoyed by all the little problems that others are causing. If you see fleas on another person then it can indicate that you are annoyed with that person and that there could be a problem for you. On the positive side if you have pets, dreaming of fleas can also be your mind's internal warning system, telling you it is time to make sure your animals get treatment against fleas.

FLEET

Decision changes. To see a fleet of ships or aeroplanes indicates that you need to make some changes to your business plans. If you dream of a fleet of aeroplanes then an immediate decision has to be made. This could also be an augury of pending war on the horizon in foreign countries.

FLOOD

Emotional obstacles. Dreaming of a flood is indicative of emotional issues that need to be sorted out. If the flood is gentle, not above knee height, and quickly recedes then your problems will be easily

solved. If the water is muddy and the flood chest-height then it indicates the problem will be harder to resolve. If you are swept away in the flood, this suggests that a person is using you for their own their own emotional selfish needs.

FLOUR

Domestic contentment. To dream of buying flour indicates that you may be feeling under the weather, but if you are baking flour then it suggests domestic happiness and contentment, perhaps that you are preparing for a family get-together. If someone else is baking or preparing flour then it implies that you will be visiting a member of your family.
➠ *Bread*

FLOWER

Good fortune. To see flowers in your dream generally brings the promise of good fortune and especially romance. Flowers wilting indicate a relationship dying. In business dealings it is a warning not to be over confident. Artificial flowers mean that you could be acting against your own beliefs and you need to think carefully about your motives, unless of course you suffer from hay fever when this dream indicates that maybe you are being over-cautious in a situation.

ABOVE: Seeing flowers in your dream symbolizes romance and good fortune.
LEFT: Floods, like Giuseppini's Deluge, reflect the dreamer's emotional issues.
FAR LEFT: Tropical fish such as the Royal Tang represent ephemeral pleasures.

FLUTE

Domestic issues. To hear a flute being played in your dreams means that you are happy with your domestic arrangements. However, if you are playing the flute, this means that you could be involved in an embarrassing situation.

FLY

Flies are enemies. If flies appear in your dream, as well as representing disease and infection, they can also mean that enemies are gathering around you. They are generally weak and jealous, but if you defeat them in your dreams then you will defeat them in life.

➡ *Annoyance*

FLYING

New experiences. Flying in a dream is very common; it represents our ambitions and indicates a need for new experiences. If you are flying at a great height then it signifies the achievement of your ambitions. Flying upwards indicates that you are rising up to reach your target, whereas descending may indicate that you need to re-appraise your goals.

If you believe that you are pedalling upwards then it indicates that hard work is required to achieve your goals. If you have wings then there are people to support you on the way and you will find a much smoother ascent to your ambitions.

If you dream of being shot at while flying it indicates that someone else could be working against your interests. If you fly over buildings in your dreams it indicates that you have ambition to progress in your work or change jobs. Flying over water suggests the desire for a new sexual relationship and this sort of dream is often at the start of a new relationship.

Just floating means that you are content and want to sit back and enjoy life as it is now. Flying into space indicates that you wish to have some time to reflect on your emotional situation and that although things are going well you need to think about long-term objectives.

FOAL

A new project. To dream of a foal indicates that you are about to start a new project which will be successful.

➡ *Horse*

FOG

Problems. To see fog in your dreams means that there is a problem in your life. If the fog is at sea or seems to be coming off the sea, this indicates that you have an emotional problem to sort out. If it is foggy on land, this indicates problems at work. If the fog clears or you hear a foghorn then it indicates that the problem will disappear in the course of time time.

FOOT

Journeys and obstacles through life. If you have an itch in your foot in your dream then you are about to go on a journey. If your feet are just painful then it means that you have family problems. If you imagine your feet are on fire or burning, then someone is jealous of you and is out to cause you problems. Cold feet mean that you are having reservations about a relationship.

If you look down upon your feet in your dream and they are not your own then it means that you will soon have new friends. If someone steps on your feet then there is gossip around you. If you dream that your feet are covered in mud, then a financial opportunity will arise, but you need to be careful that others do not take advantage of you.

If your foot was broken in your dream then it would indicate that your financial loss was caused by your own carelessness. Seeing lots of feet in a dream means that finances really need to be sorted out quickly and the dream is letting you know that you should do something about it. If you kiss someone else's feet then it indicates that you will have to gain a sense of humility in your dealings.

The worst dream to have of feet is when they are suddenly very swollen, as this implies a scandal is near. Divorce is also associated with swollen feet.

To dream that you have three or more feet implies that you may lose the use of one foot unless you are careful. It also means that you will be in charge of many people.

To see men and women dancing barefoot signifies new friendships and happiness. If the music is not to your taste then it would indicate that the friendships would be from a new circle of friends.

FOOTBALL

A windfall expected. To dream of playing football is generally good news as it signifies the possibility of a financial gain. However, to be stuck on the reserves bench means that you need to be choosier with friends.

FOREIGN LANDS

A need for a break. If you dream that you are in a foreign country then it is an indication that you have aspirations towards new adventures. This dream tells you to persevere and you will achieve your wishes, although you need to make sure that you take it at a gentle pace. To meet someone foreign in your dreams is always considered to be a fortunate omen.

FOREST

Obstacles and opportunities. The meaning of the forest will depend very much on the situation. If you are alone in the forest then someone will let you down. Hiding or being lost in a forest indicates obstacles that you must accept and face to be able to proceed; you may have to undertake a long journey to resolve the issue. On the other hand if you feel that you are enjoying the forest walk then it can indicate that you will gain status and fame.

➠ *Tree*

FOX

Foxes represent guile. Cunning is a word we often associate with foxes, and in dreams it means that you have to show the skills of the fox in your current situation. Vixens represent women with vixen-like traits.

➠ *Hounds*

FRECKLES

To dream of seeing freckles on a person, particularly if they are of the opposite sex, indicates strong sexual attraction; though for a woman to see them it may mean that she has a rival in love. In other situations it shows an embarrassment in some areas of your social life.

LEFT: A Thai wooden statue of a flute player. A flute played in your dreams indicates domestic satisfaction, although if you are playing the flute yourself it may indicate that you will have to endure an embarrassing situation.

FRIDGE

Coldness. If your dream includes a fridge, it is a representation of how you feel at the moment and may reflect a coldness felt towards your partner. That is, providing the blankets have not fallen off you in your sleep.

FRIENDSHIP

Friendships in a dream reflect real-life friendships and indicate a happy and active social time to come. New friends in dreams often represent a new circle of friends rather than a particular person and might symbolize a new interest that will be taken up or a club that you will join.

FRIGHTENED

Success. Being frightened in dreams is about learning to cope with the situation. As you overcome the situation you will not be frightened anymore. A successful outcome is assured and your fears are nothing to get worried about. If you dream of frightening someone else then you may get an unexpected fright yourself from an unexpected source.

FROG

Frogs indicate success. Frogs are lucky in dreams as they represent luck in life and love. In a love situation frogs can indicate a long and happy relationship. The frog lives on land and water, which means that you are able to adapt easily to the situations around you.

FRYING

Problems in love. If you dream that you are frying then it indicates that there are issues in a relationship that need to be resolved before they become too intense. There may also be another possible relationship on the horizon, but you must be careful here not to jump from the frying pan into the fire.

FUNERAL

Change. To see a funeral, or even your own funeral, means that you are very worried and stress is at a high level. However, things are going to change for the better very soon. Like death dreams a funeral dream means that you are going to be able to leave past problems behind.

FURNACE

A hot furnace in your dream is a good omen and if it is burning brightly this will add to your luck. If the furnace is standing cold or is poorly lit then this can indicate problems with your children. If you fall into the furnace in your dream then business problems are likely to come your way.

FURNITURE

Home issues. Furniture in a dream represents the home and the state of the furniture will reflect the state of your relationship within the home. If you dream of newer furniture than you have then it indicates that finances are about to improve. If the furniture looks shabby then it can be a warning against being frivolous with your expenditure. If you are surrounded by antique furniture then the dream is suggesting that you are happy with your relationship, though if it is in need of repair it indicates that you are not happy but that you feel there is nothing you can do about the situation. Bookcases indicate that you share a desire for knowledge. If you dream of looking around furniture shops then it indicates that there will be some adjustments in your life that you are uncertain about.

FURS

Prosperity. If you dream of dealing with or wearing furs then it indicates that you will do well financially. It is also a warning, however, that you should not get involved with arguments at the moment as you may not win. The type of animal that the fur once belonged to gives some insight into the nature of the argument.

GALLERY

Contentment is on its way. To dream you are wandering through an art gallery means that a period of peace and contentment will soon be with you, which will help you to relax. The pictures you view in your dream will give you an insight into the areas of your life that you need to escape from. However, if you are involved in the visual arts, or are in the process of investigating a creative idea, this dream strongly implies that the artists that you are drawn to in the gallery will hold the key to your creative unfolding and even direction. Therefore, seek further information on the artists under review.

GAMES

Achievement. Games in general signify hope and expectation of achievement. Solitary games, such as chess, indicate that you have to be responsible for yourself, whereas a game involving a team, such as football, is a wish for success with your peers. It also suggests a wish to be accepted by others.

GARDEN

A pleasurable time. Seeing a cared-for garden in full bloom means joy and romance will be entering your life and you will feel elated over the weeks ahead. An unkempt or overgrown garden means that you have been neglecting your duties lately. A vegetable garden means business success.

➠ *Gardener, Home, Mansion*

GARDENER

Effort. Dreaming of being a gardener indicates that although you will need to put in a lot of effort, you will find that in the end it is rewarded and that you will reap the benefits. To see a gardener hard at work denotes that you will soon enjoy the rich life because of your past willingness to adapt.

➠ *Garden, Lumberjack, Shears*

GARGOYLE

Embarrassment. If you dream of a gargoyle it is likely that some embarrassing revelations are about to be made. You should not worry about this unduly, though, as there will be no long-term detrimental effects and you should just perhaps laugh the situation off.

GARLIC

Protection. Garlic has long been associated with protection from vampires, and in a dream garlic indicates that you have protection from people doing you some harm. If you dream of eating garlic with a partner it suggests that you are more interested in financial stability rather than love.

➠ *Vampire*

TOP: *A beautiful garden with monkeys, from a painting by Valmiki Udaipur.*
ABOVE: *A Notre Dame gargoyle enjoys a panoramic view of Paris.*
LEFT: *Furniture in your dream reflects your home and your relationships there.*
FAR LEFT: *A Red-eyed Tree Frog, which represents luck in life and love.*

GARTER

If your garters are loose then it can indicate unwanted companions. If you lose one and it is handed back by a friend then everything will be fine, but if it is your partner that gives you the garter this represents emotional difficulties. Dreaming of displaying your garters to all means that you are unhappy with your relationships at the moment, but it is also a warning that perhaps you are being to indiscriminate with your affections.

➠ *Prostitute*

GAS

Warning. Gas appearing in a dream is a warning omen, hinting at scandalous gossip which may be about you. Seeing a gas man in your dream, or lighting a gas appliance, suggests that finances need to be watched. Gas explosions signify an urgent need to curb talk and act on the difficulties, both in your finances and relationships.

GATE

The next step. A gate in a dream signifies the next part of your plan. It represents an obstacle, but one that must be crossed. If the gate is open then the path ahead for you is clear; if closed then it simply means that you will have to make more of an effort, but you will achieve the same results.

GAVEL

Justice. If you see a gavel in your dream it indicates that you will be able to right a wrong. It is also a warning not to treat others too harshly. You will need to show compassion and understanding coupled with a sense of tolerance if justice is to be fairly and objectively administered.

GENITALS

Sexual feelings. As one might suspect dreaming of your genitals has a bearing on how you feel sexually at the moment and as long as they look healthy and normal then it does not represent a problem. If you dream of unhealthy or diseased genitals then it could mean that you are being promiscuous at the moment: this is a warning of what could happen if you continue to

have sexual relationships without taking the correct precautionary measures. If you dream of showing your genitals to others – in private or public – it may show an inclination towards exhibitionism. Pain in the genital area indicates the need to see a doctor.

GIANTS

Listen carefully. If a giant appears in a dream it means that you are about to hear or be told something to which you should pay great attention. The giant, of course, signifies a matter of great size and import and the news will have a significant effect on your life.

GIRAFFE

Look at the overall picture. The giraffe is known for its ability to see from a height and therefore in a dream is telling you to look at the overall project. Try and look at things from a detached, higher perspective and you will see the solution.

GIRL

Prospects. If a man dreams of a girl, then this dream could signify romantic encounters. However, regardless of your sex this dream brings new prospects and news. A man dreaming of being a girl can mean that he is a bit confused about his sexuality.

GLASS

Celebration. Drinking out of a glass or a goblet indicates that you will shortly receive news of a celebration. If the glass is broken then you are not happy with the situation.

GLASSES

Change of viewpoint. To see glasses on someone that does not need to wear them indicates that your relationship will change. If you do not wear glasses and you put a pair on in your dreams then it indicates that you need to look around you, as you are oblivious to something important that is taking place in real life. Changing into dark glasses indicates that you will find a new interest that will illuminate an unseen talent that you have.

➠ *Face, Shop*

GLOVES

Security. Gloves in dreams are said to represent how we feel in regard to emotional and financial security. New gloves indicate financial security and as you can imagine losing gloves represents the loss of security. Finding a pair of gloves indicates that someone will help you with your current problems.

BELOW: Pouring liquid gold, a symbol of fame and fortune.
BELOW LEFT: A goat in a dream warns you of hard times at work.
LEFT: A glass or goblet in your dream indicates an imminent celebration.

GOAT

A warning about business involvements. If a goat appears in your dream you need to be wary as the going could get tough. The goat represents the astrological sign of Capricorn, which refers to the goat as a symbol of ambition. If the goat is helping you in your dream this is a positive sign. However, if the goat is behaving in an unruly manner something or someone is hindering your progress in life.

GOLD

Fame and fortune. Gold in dreams is very significant, but the meaning of your dream will depend very much on how you discover the gold. If you are trying to find gold either by panning in a river or stream, or by just looking around for it on the ground, this means that you can effect a beneficial change in your circumstances by taking action. If, however, you are trying to find gold by mining, this indicates that although you will be successful with a financial venture there could be a lot of family squabbling.

If you dream that you find gold that turns out to be something different then you may have found fools' gold. This means you should look in your heart, not just at your bank balance, to find the right direction in life.

Losing gold in your dream indicates the loss of money. However, hiding gold indicates that at the moment you are putting finances before anything else and this is causing problems in your relationship.

Gold in nuggets or coins represents financial rewards and prosperity. Gold in clothes such as golden-coloured embroidery often indicates a rise in status and authority.

➠ *Money, Ring*

GOLF

Romantic affairs. Even though golf is quite a solitary game, in dreams it represents a new romantic liaison. To putt a hole in one would imply immediate and mutual reciprocation of love. To struggle but eventually finish the round implies time is needed to develop the bonds. To find yourself in the bunkers of the course implies an overzealous nature and carelessness in your approach, so think before you drive the club.

GOOSE

A message of joy. A dream of geese, or even a single goose, indicates good news in a message you will send to someone. This dream is particularly appropriate if you are planning to write a letter to a loved one, as you will be in a very articulate mood, and will express your emotions with feeling.

GOOSEBERRY

Fertility. Dreaming of gooseberries is a double-edged dream because although it predicts fertility, it also brings with it indiscretions and misbehaviour, perhaps suggesting an affair that becomes out of control.

GORGE

Emotional obstacle. If you come across a gorge in your dream it means that you have to face up to a very deep and emotional situation. If you can find a way to cross the gorge then you will be able to find a way to patch up the relationship difficulties you are facing.
➡ *Falling*

GRADUATION

Success. If you see yourself graduating in your dream it indicates success. To witness a graduation ceremony suggests there will be an increase in your social and business affiliations that will confer a higher status upon you.
➡ *Teacher, University*

GRAIN

Success. If you dream of grain then you will succeed in your new and hectic business plans. Finances will take a rise over the next few months and profits will be increased to new levels.
➡ *Wheat*

GRANDPARENTS

Advice. In most tribal traditions grandparents are considered fountains of wisdom and knowledge in a dream and it is important if you dream of your grandparents, as they are giving you a message that should be acted upon. If your grandparents have passed away then it may indicate that they are contacting you as a spirit or ghost.

GRAPE

Joy. Dreaming of grapes is an indication of joy and hints that a celebration party will go extremely well. Green grapes are considered better than black in terms of the intensity of the celebration and its significance. There is, however, a hidden warning in such dreams against overindulgence – suggesting that success can go to your head and that you may become intoxicated with a sense of self-importance.
➡ *Vine, Wine*

London & Coventry Photo Co. COVENTRY

GRASS

If you dream of grass then it is a good sign and indicates that your projects will be successful. However, if you dream of cutting grass then you will receive unpleasant news from a friend that will make you feel sad for a short while.
➡ *Lawn*

GRASSHOPPER

Confusing messages. If you dream of seeing grasshoppers, it means that you are being given misleading messages from other people. It is advisable that you seek competent professional guidance, as issues hanging in the balance require tact and diplomacy.

GRAVE

Sad news. A grave in a dream represents sad news, although not necessarily death. A grave with flowers indicates a broken promise, while a grave in disrepair is said to indicate a broken heart. If you dream of someone digging a grave, then there are people around you that may not be all that they seem.

GRAVY

Prosperity. If you dream of gravy – particularly if it is in a gravy boat – then you will find great prosperity. This dream can also be taken as a warning not to be overindulgent; if you pour too much gravy over your food in your dream then it is an indication of extravagance.

GREASE

Mistakes. If you find your hands or clothes covered with grease then this is a warning that you must hold fire on decisions that you are about to make – they will not work well for you in the long run. Other people smeared in grease suggests that you would do well to remove yourself from any awkward delegations in which you do not have a say as soon as possible.

GRINDSTONE

A friend to help. If you dream of sharpening your knife on a grindstone then it signifies that someone will help you in your endeavours. Nevertheless, hard work is involved and you will have 'your nose to the grindstone'.

GROCER

Successful negotiations. If you dream of meeting the grocer in your dreams then it indicates that you are just about to start negotiations in your business which will prove to be pleasant and will result in long-term business establishment and stability.

GROCERIES

Success and luck. To dream of doing the grocery shopping indicates that you will succeed in your endeavours, as long as the fruit or vegetables in your dream do not appear mouldy. This would signify problems and regrets in the form of decaying of an opportunity through lack of spontaneous action to take advantage of the good fortune when it appeared.

GROOM

Legal notices. To dream of a groom indicates that there will be some legal issues to be sorted out in connection with the family before any new venture or marriage can go ahead.
➡ *Celebration, Wedding*

GUARDIAN

Financial help. If you dream of a guardian then it indicates that this person is willing and able to offer you help in your current situation. You must make the first move, though, and contact the person you see as the guardian to ask for help.

GUIDANCE

Help yourself. If you dream that you need guidance from someone else during your travels it is a sign that everything is not quite clear in your mind but if you allow your intuition to work you will find the right direction.

ABOVE LEFT: Romans pressing grapes, a symbol of celebration.
LEFT: A young woman poses in mortar board and gown for her graduation photograph, amid the clutter of a victorian photographic studio.
ABOVE FAR LEFT: The god Brahma rides on a cosmic goose.

GUITAR

Appreciation. It is quite common to dream of playing a guitar, perhaps as part of a rock group. More than anything this dream reveals a desire to be appreciated. Playing a guitar is also coupled with the wish for a sexual adventure and might indicate a period of passion.

GULL

An overseas messenger. If you dream of seagulls be aware that you may receive unfortunate news from overseas. Also, this is a time when you need to be careful and not too trustful of persuasive, questionable schemes. If the gulls are flying over the sea it indicates that you are unclear about your feelings regarding an issue overseas

GUN

Distress and worries. Guns in a dream denote distress and severe times of worries, brought about by external pressures relating to people's opinions of you. If you used the gun and killed someone in your dream it means that you will lose respect from your peers, whereas if you saw someone else with a gun it means that people with evil intentions will cause you many worries and may even cause you sickness requiring medical help.

⟹ *Killing, Shooting*

GUTS

Depression. Although pain in the guts can be a symptom of ill health it can also indicate that you feel depressed and are not sure of your direction in life. To see the guts of animals indicates that you need to take a long look at digesting some lesson or information before you proceed any further. Ulcers imply anxieties and stresses brought about by adverse demands on your time and energy.

⟹ *Pain*

GYMNASTICS

Take care. Seeing gymnastics or exercise in your dreams indicates a need to be careful and not to overdo things; not necessarily from an exercise point of view, but in life in general. You are trying to do too much at once and are acting too impulsively.

GYPSY

Unsettled. If a gypsy appears in your dream it means that you feel unsettled about something. This dream might indicate a move and certainly you feel restless. A dream such as this is generally good luck, although you may experience some difficulties to start with

⟹ *Gold (coins)*

HAEMORRHAGE

Avoid controversy. If you see yourself bleeding heavily in a dream it indicates that you need to avoid confrontation with friends. If the blood appears to be coming from a wound then it indicates bad business dealings particularly from abroad. To see someone else suffer a haemorrhage indicates your help will be called upon soon to sort out and heal a situation.

HAIR

Represents the spirit. Hair is important in dreams as it is a good indicator of the way you are feeling. If the hair feels and looks good it indicates that you feel good as well. If in your dream you are looking at the state of your own hair it can mean that you are unhappy with it.

Hair that is thinning or unhealthy in your dream indicates confidence problems. If you are forever combing your hair it indicates that there is an annoying problem; however, you will be able to sort it out but it will take time. If someone else is brushing your hair then it indicates that you will need someone else's help to resolve the situation.

If someone has tangles and dirty hair (including yourself) this indicates that the person is going to go through some pretty torrid times financially. To see a strange lady with beautiful hair suggests a new friendship is on the way, and if you are male, the possibility of a romantic opportunity. Long male hair in a dream is said to signify cowardice.

If you are kissing someone's hair then it means contentment in the relationship. If you are eating it, on the other hand, then it means that you need to place careful attention on events happening around the home.

If you dream that you are at the hairdresser's having your hair cut then it indicates success in a new venture. If you are cutting someone else's hair then it indicates a successful partnership. To have your hair plaitted or have hair extensions added is good news but not so good if it is someone else's hair, as this leads to arguments.

A woman curling or colouring her hair indicates an improvement in relationships. If bleaching is involved it indicates a relationship that you might be rushing into.

The colour of the hair is important. Male hair turning black and curly indicates that you will be deceived. Going grey or seeing grey hair is an omen that someone in your family is ill and could do with your support. To gel your hair in a dream means that there is a chance of prosperity on its way, but to perfume your hair would indicate vanity and does not bode well for friendships.

Red hair means unfaithfulness and changes, though it can also mean a very passionate start to a relationship. White hair indicates happiness and enjoyment, as if the cares of the world have been put behind you. For a woman to dream of her or someone else's hair turning into flowers foretells news

of a loved one from a distance, though if it changes into snakes then someone is about to do you a very great injustice.

To see yourself or someone else in a wig indicates that you would like to change your identity and this dream often indicates a change of friendships and social groups; however, losing a wig indicates derision and people finding out things about you that you wish to remain a secret.
➡ *Doctors*

HAIRDRESSER

A sign of your health. If you dream that you are visiting your hairdresser (particularly if you are a woman), if you are pleased with the result it indicates healthy times. For a man a visit to the hairdresser may mean an indiscretion with a female. If you dream that you are the hairdresser and that is not actually your profession then this is a request for help from someone.
➡ *Hair*

HAM

Good luck. Ham in a dream promotes good luck, particularly in business prospects, although there is also a warning that you should take care when dealing with others as one or two people may be underhand in their business dealings with you.

HANDS

Creativity. Hands in dreams represent creativity. The meaning will be dictated more by what the hand is doing or touching than anything else. If your

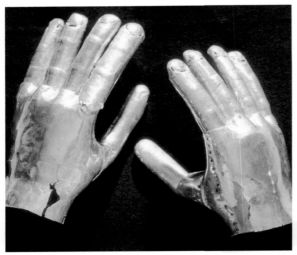

hands are doing things in a dream (e.g. working tools, painting or drawing) it indicates that you will be using your skills in a work opportunity that will provide long term rewards for you.

If the hands you see in your dream are grubby, then it indicates that you need to watch how you present yourself to others. Bent or old hands represent the easing of a financial burden, though you will have had to work hard for it. If it is the left hand in the dream it indicates romantic involvement that will fall apart due to deceit. If it is the right hand that is bent it denotes falling prey to the deception of others.

If your hands are covered in blood then it indicates a family argument that needs to be resolved, and washing your hands indicates that you are able to take control of the situation. Otherwise, injured hands just mean that you are likely to suffer some setbacks.

HANGING

You will be rewarded. This dream generally brings good news, providing that you are not the hangman in your dream, which signifies you will let someone down. You should also refrain from taking action against others.

HARDSHIP

Financial balancing. If you dream that you are in hardship it suggests that it is time for you to sort out your finances, as money is starting to flow out quicker than it is coming in and credit card bills are likely to be piling up. The good news, though, is that these problems can be sorted out now before they get worse.

HARE

Hares indicate change. Hares have a strong mythical connection; witches in the Middle Ages were often accused of changing themselves into hares to steal milk from the local farmers' cows. Dreaming of hares means that there are some unexpected changes in store for you.

➡ *Hunting*

HARLEQUIN

The Harlequin, also known as the Jester, links in with the fool of the Tarot. This dream indicates that you are about to start again, leaving behind the past and starting on a new road. It is time to analyse what is right and what is wrong in your life: anything that is wrong needs to be left in the past.

HARP

The progress of time. If the strings of a harp break in your dream this indicates that you want to stop time in your relationship; maybe you feel that you cannot continue in the relationship and that it is time that you broke free from your partner. If the harp carries on playing in your dream you have the ability to stay the course.

➡ *Magic and the Occult, Orchestra*

HARVEST

A guide to your rewards. If you dream of a good harvest or harvesting it indicates that you are soon to see the rewards of your efforts over the last six to 12 months. A poor harvest portends associations that are connected to you and have one goal in mind, and that is to exploit you, so you may have to box clever for a while if you are to avoid being taken for a ride.
➠ *Field*

HASSOCK

To dream that you are kneeling on a cushion or hassock means that things will become easier for you in the near future. The problems you face with others will shortly be resolved and you will feel that you will be able to get on with your life.

HAT

Your appearance to others. The interpretation of hats in dreams depends very much on what the dreamer is doing with the hat in the dream. Losing your hat in the wind indicates a recession is about to hit your business interests, while leaving your hat somewhere indicates a careless attitude to money. If you have a new hat good luck will follow; however, if the hat in your dream is too small for you this indicates conceit and overconfidence. A hat that is too large suggests that you feel unsure of your thoughts. A top hat signifies an increase in status.

HATRED

Beware of your responses. To feel hatred against a person in your dream is a warning that you are being too critical. If in your dream someone is issuing hateful vibes towards you then you will find that friends will rally round to support you in any problems that you have.

HAY

Financial pressures. Seeing hay in a dream is a warning that you need to tighten your belt and save some money. You may feel that you are all right at the moment but things are going to get tough down the line so you need to make sure you have something to fall back on while you can.

ABOVE: Harvesting, from August of an early fifteenth-century German tapestry, depicting the labours of the months.
LEFT: Thomas Eller as Harlequin, indicating new beginnings.
ABOVE LEFT: A pair of golden Peruvian burial gloves.

HEAD

Where the head is prominent in a dream it is a message to focus the mind and bring your thoughts together: consideration must be given to what else is going on in the dream in order to discover which details are relevant and which are not.

If the head is floating without a body it indicates that you need to use your head at the moment. Perhaps think before you act. If the head is larger than usual then although there may be good news (in particular involving promotion) you need to be careful about being over-confident.

If on the other hand your head is smaller than usual then it indicates that you will achieve more than you think.

A pain in the head indicates that you should keep your secrets to yourself; however, if you dream that your head is on fire then it can indicate that you are being too aggressive or hot-headed.

If your or someone else's head appears to be on your body backwards, it indicates that you will need to look back over the past and resurrect an old passion, be it business or romance. If you do not recognize the head of the person this indicates that you are likely to meet an intellectual soon.

A child's head in a dream indicates financial success in the future. The age of the child will give an approximation of how long it will take, so.if the child's head appears to be around 10 years old then it will take eight years for your project to reach fruition; the same length of time that it will take for the child to mature. If the head is disembodied, however, and appears torn from the trunk then it brings with it disappointments and problems.

If your dream consists of the image of your forehead it indicates that you will achieve help from an unexpected source. If you dream of touching or kissing someone's forehead then it indicates a very happy relationship.

If your forehead in your dream is made of metal or stone then you will have an enemy that you cannot make amends with. An injury to your forehead indicates a need to watch financial matters over the next few months.

➥ *Bathing, Brain, Hair, Hat*

HEADACHE

Privacy. To dream of a headache means that you need to keep something private. Half of you feels that it would be a relief to tell someone but the other half is telling you that it would do more harm than good. You need to keep quiet about the issue at the moment.

HEARSE

Promotion. If you dream of driving a hearse it means that you will be rewarded with a promotion in your job, where you will take on more responsibility and be aided by others. If the hearse is drawn by a feathered horse this indicates a marriage is near.

HEAT AND COLD

An indication of feelings. Hot weather in your dreams is considered a good omen, as it brings with it success and opportunities. Cold weather means that you feel depressed about a situation and in a dream represents the need for hard work. Wet weather brings emotional problems that need to be resolved before you can move forward.

HEAVEN

 Change. To dream of heaven or paradise indicates that you are preparing for changes in your life; these may not be easy to cope with, but you will have to embrace them if you are going to be able to relax and enjoy the future.

HEDGE

Meeting other people. A hedge represents an obstacle and therefore to jump through or walk through a hedge indicates that you will succeed in your undertakings, which will involve others. For someone to walk though the gap in a hedge indicates a new find that will break down the barriers that you often put up. Cutting or clipping a hedge indicates preparing for a social occasion.

HEDGEHOG SEE PORCUPINE

HEELS

Sudden changes. If you dream that you break the heel of a shoe in your dream then a long-term friendship will suddenly break up. Dreaming of repairing your own heels represents problems at a party. Dreaming of wearing platform heels indicates that you want to be noticed.

➡ *Boots, Clothes, Shoes*

HELICOPTER

Escape. If you dream that you are in a helicopter then it indicates that you are trying to escape the current situation. This dream warns you that you should also think of the needs of others who have supported you in the past.

➡ *Flying*

HELL

Fear. If you dream of being in hell, it indicates that you may be acting against your true beliefs in a particular circumstance, and the dream is a warning against acting purely for financial gain, hinting that your behaviour may cause you to lose friends.

HELMET

Problems. To see someone wearing a helmet in a dream indicates that someone else is hiding their true motives from you. If you are wearing the helmet in your dream then you need to organize your plans properly and try not to be a scatterbrain. Often you are putting up a block and other people are unable to help you because you are hiding information from them.

HEMP

Stick with what you know best. To dream of fields of Manila hemp or hemp used for rope-making indicates that you can feel too tied to what others want you to do; however it is in your best interest to stick with the work. If you cut yourself while collecting hemp then a quarrel is sure to follow.

HERBS

Recovery. To dream of herbs means that you may be feeling under the weather. The herbs dreamt about may be the most suitable ones to help you recover from what has been an exhausting time for you. To see a variety of herbs indicates that you will experience a period of petty annoyances, but that success will be yours if you avoid excessive displays of anger.

➡ *Witch*

ABOVE: A bronze Corinthian-style helmet from 500 BC, Haghia Paraskevi.
TOP: Hell, in which decencies are respected and undergarments are compulsory.
ABOVE LEFT: The elect arrive at the gates of Heaven and are greeted by angels.

HERMAPHRODITE

Self-indulgence. To see yourself as a hermaphrodite is considered to be a warning regarding overindulgence, not just sexually but also recreationally, for example, by experimenting with drugs. It can also mean that you feel confused about your own sexuality: take a balanced perspective on life and see things from the point of view of a member of the opposite sex. For men this means developing your feminine receptivity and intuition, and for women it indicates the dynamic forcefulness of male aggression to succeed.

HERMIT

Enlightenment. If you dream of being a hermit it marks a time of self-imposed introspection. Through pensive marshalling of your thoughts, with a view to long-range ideals and goals, you will gain self-knowledge and emerge enlightened and with clarity about your future realities.

➡ *Labyrinth*

HIDE

Protection. The hide of an animal is a representation of protection and clothing, which in dreams gives you the strength of that animal. In magical beliefs and ancient cultures witch doctors dressed up using the horns and hides of the animals they wanted to emulate and gain the powers of. By doing so they felt that they could take on their appearance and physically change into them. Many of our legends of werewolves have a link to this belief.

HILL

Obstacles and achievement. Hills in dreams represent obstacles to overcome. The general guidelines to understanding this type of dream is that if you reach the top of the hill you will achieve your goal. If you give up halfway or try walking round the hill then you are trying to avoid the problem. This will only compound the issue and it will return later if you continue to avoid it.

➡ *Climbing*

HIPPOPOTAMUS

Perseverance and stamina. A dream featuring a hippopotamus indicates a need for perseverance. It can also be an indication that you feel unhappy with your own body and can be a warning to change your eating habits.

HISTORY

Reliving the past. There are two sorts of historical dreams. The first type is retrospective and normally suggests you are feeling anxious about the present and are therefore seeking solace in a past time where you felt safe. The second type of historical dream is where a message is conveyed to help you prepare for the future which draws upon your past knowledge or experiences; often this is modified in the light of current experiences. This may be lead to an unexpected new opportunity. In many cultures feeling a strong affinity with a past event in a dream is believed to be associated with regression to a former life.

HOLIDAY

You need a break. To dream of being on holiday indicates that you need to take some time away from your work to relax and enjoy yourself. Don't worry because all of the effort that you have applied to your current undertakings will be rewarded.

➡ *Travelling*

HOME

Satisfaction. To dream of your home in a pleasant situation means that you are content with the way things are. It indicates a wish to keep things stable in your life.

HOMICIDE

Repressed anger. To dream of committing homicide is a warning that you are allowing yourself to react too quickly to events. It is a time to sit back and take steps to sort out problems that you have at the moment with friends and partners.

HOMOSEXUAL

Insecurity. A dream of this nature is common regardless of your sexuality and indicates that you are thinking about sexual experimentation. If a heterosexual person dreams about homosexuality regularly this reveals an underlying insecurity and non-communication with the opposite sex and also indicates a strong desire to emulate and imbibe the qualities of the person you were entertaining in your dream. If you are a homosexual then this simply strengthens your erotic desires for the person you saw in your dream.

ABOVE: Pamalican Island in the Philippines, an ideal holiday destination.
LEFT: Glastonbury Tor; hills in dreams must be climbed to achieve your goals.
ABOVE LEFT: An Etruscan statue of a hermaphrodite.

HONEY SEE BEE

HONEYSUCKLE

Domestic happiness. In a dream honeysuckle represents domestic bliss and happiness. Your marriage is indicated to be long and happy and any business transactions undertaken in the few weeks after dreaming of honeysuckle will also work out well.

HOOD

Deception. To wear a hood indicates the need to hide. So if you are wearing a hood in your dream then you are trying to hide from someone. If someone else is wearing a hood then they are hiding from you. In all, this means that you are going to have to be more careful about who you trust.

HOOP

A dream of liberation. To dream of playing with hoops or seeing hoops means that you want to escape from your current situation; to break free from any restrictions. You also want sexual freedom from others that are spinning their charms on you.

HOPS

Energy. If you dream of hops growing then it indicates that you will have the energy to fulfil your work commitments, which will lead to success and a profitable time. If you see hops being picked then the augury is one of rapid movement into a passionate exciting affair, but note that this will be short-lived.

➠ *Brewing*

HORIZON

Success. The horizon represents the future and your personal ambitions. To dream of a new horizon means that you will achieve success and peace. A distant horizon is more favourable than a near horizon as it means the goal will be achieved quicker.

HORN

Warning. A horn is a warning, regardless of whether it is a car horn, foghorn or a musical horn. The horn indicates loud, over-exuberance and bombastic behaviour, which you will need to curb if you are to maintain your dignity. The exception is if the horn was blown at an appropriate venue, such as a football match, where you were cheering on the players, in which case it heralds a period of social gaiety and playfulness.

HORNS

Sexual fulfilment. Horns in the past, and still today in some cultures, have been used as a symbol of sexual potency, particularly for males. Therefore if you are a male and have had this dream you may have an underlying concern regarding impotence and so this dream is compensatory in nature suggesting that you seek medical counsel.

HORSE

Horses represent speed and power. We still use horses as a measurement of power in transport, and in dreams they can signify the same thing. Therefore to see a galloping horse is a sign of success. If you are fearful of the horse in your dream then it indicates that you are fearful of an experience in your life.

If you are riding the horse and are in control, status awaits. If, however, you are riding an uncontrolled horse, then your dream indicates that you are literally being taken for a ride: look at relationships and business issues very closely. If you dream that you are thrown from a horse then it indicates a rival is going to cause problems for you.

If you are riding a horse that constantly bucks, it could indicate that you have a back or joint problem: this is your body's way of reminding you to pay attention to your health. If the horse kicks you, it is a warning that you should be aware of your actions and of those around you. It is in effect a kick up the backside.

To dream of putting a bridle on a horse, indicates that you are about to take on an unwanted task, but once you have completed the task you will be glad you made the effort. To see a horseshoe is a lucky symbol, and some luck is about to come your way. However, if the horseshoe does not fit the horse, you may be found guilty of embezzling funds. If you are able to shoe the animal then success will come to you, even if it requires plenty of hard work. You will also find that your success turns out better than you planned.

If a small pony appears in your dream, it indicates that you are about to invest in something that will have success, though you are advised to start off slowly and only invest a modest amount.

The colour of the horse is also significant in a dream: a white horse promotes the message and brings hope, whereas a black horse indicates delays. If you see black and white horses together, it is an indication that you need to ensure that you look at both sides of the issue. To those at sea, dreams of white horses mean that the weather could take a turn for the worse, as the white crests of waves on the sea are called white horses.

Colours in between black and white can lead to confusion. If you see Spanish or Arabic horses, this relates to romantic issues.

A stallion indicates success and someone with a powerful personality who will help you. If you dream that you are riding bareback, without a saddle or reins, and are amongst another group of horse riders, it indicates that you have many helpful friends.

To dream of a heavy horse pulling a plough indicates prosperity and rewards in financial endeavours. If, however, the horse is having difficulty, then you too will have to face obstacles.

To dream of a stable brimming with horses is a warning against greed, whereas a dream of an empty stable shows an opportunity for financial improvement.

Horses in dreams, particularly for women, can also have sexual connotations; it is worth assessing current partnership issues that need to be resolved at the moment.

Traditionally, it was thought that if women dreamt of a black horse, she would want a husband that was strong, protective and dominant; however, if it was a white horse in her dreams, she would choose a partner that she could dominate. To a certain extent you will also find this true of a girl who has a horse as a pet.

If you are at the beginning of a relationship then to dream of riding a horse uphill means that the romance will blossom and grow; on the other hand, if you are riding down a hill, then the relationship will follow suit and be downhill from now on.

If you dream of using a whip on a horse, it indicates that you wish to dominate another person; it possibly also means that you wish to hurt them. This dream can act as a warning as it may indicate that you are abusing someone else's trust in you.

➡ *Donkey, Foal*

ABOVE: Status must await this rider, who has his horse perfectly under control.
LEFT: A Rocky Mountain Big Horn Sheep, issuing a warning to dreamers.
ABOVE LEFT: The horizon in a dream represents your future and ambitions.

people, discussing an intellectual hobby of yours into the long hours of the night.
➡ *Eating, Root*

HOSPITAL

Overloaded. If you dream that you are being taken to hospital it indicates that you cannot cope with the situations around you at the moment. You are perhaps very run down and tired and could do with some rest. There is a need to ensure that others take some of the pressure off you. If you visit someone in hospital in your dream it means that someone is in need of your help.
➡ *Doctors*

HUGGING

Reassurance. If you hug someone in your dream you are looking for reassurance and their support. If it is a gentle hug you are simply asking them for support; a stronger hug indicates that significant changes are in store for you. If you are hugging a stranger, though, these changes may not be what you expect.

HUMILIATION

Arrogance. If you have a fear of being humiliated in your dreams it is an indication that you may well be displaying arrogance at the moment and this is likely to lose you some friends. Take heed of this warning for it will prevent unnecessary errors due to vanity and pride; it will help you to see the real complexities involved in the situation and facilitate a successful outcome.

HORSE CHESTNUTS

Problems with children. To dream of horse chestnuts indicates that you might be worried over problems a child you know is having at school. It will be important for you to check whether the child is being bullied or there is some other reason for school problems.

HORSERADISH

Intellectual discussions. If you dream of eating horseradish then it means that you will shortly have the opportunity of meeting with like-minded

HUNCHBACK

Luck. To dream of a hunchback is good news. You are able to look deeply at your problem – not just what is on the surface – and will be able to come up with a long-term solution.

HUNGER SEE FAMISHED

HUNTING

Hunts signify problems and resolutions. Unless you are planning to go fox hunting, dreaming of hunting foxes and hares will bring bad news and problems that you will not be able to overcome. On the other hand, hunting large animals such as stags or buffalo represents good luck and issues that are surmountable – so persevere.

HUSBAND

Contentment. To dream of your husband if you are married shows contentment in the relationship. However, if you dream of a husband when you are not married it means that your are about to fall out with your partner, particularly if the relationship has just begun.
➡ *Wife*

HYACINTH

Separation. Hyacinth in a dream is an indication that you will soon be separated from someone that is close to you, due to unexpected events. In the end this separation will benefit both of you.

HYENA

Someone is laughing at you. Just like the tradition of the laughing hyena, someone is laughing at your efforts and could be putting obstacles in your way. Be warned, someone is not as helpful as they may seem and you need to be wary. In some cultures evil spirits were able to transform themselves into hyenas.

HYMN

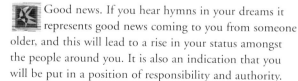

Good news. If you hear hymns in your dreams it represents good news coming to you from someone older, and this will lead to a rise in your status amongst the people around you. It is also an indication that you will be put in a position of responsibility and authority.

BELOW: A choir of monks singing, from a fifteenth century English Psalter. Their hymns in a dream could be an omen of good fortune.
LEFT: Horse chestnuts hint that a child may be having problems.

HYPNOTIST

Let secrets remain in the past. To dream of being hypnotized is a warning that you should not interfere or reveal an incident from the past that you feel guilty about. Even if you want to confess, you should avoid doing so, as the truth could hurt others.

HYPOCRISY

Guard against your own thoughts. If you find that you are being hypocritical in your dream then you should make sure that you do not make hasty judgements against others, as that is not going to win you friends. This dream can also be a warning to check your health if people are making hypocritical attacks towards you.

ICE

Warning. If you dream of walking or especially slipping on ice, it is considered to be a warning that you need to pay attention to you finances or you

could get into trouble. An iceberg indicates that you are facing a hidden obstacle. To see an icicle or ice-covered trees, however, indicates that, given time, your dreams and aspirations will come to fruition.

ICE CREAM

Business success. If you dream of eating ice cream it suggests some small business successes shortly. Ice cream can also mean that family life is good; however, to see melted or spilt ice cream indicates that there could be some family tensions in the air.

IDLENESS

Start taking responsibility. If you dream of being idle it is a warning that you are not putting enough effort into work at the moment and that an

embarrassing exposé will be greeting you soon from those in authority. If someone else is idle in your dream then you have to make an effort to confront the persons in question to discover the source of incompetence.

INDULGENCE

Greed. To dream of indulgence with food indicates that you are going to need to keep a careful rein on expenditure. You may have been a little greedy in the past few months and now you will have to be more careful.

INJURY

Hostility. If you dream of being injured it indicates that others are showing unnecessary emotional hostility towards you; however, this situation is unlikely to involve any physical violence. If you dream of an injury to another person then you need to examine your relationship with them to enable you to resolve the problems pleasantly.

INSANITY

Realisation. If you dream that you are going insane it indicates that you are becoming more realistic about your direction. This dream reveals that you want to turn over a new leaf and go in a new direction in relation to work or a relationship. Often this dream means that you want to make life-changing decisions that will have a positive effect on you as a person but might seem insane to other people. If, however, someone else in your dream is going insane then it is a warning to expect a sudden change of circumstances.

➡ *Labyrinth, Maze*

INSECTS SEE BUGS

INSULT

Loyalty. Funnily enough, whether your dream involves giving or being on the receiving end of insults, this dream indicates that you are trusted and loyal friends will help you whatever problems you have.

INVENTION

Achievement. To dream of an invention or being an inventor indicates that you will achieve great success. To meet an inventor means that you will find associates to help you in your unique endeavours. If you are the inventor yourself, then a phase of extraordinary thinking is about to elucidate an answer to a particular enquiry.

➠ *Apprentice, College, Lecture, University*

INVISIBILITY

Change. Dreaming you are invisible means that changes are about to occur over which you will have no control. If you dream that you are invisible in someone else's house then this may indicate that you are psychically picking up on a particular experience they are having or situation they are in.

IRONING

Profitability. If you dream of ironing – whether man or woman – it indicates that a new enterprise will be profitable. If you scorch your ironing then it is a warning to look out for someone else who is trying to take your place.

ISLAND

Isolation. If you dream that you are on an island then this represents a need for time to yourself to reflect on your circumstances. It may be that you have a number of issues that you need to address and need time to think. If you are rescued from an island, or manage to gain freedom through your own means, you will be able to overcome the issues.

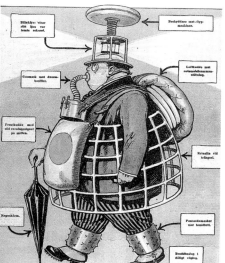

ISOLATION

Worries. If you dream that you are isolated it means that you havecomplex and personal issues on your mind that you are having difficulties explaining to others. Perhaps if you tried to talk to your friends you would find that they would at least listen, and therefore, share some of the pressure that you have been dealing with alone; they may even contribute towards sorting out the bones of contention.

ITCH

Worrying. If you dream you are itching then it indicates a worry; however, there is no use worrying over this situation as there is nothing you can do about it until it is over. If someone else is itching in your dream then it is an instruction for you to try and help that person overcome their fears.

➠ *Bug*

BELOW: Kata Beach on Phuket Island, Thailand – a symbol of isolation.
ABOVE: The Far-sighted Man, prepared for every accident.
BELOW LEFT: Icicles signify that your dreams will eventually come true, if you give them enough time

IVORY

Ivory and elephants represent memory. In dreams ivory represents a memory brought up from the past, particularly concerning the home. Perhaps something that you have forgotten about in the house needs taking care of. Something is broken so you should fix it.

➠ *Elephant*

IVY

Friendship. If you dream of ivy, whether growing indoors or out, it indicates that there are a lot of people around you who are willing to help you sort out problems, whatever the issue – you only need to ask and the help will be there.

JACKET

Financial opportunities. If the jacket you are wearing in your dream is new this represents new business opportunities. Wearing someone else's jacket indicates that you are going to ask that person for a financial loan. A torn jacket suggests that your children will rebel against you. A bright jacket indicates that you have an optimistic disposition concerning the weather, whereas a dark jacket indicates that you do not like having to succumb to the elements.

➠ *Colours*

JADE

Intuition. If you see the green stone jade in a dream it means that you should trust your inner intuition. Look at your problems and trust your feelings, as your instincts will tell you the right way to proceed. Jade also represents our ancestors, so it may be that we are receiving helpful advice from departed relatives.

JAIL

Obstacles. A dream about a jail represents obstacles that you are facing and need to get out of. If you succeeded in your dream to escape from jail then it indicates that you will be able to extradite yourself from a problem in your life. The longer it takes you to get out of jail the harder it will be, but you will overcome the situation.

➠ *Trapped*

JAILER

Lack of support. If you see a jailor in your dream it means that a friend will let you down when you need them. Likewise, if you dream of jailing someone else then just when they need your help, you are likely to let them down, unless you take note of this dream and act to the contrary.

JAM

Appreciations. Jam on the table indicates contentment with a family situation. Friends and family will also appreciate the amount of work that you have done lately for them and will be keen to help you out of any difficulties that you are now facing.

JANITOR

Problems with children. If a janitor appears in your dream, regardless of whether it is you or somebody else, it indicates a problem with children that will need to be sorted out. Lots of little things are annoying you at the moment and are preventing you from making long-term plans. This dream is warning you to look at long-range goals and leave some of the smaller things until later.

JAR

Celebration. A jar represents a celebration and enjoyment of a social occasion. If you are having difficulty taking the lid off the jar it may be that you are having difficulty communicating with others.

JASMINE

Romantic events. This flower in a dream is an indication of a new romance that is going to start and blossom, bringing joy to your heart and imagination. To be aware of the smell of jasmine either on a person or in a garden suggests that your creative talents require an input of passion to acheive the desired outcome.

JAW

Avoid talking out of turn. If you get jaw ache in a dream or you dream that you cannot seem to move your jaw it means that you should be careful of what you say. You are likely to say the wrong thing to the wrong person at the wrong time and this is going to cause unpleasantness that could be avoided. To see the jaws of others, however, represents healthy finances.

ABOVE: Wincarnis Old English wine jelly, representing social pleasure.
RIGHT: A court jester, who symbolizes origianlity in a dream.
LEFT: Edvard Munch's emotive depiction of Jealousy.

JEALOUSY

Problems. If in your dream jealousy concerns another person in a relationship then you can expect problems in your relationship. If you are jealous of another person at work because of their career then you are heading for career problems. If the jealousy is being directed at you, however, you will be able to turn the problem into an advantage.

➡ *Sparrow*

JELLY

Social pleasure. To dream of making jelly indicates a get-together soon of family and children. However, to dream that you are eating jelly indicates that you feel that all your time is being taken up with unimportant things.

JESTER

Originality. A court jester was the only person that could make fun of royalty without repercussions. In a dream the jester means that you can turn your ideas on their head and head in a new direction, with or without your past. You have the ability to see things with fresh, innovative ideas.

JEWELLERY

Jewellery is generally a good omen. Being given jewellery or giving it to someone else indicates love and affection and is a good omen of things to come. If you dream that you are stealing jewellery then it indicates that you need to take very good care of your business at the moment. If you lose jewellery then it indicates an obstacle, and if you are able to recover it, then you will be able to resolve the problem.

A tiara in a dream is indicative of a crown and therefore represents honour and a rise of status. Amulets are symbols of protection or of magical spells; the exact meaning will depend on the type of stone but it does indicate a need to make some decisions.

Earrings are of course related to the ear and mean that you need to listen carefully to what is happening to enable you to take advantage of the situations around you. However, this dream can indicate that you need to be careful of repeating something you heard to others.

If you dream you have a stud in your tongue then it indicates that you have to think before you talk. If a man dreams of wearing earrings it is actually good news as far as job opportunities are concerned.

Beads are good news financially if you receive them, however, if your string of beads breaks, or you lose some then it can indicate money being lost. Necklaces are good for romance, providing the necklace does not break or get damaged, which represents quarrels. On the whole, necklaces show that love will blossom and strengthen.

If you dream that you are given a locket, this is good news for relationships as it indicates a long commitment and marriage, and lots of children.

Bracelets in dreams stand for long-term friendships and relationships. It is a fortunate time for you as long as the bracelet in your dream is not broken, which indicates the loss of friendship. If you have just met a new partner and you have dreamt of a bracelet, this dream foretells that your engagement is in the near future.

Rings of course stand for engagements, marriage and commitment in long-term relationships. To give or be

given a ring is of particular significance as this indicates a forthcoming marriage or engagement. If you lose a ring then it does not necessarily mean the opposite, i.e. that a long-term relationship will be broken, but instead can mean that you will have good news in business.

Rings do not have beginning or an end and stand for the eternity of a relationship. To see two rings intertwined in a dream indicates the start of a very close and long-lasting relationship. To dream of broken rings is a signal of a broken relationship and broken hearts.

If you dream of a jewellery box and you take the jewellery from the box to try it on, this means that you feel you are stagnating and not getting out and about enough. To put the jewellery in the box indicates that you are happy being at home and want to be able to spend some quality time with your family, away from everyone else.

Dreaming of costume jewellery indicates that you are concentrating on your own vanity too much and that you may not have the right attitude at the moment. It indicates falseness and that you are creating an image that is not really you, but will be found out sooner or later.

JEWELS

Truth. Jewels in a dream represent truth and will very much depend on the type of stone and its colour. The shape of the jewel is also important and broadly speaking a round or heart shape will relate to romantic issues, whereas rectangle shapes seem to be more practical in nature. The wearing of jewels in your dreams means that your status will increase in the eyes of others.

BELOW: Jewellery from the Cheapside Hoard, found by a workman in 1912.
LEFT: The amulet of eight trigrams, worn by Chinese children for good luck.
FAR LEFT: Empress Farah of Iran's Diadem, which contains 294 diamonds.

JILTED

Fear and anxiety. If you dream of being jilted at the altar – or elsewhere – then it suggests you have a fear that your partner will leave you. Despite this, such a dream often means that the relationship is strong and your fears unfounded.

JOCKEY

 A proposition. If you are female and have dreamt of being or seeing a jockey, this may mean an indecent proposition. If you are male it means you may have to rein in your confidence.

➠ *Horse*

JUDGEMENT

Understanding. If you dream of the day of Judgement or if you play out the judgement in

a court of law in your dream, it is an indication that you are about to gain an understanding of your need to change your viewpoints in order to progress.

JUG

 Friendship. To dream of full jugs indicates fun times with friends that are inspirational and have a bias towards health and fitness, whereas empty jugs portend a new acquaintance that will generate sparks which will blossom into a whirlwind romance.

JUNGLE

Warning over resources. If you are in a jungle in your dream then it indicates that you feel that you

are trying to do too much. Your resources are low and it is important that you watch finances and take note of what other people expect of you. You could be running out of time and energy.

➠ *Lost*

JURY

Use your intuition. To dream of serving on a jury is a message that you should rely on your own instincts and intuition to deal with a current issue. If you do then you will get the right verdict. To dream of appearing before a jury indicates that you are about to receive a reward for all the work you have put in lately.

JUSTICE

If you feel that you have achieved justice in your dream then it indicates that you will achieve some recognition soon. If you are delivering justice to another person then it is a warning regarding your own arrogance and that you need to think carefully before you criticize someone.

KALEIDOSCOPE

Swift change. Kaleidoscopes in your dream represents fashions and fads in all their fleeting transience and fickleness. Although the changing patterns are swift and delightful, they are only passing phases. So be prepared for a spell of bouts involving swings in your moods and tastes.

KANGAROO

Thrift. Kangaroos hopping at speed indicate thrift and economical use of power. If you felt drawn to the joey in the pouch, then you are looking for the security that you had as a child. Kicking kangaroos indicate stiff rivalry and that you may need to prepare to defend your viewpoint against hostile critics.
➠ *Hide*

KEG

Stand on your own two feet. To dream of a keg indicates that you need to be self-sufficient and to enter the social arena again. If the keg is full it indicates that you will experience reversals in your current undertakings. If the keg is empty, though, you can expect your prosperity to fluorish very soon.

KETTLE

Contentment. A boiling kettle indicates contentment within the family home. If it is broken then there are financial issues affecting the family that need to be resolved.

KEY

Solutions. Keys are very important in dreams, as they represent solutions to problems. To be given a key means that you will receive help; likewise, to give a key to someone else indicates that you will be helping

them. Unlocking a door with a key can indicate that a new opportunity will present itself. If your key unlocks a casket then this indicates sexual involvement with someone. If, however, you find a keyhole and do not have a key, it indicates something that is not meant for you – even more so if you look through the keyhole.

KIDNEYS

Take good care of yourself. To dream of your own kidneys means that you may require a health check: you could have health problems because of overindulgence. Eating kidneys, however, is an indication of love affairs of a clandestine nature.
➠ *Urine*

BELOW: A twelfth century fresco of Saint Peter, with a very important key.
BELOW LEFT: Dufresne's Forêt Tropicale, *warning of financial difficulties.*
BELOW FAR LEFT: Le Jugement, from a 1920s pack of Tarot cards.

KILLING

A period of misfortune or stress. If you dream of killing someone, whether on purpose or by accident, then you need to curb your temper. This type of dream indicates that you may be facing a period of emotional stress. However, killing animals in dreams generally means good news will come your way: you will be successful, overcome obstacles and achieve all that you desire. To dream of killing someone also indicates that you are under a lot of emotional pressure at the moment. There is a need to make sure that you are not overreacting with people and it could mean that you have an anger control problem. This dream is a wake-up call to get to the root of your stress before you unintentionally hurt someone.
➡ *Battle, Shooting*

KINGFISHER

A sign of good fortune. Dreaming of a kingfisher indicates that success will be yours soon: the waiting has been worth it! With that success prestige will follow and others will value you, and your efforts, much

more. To see this iridescent fellow diving for fish means that you would benefit from taking a risk in a business proposition – but be precise and meticulous before diving into the depths.

KISSING

The meaning of this dream lies in the kiss and the type of kiss will determine the outcome. A gentle affectionate kiss to a loved one is just an expression of affection; however, if the kiss is nonchalant and given with no meaning then it indicates that you have a false friend.

KITCHEN

Social state. The kitchen in a dream represents how we feel about the current family situation. The newer, cleaner and more comfortable you feel the kitchen is in your dream; the more you feel happy about your family situation.

KITE

Be careful not to overload yourself. To dream of one kite is good news and indicates a successful venture; however, if you see many kites in your dream it means that you are overburdening yourself and you could lose out, particularly if the kites are swooping.

KITE FLYING

Flying a kite represents our hopes and ideals. Whether we fulfil these goals depends on the way

that the kite is flying in your dream: if the kite is soaring high in the sky then you will be successful. However, if you are unable to launch it into the sky, or if it continues to crash, then fulfilling your hopes and dreams will be problematic.
➠ *Wind*

KITTEN SEE CAT

KNAPSACK

A journey. A knapsack or rucksack in your dream indicates a journey that needs to be made. Although it can mean a holiday, it also suggests that you wish to leave the trials and tribulations of those that are hampering you and start again. An empty knapsack means leaving behind financial opportunities to do something that you want to do for your inner soul's sake. A full rucksack indicates that you have financial opportunities connected with travel.

KNITTING

Contentment. To dream of knitting is a sign that you are contented. Conversely, dropping a stitch or having to unravel indicates that there will be some domestic arguments.

KNOCKER

Financial risk. Dreaming of a door knocker suggests that you might be worried about finances. To knock on someone else's door indicates a meeting with them to discuss financial issues, or a new business opportunity that is about to be proposed.

KNOTS

A reminder. A knot represents something that you should not forget to do. It also represents an obstacle, and as long as you succeed in untying the knot, you will succeed in resolving the problem. If you live by the coast or work at sea then it is an indication of windy weather to come.

LABYRINTH

Emotional decisions. The labyrinth in a dream is an indication that you are facing obstacles in your emotional life. Decisions need to be made and the ease with which you find the way out of your dream labyrinth will dictate how easily you will be able to overcome those obstacles on waking. To get to the centre of the labyrinth bodes well for self-discovery and aspects relating to self-actualization.
➠ *Map, Maze*

ABOVE: A Roman mosaic of Theseus fighting the Minotaur in the Labyrinth.
LEFT: A soaring kite suggests that the dreamer will be prosperous.
FAR LEFT: A Kingfisher in your dream indicates that success is worth the wait.

Getting to the top of the ladder indicates that you may also gain prestige and recognition: you have achieved your aims. If you are using a ladder to climb to the top of a house it can suggest that you are about to obtain the house of your dreams. If the ladder is by office blocks then it indicates the achievement of the top position in your workplace.

If you get to the top of the ladder and start to suffer from vertigo it can mean that you are afraid of taking on the responsibilities that have been placed upon you by others. It can also imply that you may be afraid of the dizzy heights of success.

If you are going down a ladder then it means that you have to rethink your plans. If you get struck by a ladder it indicates that you will have an argument with someone in a work situation. Depending on what happens in the dream this could lead to a confrontation with your boss that will need to be resolved. A ladder breaking in front of you means that you will be faced with an obstacle but you are able to avoid it. To walk under a ladder indicates that you will have to deal with extra pressure at work.

If you dream of walking along with a ladder then it indicates that you will be called upon to help a friend.

LADDER

The ups and downs of life. Ladders are very simple metaphors in dreams – symbolizing the trials of life. To climb up a ladder signifies that you are getting to the top of something. If a rung breaks then this represents slip-ups, but if you are able to regain your step it indicates that although experiencing a temporary setback you are able to move upwards and onwards in life.

The height of the ladder will represent how far you have to climb to reach your goal, and how easy you find the climb will indicate the degree of ease or difficulty you will experience in the pursuit of your ambitions.

Using an escalator in a dream indicates that you are moving swiftly on to your target and will reach it that much quicker, though of course the descent can be as equally quick, though generally smooth.

Using a ship's ladder or rope ladder indicates that a relationship that you are involved in needs looking at closely; if you are able to work your way up the ladder on to the boat then it indicates that you will be able to sort out your emotional difficulties that you are experiencing in the relationship.

LADLE

Domestic happiness. To dream of a ladle, means that you will be lucky in family life with plenty of children around you to keep you busy. This is a dream about your wishes for a family.

LAMB SEE SHEEP

LAMENTING

Sorrow. If you find you are lamenting the loss of a friend or relative that you have fallen out with in your dreams then it means that you will need to try and make contact, as your help to them will bring a stronger friendship for the future.

LANCE

Enemies. To see a lance in your dreams means that someone is trying to attack you. More

BELOW LEFT: A knight with a very fine lance heads for battle.
LEFT: Dreaming of a ladle indicates a happy home and family life.
FAR LEFT: A Byzantine icon dating from the late twelfth century, depicting the heavenly ladder of John Klimax.

often than not this attack will be verbal rather than physical. Someone else's careless words may have caused you emotional heartache; they have misjudged you so don't take their words to heart. Stand up for your beliefs and soon an apology in some form will be heading your way.
➠ *Fight*

LAPIS

Honesty. If you see the deep blue colour of lapis in your dreams it means that you have to be honest with yourself and others about a particular situation. If you do this then success will result but you may have to dig deep to uncover the truths. This is also a time for learning about yourself and others who may appear in the dream.

LARD

Tough negotiations. Dreaming of lard indicates that you have some people around you who are trying to persuade you do something that is not in your best interests. You need to stick to your guns and not allow them to influence you, otherwise you could be at a financial loss.

LAUGHTER

Sorrow. If you are laughing at others in your dream it indicates that you might have to deal with an unpleasant episode in the next few days. The exception is if you are laughing at children, which brings news of financial rewards. Also take into account the situation of where the laughter occurred; if the laughter seemed inappropriate then you will not be laughing in a few days.

LAUNDRY

Gossip. The saying that you do not wash your dirty laundry in public also applies to dreams. So if you dream that you are in a laundrette it means that

people will gossip about you. If you dream of washing your own laundry it indicates that although there is hard work in your domestic life everything will come through in the end. If you dream that your laundry remains soiled even after having used the best soaps, prepare yourself for a rocky emotional spin involving a family argument that you will not be able to resolve quietly.

LAUREL

Overconfidence. Although laurel in a dream is a good omen in that it promotes success you will need to be careful as the success can result in overconfidence and the successes gained can so easily be overturned.

LAWN

Contentment. If you dream of walking across a freshly cut lawn it indicates that you are content with life. To sit on a lawn in the summer indicates that a new romance is about to enter your life. If the lawn seems ill-managed or neglected, this presages hostility around you. Any changes that you were planning may benefit from a short delay until these forces no longer pose a threat to your security.
➡ *Grass*

LAWSUIT

Argument. A lawsuit in a dream represents an argument. If you win the lawsuit then it means that you are likely to lose the argument and vice versa. If you dream of starting a lawsuit then it is a warning not to do so as your reasoning is wrong.

LAWYER

Wasted money. If you dream of hiring a lawyer in your dream then this is a warning not to waste money at the moment. If you dream of being a lawyer this brings fortuitous news of money.

LAZINESS

Relaxation. If you dream of being lazy then it can indicate that you have been working too hard recently and that you need to relax and take time out. If you dream that other people are telling you that you are lazy then there could be an element of truth to their jibes.

LEARNING

New skills. You are about to take up new studies and skills. The degree of ease or difficulty that you experience in learning will indicate how quickly you will adjust to the new environment.

➡ **Books, Certificate, College, Library, University**

LEATHER

A positive omen. Leather is always considered a good omen in a dream and generally promises successful business and romantic liaisons. Ornaments made out of leather indicate a very strong marriage or commitment.

LECTURE

To impart information. Attending a lecture in a dream suggests that you are about to learn something new, but that you will not be particularly brilliant at this subject. Delivering the lecture, however, implies that you will achieve great success with the new skills or subject you are about to learn.

LEECHES

Overdemanded. If you dream of leeches it means that a lot of people are demanding your help and attention. You need to be careful as others could take advantage of you. If you dream of having

BELOW: Problems with legs in your dreams could indicate hampered decisions.
BELOW LEFT: Freshly cut lawns represent the dreamer's contentment with life.
FAR LEFT: Three 1960s teenagers use a laundrette as a place to socialize.

leeches for medical treatment then it indicates that you need to look after your health, or that of someone else, by way of removing parasitic friendships.

LEG

Signifies decision-making. A leg in your dream indicates the ability to make a quick decision and move in a new direction. However, if there are problems with the legs in your dream then it means that opportunities and decisions will be hampered. Skinny legs indicate embarrassment

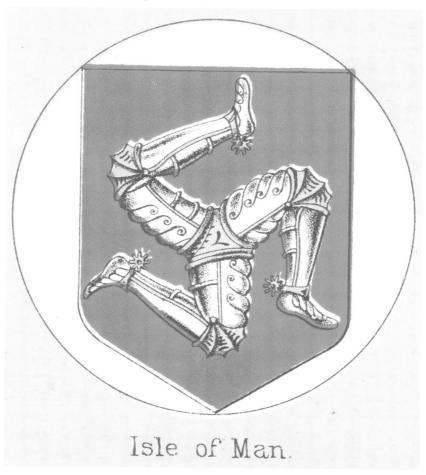

Isle of Man.

LEMON

Financial issues. Lemons in a dream can suggest you need to be aware of finances. It is time to tighten your belt and take a more economical approach to your household budget. If you dream of sucking on a lemon then you need to be careful that you do not cause an embarrassment to yourself or to others because of your limited finances.

LENTILS

Relationship issues. If you dream of lentils then it indicates that you and your partner are having arguments and that you are sure the other person is deceiving you. Your parents, though, are trying to get you to work at the relationship which they feel is in the best interests of everyone. It is not in your best interests and you need to decide for yourself.

LEOPARD

Dangerous rivals: a leopard attacking you in a dream signifies opposition, so be careful where you place your confidences. To kill a leopard means that you will outwit your rivals.

➠ *Death, Hide, Hunting, Killing*

LETTERS

Messages. Letters in a dream at their most basic indicate that you are about to receive a message. If you see a letter of the alphabet then it is shorthand for a word or a person; they may have that letter as the first letter of their name, for example.

To receive a letter is good news as it brings a message from someone close to you. In your dream the letter may indicate extra information if you can read it. If the letter brings problems then it may bring a struggle in waking life. If the letter is from a bank then this would indicate financial difficulties that need to be resolved.

Sending a letter means that you need to get a message over to someone. If it is a friend or a relative then it can mean that you are having difficulty explaining to them something that is going on. A letter being sent to a partner can reveal frustration in your relationship; it can also indicate emotional or sexual problems which can be difficult to discuss with each other. In this case the dream is suggesting that you approach your partner and talk about the problems before you drift even further apart.

To write love letters to unknown people may indicate that you wish to inform someone about an affair that you regret. By sending the letter in your dream you feel that you have confessed and will not need to actually confess when you wake.

To receive letters from people who you do not know suggests that things could be uncomfortable for you at the moment. To send letters to people you do not know indicates that you are jealous of someone. Someone handing you a letter instead of receiving it through the post means minor problems.

If the letter is work-related then it would indicate that there are problems in your working environment. A letter which is unsigned and unnamed indicates that you are about to be attacked physically or verbally from an unknown person.

If you fail to read a
letter then you will lose
out on a business deal.
Receiving or sending a
torn letter will result in
business problems.

If you have just
taken or are about to
take an exam then it
may mean that you are
just anxious about the
results. If the letter gives
the result then it is better
to dream of poor results
than good. If, however,
no exams are due then it indicates that you may be about
to take a course of some sort.

The colour of the paper and ink will bear some
influence on the dream. For instance, green ink or paper
denotes that the dream relates to love and relationships.
Blue ink will give support, while red ink means that
action needs to be taken.

If you do not read the letter but throw it away then it
means that there is something you really need to talk about
to a friend or a partner as you need their forgiveness.

If the letter you have found is hidden behind some
books, for instance, then it is a warning that you do not
trust someone. It could be that you feel a partner is
having an affair. Finding a lot of letters means that the
problem could be with you and there are some guilty
admissions that you need to make.

Dreaming of rare stamps indicates a good financial
year ahead for you. Foreign stamps will bring new friends
that will help you in your work. Putting stamps onto an
envelope will mean that your status in society is about to
increase.

Talking to the postman in your dream is construed as
ill-luck as it means that you are about to enter an affair
and be found out about, which will cause problems for
you and your family.

Finally, it is important that on reading the letter you
take note of what is said to you first thing when you wake
up as that will dictate what you should do in relation to
your dream.

BELOW: Libraries in dreams indicate a quest for knowledge.
LEFT: Letters from Sir Francis Drake to Elizabeth I, from March 1587.
BELOW LEFT: Dreaming of a leopard refers to dangerous enemies in your life.

LETTUCE

Jealousy. You will have to watch out if you dream
of eating lettuce, as you are showing signs of being
jealous of someone else's position; if you are not careful
you will end up in an embarrassing situation of your own
making. To see lettuce growing suggests that you may
gain a savoured prize that has been in your sights for
some time.

➨ *Eating*

LIBRARY

Knowledge. If you see a library in your dreams it
can indicate that you may be about to take up a
new study or hobby. It also indicates that you are not
content with your present circumstances and intend to
change. To be inside a library heralds interests and
hobbies that will involve going back to college or taking
up a new course of education.

➨ *Learning*

LICE

Catching an illness. To dream that you are infected with lice can indicate that you are coming down with an illness. It is often found that dreaming of lice indicates that your body is developing an allergic skin reaction. Dreaming of lice on animals indicates hardship and financial problems.

LIFT

Success. To dream of going up in a lift indicates swift promotion and career opportunities: expect to hear news soon of career enhancement. If the lift is on its way down, then it indicates a time for rethinking your career plans.

LIGHTNING

A bolt from the blue. Dreaming of lightning indicates that you will soon find yourself in the middle of some unexpected events. However, just as everything feels fresher after a thunderstorm, so your dream represents a renewed vigour and a continuation of some old projects, as well as the start of some new ones.

➡ *Storm, Thunder*

LILY

Happiness is presaged if you see or are given lilies in a dream. If the lilies are wilting or poorly

Here stately Lilies, pale and proud,
In vesture pure as summer cloud;

presented, then the signs are that a relationship is about to enter a difficult phase, involving stubbornness and a lack of compromise by both parties.

LIMOUSINE

A dream involving a limousine indicates that there are going to be people around you to help you and that you will achieve whatever goal you have in mind comfortably and will enjoy the journey. If you are the driver, though, then the work seems to offer luxuries to others more than it does to you.

➡ *Bus, Road*

LINEN

Income. Dreaming of linen usually signifies prosperity, so much so that if someone approaches you dressed in linen in your dream it represents the opportunity of an inheritance. If your linen was spoiled, however, then expect your income to spiral downwards.

LION

Pride comes before a fall. Lions are the king of the jungle and in a dream can represent royalty. They are also a warning that you need to be protective of your family, but not to take pride too much as a virtue, otherwise problems will come your way.

LIQUOR

Flattery. To dream of drinking liquor is an indication that you might take someone's flattery too much to heart. You need to remain realistic and not just base your opinions on what others think of you. To see liquor barrels leads to the blossoming of your assets at the expense of domestic stability and happiness.

LITERATURE

A record of new actions. The type of book you are reading in your dream gives an indication of the area of your life you need to work on. Reading a romance novel in your dream, for example, suggests that you need to pay attention to your love life. Reading an academic or non-fiction book is a warning that perhaps you need to broaden your horizons by taking a course or perhaps rethink your work situation.

BELOW: The colourful Agama lizard, common in central Africa, basks in the early morning sun.
BELOW LEFT: Seeing lilies in a dream can signify stubbornness.
BELOW FAR LEFT: The Chinese goddess Tien-mou, the Mother of Lightning, sends electricity down from the clouds.

LIVER

A liver that is not functioning properly foretells of a quarrelsome, overcritical person who will enter your life, bringing disharmony and unnecessary problems. To eat liver in a dream indicates that a deceptive individual may come between you and your loved one. Prepare to root out the troublesome person that will gnaw at your patience.

LIZARD

An insincere acquaintance. Lizards represent untrustworthy foes that you need to be on guard against. Lizards do have acute hearing, so the dispute could be caused by something that a friend heard.

LOBSTER

Repayment negotiations. If you see a lobster in your dream it means that you will have to renegotiate loans. If you are eating the lobster then these negotiations will be successful.

LOCK

Legal activities. If you dream of a lock it indicates that you will have some legal activities to deal with. To pick a lock is a warning that you must not allow yourself to get involved in activities that you know to be dishonest or conducted in an underhand way.

LOCOMOTIVE

 Achievement. To be driving a locomotive means that you are well on the way to achieving results, although take care not to get carried away with early progress. If a locomotive plays just a cameo role in your dream then expect a visitor who will further your career.

LOCUST

Loss of business. It is thought that locusts in a dream signify devastation. To see a swarm of locusts indicates you do not have enough time to prepare, and in the modern world it is an indication that you are trying to take on too much.

LODGER

Secrets. If you have a lodger in your dreams it indicates that you have some secrets that you are trying to hide; public knowledge of these secrets might cause considerable embarrassment to friends and family. They tend to involve extramarital affairs.

LOOM

One step back to move forward. To dream of a loom means that you will need to adjust your current situation even if this means taking a change of direction. You are feeling irritated but everything will work out for you in the end. To see a loom in your dream with no one working it, however, implies that you are being too stubborn at the moment.

LOST

Find a new direction. If you feel that you are lost in a dream it indicates that you feel that you have lost your way in life. You are in a situation where you need to find a new direction for yourself. If you are on land then it is likely to be a career direction, whereas if it is at sea then it is an emotional direction. The dream itself and whether you find a direction to go in and how easy that is, will influence how easy it is to find a new direction when you awake.

➡ *Crossroads, Unknown Places, Wandering*

LOUNGE

Security. The lounge in a dream represents your home and your security. The more comfortable the room in your dream, the better you feel about your home situation. If the lounge feels crowded then it is an indication that you wish for more time to yourself.

LOVE

Happiness. To dream of falling in love reflects a desire for happiness and affection if you are single.

If you have a partner, this dream reflects an increased bond between you. If you see other people making love then this indicates that your life will go well.

LUMBER

Effort with little gained. If you dream of lumber (piles of wood) it indicates that you will have to put a lot of effort into activities with very little gain. However, if you see the lumber burning then it suggests that you will receive some money from an unexpected source.
➠ *Lumberjack*

LUMBERJACK

Effort. If you are male and a lumberjack appears in your dream it indicates that putting some effort into a job will reap the rewards you desire, although it may take some time. A woman dreaming of a lumberjack indicates that she is about to or wishes to meet someone from an agricultural background.

LYNX

Warning of a woman. The lynx represents an enemy, mostly in this case as a woman. It is a symbol of hidden hostility, so when you wake you will need to find the woman with the evil influence.

LYRE

Engagement. If you are male and you dream of a lyre; it means that you will meet a new business partner, however, if you are female and have this dream, as well as acquiring a new business partner, you could stumble upon love.

MACHINERY

Anxiety but success. To see any form of machinery in a dream indicates anxiety, regardless of whether you work with that machinery in real life or not. However, the dream is positive in that it suggests that there are people around to help alleviate your concerns.

MAGIC AND THE OCCULT

Information. If you find yourself practising magic or the occult in a dream it suggests that you are trying to pick up on knowledge unknown to others, and most importantly that you will shortly attain that knowledge. If you dream of using a Ouija board then, although you will receive the information, you must use the information to help someone else and not use it merely to advance your own interests, as this would bring bad luck.

MAGNET

Sexual attraction. Dreaming of a magnet means that there is a strong sexual attraction with someone around you. Because the attraction is so strong this dream can also act as a warning – this may not be your current partner.

ABOVE: Falling in love in your dream indicates a desire for love in real life.
ABOVE LEFT: The god Pan or Silenus plays his lyre, from a Pompeiian fresco.
LEFT: A flock of sheep provide wool for spinning directly to the loom.

MAGPIE

A bird with a variety of messages. The magpie nursery rhyme has become so ingrained in our minds that its meaning is exactly the same in dreams: 'one for sorrow, two for joy, three for a girl, four for a boy' depending on the variation of the rhyme with which you were brought up. Magpies could also indicate an answer to a question that seems to be black and white but is not, so look again more closely between the lines and study the subtler colours that you find. This will prevent a myopic viewpoint and give you a refreshing depth of knowledge.

MAID

Prudence. If you dream of having a maid and you do not have one then it is an indication that you need to watch finances. This is not the time for extravagance or overspending. For a woman, dreaming of being a maid restores her credibility and confers upon her new duties that grant her increased social status.

MALICE

Help. If you see that someone is being malicious to you in your dream then you will find that you have very little to worry about in real life and that you will receive plenty of support from others. If you dream of behaving maliciously towards others, then no matter how frustrated you may feel you should try to be helpful.

MALT

Dangerous liaisons. Drinking malt in a dream indicates that you will find yourself in a dangerous situation, but that you will come to no harm. To dream of malt indicates a luxurious lifestyle that may well lead you beyond your original goals.

MAN

Masculine drive. A man in a dream brings activity and action; however, the actual meaning of the dream will depend on the situation; what the man is doing, what he is wearing and the colour of his hair. For a woman the man in the dream can represent a sexual ideal but generally represents activity and masculine drive.

MANNERS

Stalled progress. If you have bad manners in a dream then it indicates that you have stopped, or at least stalled, a project in your life that you must re-evaluate and modify to allow you to progress further. Basically, the better behaved you are in a dream, the more successful you will be in life.

MANSION

Changes in fortune. To dream that you are in a mansion means that you will need to look carefully at financial issues around you. It is possible that you will need to save money now to ensure a more secure future. To see the mansion in the distance represents the long-term financial goals you have set yourself.

MANUFACTURE

 Investment. To dream of a large factory or warehouse indicates the need for investment. If it is well-stocked it suggests that your speculations will prosper whilst a depleted or empty warehouse denotes that this is a risk that could well be a failure.

MAP

Finding a direction. You are looking for a new direction in life if you find yourself studying a map in your dreams and it can signify a physical or emotional journey. The relationship will have a corresponding

complexity to the map. How rewarding it will be is indicated in your dream by the ease or difficulty you experienced in understanding the symbols of the map.
➠ *Crossroads*

MARIGOLD

Contentment. If you dream of marigolds it shows that you will be content in life, even though you will not have much money. It seems that you will also be happy, as financial issues are not important to you.

MARMALADE

Ill health. To dream of eating or dishing out marmalade is an indication that in the morning you will not feel like eating breakfast and may feel too unwell to go to work. This dream is telling you to rest up for the day as you are below par.

MARRIAGE

Relationship issues. If you dream of the state of marriage then it indicates that your relationship is not going as well as it might. This is a warning for you to re-think whether it is really marriage you want. As an omen, dreaming of marriage at the start of a relationship suggests that the relationship will not survive.
➠ *Altar, Celebration, Ceremony, Church, Religious Icons*

MARS

Arguments. Mars in a dream brings arguments and quarrels that need to be sorted out. It is also an indication that you have the ability now to start new projects and activities. You therefore need to work with others rather than against them.

ABOVE: Van Eyck's Arnolfini Wedding, *a bad omen for a new relationship.*

119

MARTYR

Care of others. If you dream about being a martyr in your dreams it indicates that you need to be careful of being selfish and not letting others down. In general this is a warning that you need to think of others first.

MASK

Deception. To dream of someone in a mask means that you are being deceived. In real life, you may feel that this is true but do not know who the person is. When in a dream state concentrate on seeing the person behind the mask.

➠ *Theatre*

MASON

Brotherhood. To dream of seeing a mason (regardless of whether it is a freemason or an artisan working on a building) simply means that there are people around who will help when you are in need.

MASS

Support of others. To dream that you are at a church mass indicates that at the moment you feel alone and could do with the support others. An outside mass means that eventually you will gain the support you desire, but if you are inside a church it indicates that this assistance will not be forthcoming and you will have to cope alone.

MATHEMATICS

Problem-solving. Similar to anagrams, seeing sums or mathematical formulae in a dream suggests that you have problems to solve; solving them in your dream indicates success in finding a solution in your waking life.

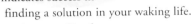

➠ *Anagram, Numbers*

MATTRESS

Comfort zone. If you are dreaming that the mattress is fine then there is not a problem – you are comfortable with a situation. However, if the mattress is uncomfortable then there are problems with the current situation and the augury is that you would benefit by saving for the rainy days ahead.

MAZE

A maze represents obstacles. Dreaming of a maze suggests that you are finding it difficult to find your way in your career. It may be that you will have to re-think the direction you want your job to take. You may even have to take a few steps backwards in order to go forward in the right direction.

➠ *Labyrinth*

MEAL

Prosperity unless alone. Dreaming of eating your meals with others is a sign of good fortune, whatever the circumstances. However, if you dream that you are eating on your own it may suggest that you should be wary of what others think of you. If the meal is breakfast then it indicates that you need to be careful about speaking too soon. Lunch indicates that you could be missing out on work opportunities. Dreaming of eating dinner or supper on you own indicates quarrels with loved ones.

MEAT

 Financial achievements. If the meat is raw it signifies that you will not fulfil your life's ambitions. If you dream of cooking meat or cooked meat on a plate then you will accomplish a lot in life; changes in the near future will help you on your way financially and you will do well.

➡ *Kidneys, Liver*

MECHANIC

Help available. If you dream of a mechanic then it indicates that soon someone will be along to help you out with your problems.

➡ *Bus, Machinery*

MEDAL

To win a medal in dreams indicates achievement. You may not receive a medal in life, but you could find that you will be promoted at work, or in some other

BELOW: Eating a meal with others in your dream symbolizes good fortune.
LEFT: The study of Arithmetic, from Caxton's Myrrour of the Worlde *(1481).*
FAR LEFT: A mask appearing in your dream is a warning of deception.

way, your work will be rewarded. If the medal is in the form of a rosette then it indicates that the achievement is transient and that the praise will be very short-lived; however, if it is in the form of a necklace then it gives the achievement longevity and your contribution will have lasting qualities well into the future.

➡ *Winning*

MEDICINE

Unpleasant start. If you dream of taking medicine, then it means that you will have to do something you do not particularly want to do, but have to. Although the results might be unpleasant to start with, the circumstances will get better in the long run. Giving medicine to other people might also be a warning that you have to treat someone else with caution.

➡ *Hospital*

MELANCHOLY

dness and failure. If you dream of melancholy in a relationship then it indicates that there are problems with the relationship and that it will fail. In all events the feeling of melancholy in a dream indicates that the actions you are taking will not have the desired happiness that you wish for.

MELON

Financial changes. If you dream of melons then you could be in for some unexpected changes of events. It is a warning that you need to be very careful with business decisions as they could lead to a heavy financial loss. It would be better to hold off any major investments.

121

MEMORIAL

Show kindness. A memorial in a dream means that you will have to show patience and kindness to relatives who are likely to be going through a bout of troubles and sickness. This dream confers upon you the role of counsellor so prepare to lend an ear.

MERCURY (HERMES)

Communications. To see the planet Mercury or the god of the same name indicates that news is on its way. This messenger brings insights and aligns synchronistic happenings that open the doors to your future. Prepare to engage in plenty of communications and maintain a flexible approach to the changing path ahead, if you wish to take full advantage of the options that will soon appear in your life. Mercury influences only last a day or two and so it is important that you act quickly.

➠ *Crossroads*

METAMORPHOSES

Change. If you dream that you can metamorphose into something you should pay attention to the creature you find yourself able to change into: this will indicate the abilities that you need to cultivate. You need to adapt and change certain aspects of your character to be able to move forward in your life. Correlate the meaning of this dream with the creature featured in your dream for a full interpretation.

➠ *Butterfly, Snake*

METEORITE

Sudden inspiration. Seeing a meteorite in a dream means that sudden opportunities will present themselves, and a chance to make the most of a situation. This effect will not last long – generally a day – so seize the chance before it disappears.

➠ *Comet*

MIDWIFE

Sickness and illness. To see a midwife in your dream means that you could be suffering from ill health. This may relate to the time when midwives were

local wise women or witches who, with their knowledge of herbs, administered treatments for ailments.

MILK

Good health. To dream of milk is a general dream indicating good health; the more milk you see, the better your health and joy will be. Goat's milk is meant to be good for financial business. If you dream of milking animals then this is even better for financial success, though if the cow is restless it may take a little longer than anticipated.

It is no use crying over spilt milk in a dream – you cannot turn the clock back. This is a dream in which you are being told to move on, and accept what you have now rather then looking back to something in the past.

If you dream of sour milk then it suggests that you had better not get too closely involved with the problems that a friend is having, as it could lead to long-term disagreements.

Dreaming of bathing in milk is a sexual fantasy of wanting to be adored and replenished in your beauty and looks.

MINK SEE FERRET

MINT

Health improvements. Dreaming of mint is quite common and it is possible that it is related to residue from toothpaste. It is also thought that mint in a dream signifies a feeling of refreshment; if you have been tired or ill recently you will find your health improves, giving you a sense of refreshing buoyancy particularly in matters involving communications.

➤ *Cooking, Gardener, Grocer*

MISCARRIAGE

Fear of failure. If you are pregnant and have dreamt of having a miscarriage then you are suffering from pangs of anxiety, understandably concerning the birth of your child. If you are not pregnant, however, then this dream indicates fear of failure. It is common among people who have had this particular type of dream to feel that they have failed their parents in some way.

MISTLETOE

Fertility. Dreaming of mistletoe for someone young is a symbol of sexual desires and fertility. It is therefore a dream of positive news to someone in a relationship. In business matters this dream heralds a need for greater patience before the rewards can be collected.

➤ *Branch, Christmas, Tree*

MOLE

Moles indicate problems. To dream of being a mole, or of seeing a mole, means there may be problems ahead. The problems are probably hiding under the surface, but will soon break out unless they are resolved. Also, someone could be being deceitful to you, and trying to weaken your financial foundation.

➤ *Dirt*

ABOVE RIGHT: If you see a mole in your dream, there may be problems ahead.
RIGHT: A hamper of mistletoe, an indicator of sexual desire and fertility.
ABOVE LEFT: Dreaming of milk can represent good health for the dreamer.

MOLE

Omen. Moles are quite important in dreams; there are many psychics who read people's characters from the moles on their body: the larger and darker the mole, the more intense the meaning. The rounder the mole in your dream, the more good fortune should come your way. A mole on the right-hand side is luckier than a mole on the left. A hairy mole indicates bad luck. Dark moles mean quarrels that may be accompanied with a bout of illness.

MONEY

In your dreams money is a way of indicating reward. To give money to others in need indicates that money will come to you in a positive way. If you receive money for hard work then it suggests good news and that you will be rewarded. Dreaming of receiving money, however, does not necessarily mean a financial reward. More often than not dreaming of receiving money is an indication of emotional security.

Dreaming of a pools or lottery win does not necessarily foretell good news. In many ways, this can be seen as a warning not to squander as money problems could haunt you in the near future.

If you have paper money in your dream and it turns into coins then this is an indication that you will have problems but they will not be large. Changing money for foreign currency implies that a windfall will come your way.

To borrow money in a dream is a warning that you need to curb your expenses and tighten your belt. Seeing your bank manager in a dream is not hopeful either and again indicates a need to watch your expenditure.

Stealing money in your dreams can actually be a good omen as it indicates that you will receive an unexpected gift. Saving money or putting the money in a safe or bank means that you will be financially comfortable in the long term.

To receive rare coins in a dream is to be given an unexpected opportunity. To receive gold coins means that, although you will not be rich, you will be emotionally very happy. To receive small amounts of coins such as pennies or cents will mean that you will succeed financially in any major investment or business opportunities that are around. If the coins are all copper then you will do well; if the coins are of silver then not so well. To dream of a large amount of gold coins means that the stock exchange may well have a major fall in value.

If you receive forged notes or counterfeit coins then you are likely to fall ill soon. Also, if you receive a bundle of notes then it promotes health and if you have been under the weather lately then your health is going to improve.

If you are male and you dream that you have found money and you are trying to hide it but cannot find a place, then it means that a woman will be the cause of a financial loss for you.

If you dream that you are holding some coins in your hand then this is a dream about the need for security and would indicate that you would soon be purchasing a house and taking out a mortgage.

➡ *Gold, Jewellery, Silver*

MONKEY

Monkeys signify enemies. To dream of seeing monkeys indicates that you have enemies around, particularly in the workplace where monkeys represent working with incompetent people. If the monkeys are shown to be aggressive then this would indicate underhand and malicious enemies at work.

➡ *Trees*

MOON

Emotions. The Moon in a dream represents your emotions and your responses to certain situations. A Moon shrouded in mist or clouds represents a relationship which you cannot get through to on an emotional level.

Which phase the Moon is in is also considered significant. If the Moon is waxing (going from New Moon to Full Moon), this indicates success in starting new projects and relationships. If the Moon is waning (decreasing from Full Moon to New Moon) then it represents the ending of relationships or the solution of problems.

A bright Full Moon indicates success and happiness in relationships. A bright moonlit night also heightens sexual sensitivity and indicates happiness and contentment in a relationship. The effect of everything is increased if you see the Moon's reflection in water.

If you dream that you are on the Moon, this indicates that you may be being unrealistic about a relationship, reading more into it than actually exists.

ABOVE: The Moon perceived as a boat by the ancient Egyptians.
LEFT: A baby Spider monkey, native to Central and South America.
FAR LEFT: Roman coins from the third century AD, a symbol of reward.

MORGUE

Take care. If you dream of yourself in a morgue then you may not be looking after your health: take this dream as a warning. Equally if you see someone that you know in the morgue in your dream, you should pay that person some extra attention and care.
➠ *Doctors*

MORTGAGE

Financial pressures. Dreaming of a mortgage indicates that you may be having difficulties with your finances. This is a dream that should prompt you into action to sort these out. Additionally, such dreams can refer to borrowings that must be kept within your limits – whether from institutions or from friends.

MORTARBOARD

Success. To see a mortarboard either on yourself or on someone else in a dream indicates that you will be successful in your studies. However, if you find that the mortarboard is too small, it may mean that you have made the wrong choice in your studies and should reconsider. If the mortarboard is too big you may need to try harder at your studies. If you are not the academic type, then this dream would indicate that there could be some financial gain if you embrace new responsibilities.
➠ *Certificate, Graduation, University*

MOSQUITO

Self-protection. To dream of mosquitoes is actually a good sign, as it means you are putting up a protective wall against others who are trying to harm you, enabling you to stand up to them.
➠ *Bite*

MOSS

Security. If you dream of a green carpet of moss it indicates that you will obtain a position where others will rely on you for their security. If it is dry or

dying it indicates that expectations of a romantic nature have been dashed and that you would benefit from looking elsewhere.

MOTH

Family problems. In your dreams, if you find moth holes in clothes it indicates family disappointment of some sort. If you see moths flying in your dreams it can mean fighting within the family. To see moths flying towards a light source implies that others will gather around you seeking your counsel and help in troubled times.

MOTHER

Emotions. Your mother calling to you in a dream can indicate that you feel you are not doing enough to help her or paying her enough attention. Otherwise a mother represents the emotional security that perhaps you need at the moment.

MOTORCYCLE

Freedom to reach the goal on your own. If you are alone on the motorcycle then it indicates that you want to achieve your goal on your own. To have a passenger means that a partnership will yield the best results.
➠ *Road, Travelling*

MOUNTAIN

Obstacles. Mountains in dreams represent obstacles to overcome. The higher and more difficult the mountain is to climb, the harder it will be to achieve your goals, but if you reach the top you will succeed. This is a dream about the need for perseverance.

MOUSE

Mice and rats represent our fears. If you dreamt of mice or rats then this reveals your fears, and the likelihood is that they will get out of control. Prepare to confront and tackle the problems as soon as possible. Mice have very poor eyesight and it is just possible that you are not looking at your problems closely enough.

MUFF

Protection. To dream that you are wearing a muff indicates that you and your interests will be protected by others. To see someone else wearing a muff means that a very strong platonic relationship will be the only source of support that you have when all others around you refuse to help.

MULBERRY

Sickness. To dream of mulberries is a warning to look after yourself as you may be feeling under the weather for a few days.

The number of mulberries you eat in the dream determines the duration of the illness. Each mulberry represents one day.

ABOVE: Perseverance is required if you dream about mountains.
LEFT: A Harvest mouse, which can be symbolic of the dreamer's fears.
ABOVE LEFT: A mortarboard in a dream represents academic success.

MULTIPLE BIRTHS SEE TWINS

MUSCLES

Lack of social contacts. If you dream of showing off your muscles it means that you need to widen your circle of friends. Painful muscles – providing you were not been overdoing it before you went to bed – indicate emotional difficulties. A woman dreaming of muscles means that extra effort is required over the next few months to get work done.

MUSES

There were nine Muses or Fates in classical mythology. Dreaming of one or several of them tells you that you are in a position whereby you can change things, but that you are not taking advantage of this opportunity. You need to look at your situation and judge what it is you would like to change, then act upon it and you will be successful.

MUSHROOM

Financial rewards. Dreaming of eating mushrooms indicates that your finances are due to 'mushroom' soon and that you will be able to cash in on your investments. You have worked hard but you will now be able to sit back and relax a little. To see wild mushrooms suggests that you may well be searching for a freer lifestyle.

MUSIC

Mood and ambience. Music affects our emotions and in a dream adds to the atmosphere, just like in a film. The type of music you hear in a dream will denote the general backdrop mood of the action. A happy, cheerful tune will inspire a happy, cheerful outlook whilst a dark melancholic tune will suggest sadness. Look up the instrument that you have dreamt of in this book to interpret your dream fully.

MUSSEL

Social negotiations. Mussels in a dream represent success in your social life and an increase in parties around the home. To eat clams is an omen denoting increasing social popularity.

MUTE

Do not do anything. The warning in this dream, if you see yourself or another person mute, is not to say anything or do anything in haste. It is time to hold back on your immediate thoughts and let things settle down. Hasty action could result in damaged relations for a long time to come.

NAKED

Secrets out in the open. If you dream that you are naked in a non-sexual setting it means that your secrets are out in the open. This is not necessarily bad news, as new opportunities will arise, providing you have nothing to hide. Seeing someone else naked is a warning of the same sort but that someone else's secrets will be revealed; however, you may not be prepared to hear them.

Being naked is about stripping away pretence and often shows your unconscious thoughts rather than thinking with the mind: it is the understanding of your emotional response to the situation that surrounds you. Other factors of the dream will give hints as to what areas need to be looked at. If you dream that you are swimming naked this represents a need to understand your emotions. The clearer the water then the clearer the solution will be.
➧ *Water*

NANNY

Trying to turn the clock back. If a nanny appears in your dream it means that you wish you could change a situation from the past. You need to be cautious of arguments with relatives.
➧ *Children*

NAVY

Victory over obstacles. If the navy appears in your dream then it indicates that you will be able to overcome obstacles that are in your way. It can also mean a holiday is in store for you once things have settled down.

MUTTON

Business achievements. If you dream of eating mutton it indicates that you will do well in financial transactions. You will find your negotiation skills blossoming and you will be able to achieve your goals without the need of major expenditure.

ABOVE: Music, represented here by Horonobu Suzuki's Lady's Toilet, *can provide an appropriate soundtrack to your dream.*
LEFT: Muscles of the human body in movement, which indicate a need for a wider circle of friends if seen in a dream.
FAR LEFT: A mushroom in a dream promises financial security.

NECK

Financial opportunities. To dream of someone's neck indicates financial opportunities. If the neck is broken then fate will not be in your favour. If you dream that your neck grows in length, you will become more involved in other people's problems; however, this will also bring arguments when you offer your point of view in areas that do not concern you.

NEEDLE

Ease or frustration. If you are threading a needle in your dream then it indicates an obstacle. How well you thread he needle will dictate how well you cope with the obstacle. If you get angry with frustration or prick yourself then you will find it difficult to cope with the situation.

NEGLIGEE

Relationships. If you are male and you dream of someone in a negligee it represents a wish to be close to that person. If you are female and you see yourself wearing the negligee it can mean that you want to be close to your partner but that you are having difficulty communicating with each other.

NEPHEW

Working together. Generally, dreaming of a nephew means that you will have an opportunity of working together in the near future and that this will be a fruitful time for your business. You should be careful to draw up boundaries, however, to make sure that the work falls to both of you equally so one party does not feel that they are being taken advantage of.

NETS (FISHING OR HUNTING)

Nets indicate the catching of different thoughts to successfully complete a project. Depending on how finely or broadly the net is woven indicates whether the details are large or small in nature. however, if the net has holes in it, then it represents wasted time and efforts through lack of attention to details in collecting or collating the information.

NETTLE

Obstacles. Nettles in dream are obstacles that you have to fight your way through. If you get through them then you will be successful but you need perseverance and effort. If you are stung by the nettles then it means that a friend may cause you embarrassment, or let you down, so prepare for a solo fight if you wish to emerge unscathed.

➠ *Thorn*

NIECE

Worries. To dream of a niece is a warning to give this person a call and make sure they are all right, as often you will find they may need your help. In the long term your help will pay off and things will work out well.

NIPPLE SEE BREAST

NOODLES

Know your limits. If you dream of noodles then this represents good business opportunities; there is, however, a need to make sure that you are not taking

BELOW: *Caravaggio's* Fortune Teller *reads her client's palm.*
LEFT: *An Egyptian fresco from the tomb of Peshedu, servant of the Palace of Truth, showing him slaking his thirst under a plam tree.*
FAR LEFT: *If you dream of a pagoda, you can expect to travel soon.*

PALM

Holidays. To see a palm tree in your dreams is an indication that you should consider booking that holiday. You have been overdoing it recently and you feel you need to relax, so now is a good time to plan holiday arrangements. You can also expect at this time news from someone abroad.

➡ *Coconut*

PALMISTRY

To dream of consulting a palmist is an indication that you need to sit down and plan your future. Important changes are going to take place shortly and you need to work out how to make the best of the opportunities. If you dream that you are the palmist then it indicates that others will be looking to you for guidance.

PALSY

Instability. If you dream that you have palsy it indicates that contracts you have recently negotiated are unstable and need to be renegotiated. If your dream indicates a friend with palsy then that friendship is unstable. Likewise, this is not a good dream to have in connection with a relationship.

PALACE

Honour. To dream of seeing a palace indicates that you will soon be honoured by those around you. If you dream of living in a palace, however, it indicates that you think of yourself too much and perhaps set yourself unrealistic goals.

PALLBEARER

Achievement. If you dream that you are a pallbearer then it indicates promotion and an increase in status. However, if you see a pallbearer in your dream, it indicates that you will upset a company or the local council.

PANCAKE

Domestic bliss. To dream of cooking pancakes is a good omen for happiness in the home. The person who cooks the pancakes in the dream is said to rule the roost and govern the home finances.

PANTHER

 A struggle or fight. Cats such as these are animals which are difficult to overcome; if you are able to track the animal down and kill it in your dream then you will succeed in your venture.

PARACHUTE

Escape. Dreaming of a parachute indicates a wish to escape from constantly worrying about your career so you can indulge your ideas and imagination. Dreams involving parachutes can also mean that relationships will be under scrutiny; the way in which you land; on your feet, back or perhaps even crash-landing on to a canopy, can be seen as a measure of your success after the critical phase has passed.

PARADISE SEE HEAVEN

PARALYSIS

Inhibition. If you dream that you are in a state of paralysis this can often be linked to sexual inhibition and emotional problems. You are going through a period where you want to fight against the current situation. There is a lack of confidence on your part and you may be unsure of yourself and your feelings towards other people. If this dream develops a regular pattern it may be wise to seek some therapy of some sort.

PARENTS

Support. Generally, parents appearing in a dream symbolize support: they are there for you and it is a message that you can go and talk to them about your difficulties and they will help you out as much as possible. If they talk to you in your dream it is important that you listen carefully as this message may be the clue to the resolution of the dream.

PARROT

Look who's talking. Parrots represent messages from gossips. If you receive a message, you should be wary of neighbours. Be careful, and make sure that you do repeat information that others would prefer you kept a secret.

➠ *Cage*

PARSLEY

Rewards for effort. If you dream of eating or growing parsley it shows that although you will have to undertake hard work you will be rewarded for your efforts in the long run. Family issues are also heightened and you may decide to add to the family.

➠ *Root*

PARSNIP

Success in business but not love. Dreaming of parsnips is an indication that business is going to take a turn for the better; however, your love life will suffer and you may need to cut back the number of hours spent in the office.

➠ *Root*

PARTNERSHIP

This can be good or bad depending on the dream. If you dream of a successful partnership then things will go well for you. However, if the partnership shows friction then there are problems to face in waking life as well.

➠ *Money*

PARTRIDGE

Love problems. To dream of partridges indicates that you have problems with romance at the moment and that you and your partner are not listening to each other: time needs to be taken to hear each other's viewpoints and re-assess the nature of the relationship.

PARTY

Good news is coming your way. Going to a party represents celebrations and good news, whereas throwing a party in your dream, represents a need for organization. Take note of the atmosphere to compare to the amount of success that you can expect. A bustling, colourful ambience indicates great triumphs, whereas a dull, bored atmosphere suggests fortunes through your own endeavours.

➠ *Celebration*

PASSENGER

Success. You should find things becoming easier for you over the next few months as everyone else is helping to make sure that things go well for you. Sit back and enjoy the attention of others and make the most of a very enjoyable and co-operative time.

PASSPORT

Remember who you are. Dreaming about a passport most obviously suggests impending opportunities for foreign travel. But it can have alternative meanings: if you dream of losing your passport then it is a warning that you are not being true to yourself and that you may be hiding your real self from others.

PASSWORD

Help is at hand. If you dream of a password then it indicates that you will be given help from an influential person. To give away a password indicates that you are being careless and this could lead to trouble in a work situation.

LEFT: A brightly coloured Macaw parrot, which symbolizes gossip and rumours when seen in a dream.
ABOVE FAR LEFT: A parachutist descends through the mist beside a castle. A dream of this nature could indicate a need to escape.

PASTRY

Decisions. If you dream of pastry then you will be faced with some crucial decisions. You will also have to be on your guard to watch out for someone who is trying to deceive you.

PATENT

Achievement. To dream of a patent or a new idea indicates that you will have success. To be granted the patent indicates that a risky venture will yield a high return. To have it deferred or rejected heralds a time of independent ingenuity in order to achieve the success augured in this dream.

➡ *Certificate, Invention, Patron, University*

PATH

A path in a dream represents a journey that you have to take. The narrower the path, the more obstacles you will have to face. If you dream of stepping off the curb then it indicates that you are being distracted from what you should be doing. Stepping back on to the path indicates that you are back on course for your original aspirations.

➡ *Accident, Guidance*

PATIENCE

Activity. To dream of patience means that activity will swiftly come and that your life will be hectic but enjoyably busy: you will not have time to sit still.

PATIENT

Patience. Sometimes in dreams images are used instead of words, and sometimes, the image represents something with a very similar spelling. This case is a classic example where the image of a patient has nothing to do with health, but is a warning to be patient and take your time.

PATRON

Protection. To dream of a patron indicates that you feel vulnerable and are in need of the support of your friends and family. If you are the patron in your dream it suggests you feel you are not receiving the respect and acknowledgement you deserve.

PAUPER

Receiving a gift. If in your dream you are either a pauper or you give money to a beggar, this then will be an indication that money is going to come to you. The only exception to this is where you refuse to give alms or charity to the poor in the dream which indicates reversals in fortune.

PEACH

Pleasure – but at a risk. Dreaming of peaches indicates that you will have to take a risk in the near future but the end result will be worth it – you just need to persevere.

PEACOCK

An omen for marriage. The peacock is an omen for meeting and possibly settling down with a beautiful man or woman. Business success is also prominent, particularly if the dream is around the time of opening a new enterprise. Peacocks in a dream can suggest a flowering of the libido energy. If the feathers were fanned out then they suggest you are seeking amorous attention, whereas if the feathers are down, they indicate modesty on display.

➠ *Pride*

PEAR

Opportunities. Seeing pears in a field or picking them represents new opportunities; if you dream of eating a pear then it indicates that you will gain an advantage by listening to what others say and then acting on that information.

PEARL

Emotions. Although classed as a gem, pearl is not a stone. In a dream pearls represent our emotions and in particular those towards our family, especially mothers and children. In a dream it means that family concerns need to be put first. If your string of pearls breaks it can mean problems within the family that need to be sorted out in a caring motherly way.

PEAS

Small obstacles. If you dream of peas it indicates that there are lots of small obstacles in your work environment that need to be sorted out. If you dream of shelling peas then it indicates a sexual incompatibility that is having a detrimental effect on the relationship.

PECAN

Social events. If you dream of eating pecans it indicates that you will be invited to a variety of social engagements in the coming week. Some of these may be lavish parties, but you will shine and enjoy being admired by others.

ABOVE: Seeing a peacock in your dream can be an omen of marriage.
LEFT: The Agiasma nature trail in Southern Cyprus, symbolizing a journey.
ABOVE LEFT: A dream involving pastry warns of crucial decisions to come.

PELICAN

A spiritual message. Dreaming of pelicans is an indication of your ability to nurture others in a spiritual way. Pelicans in your dream indicate someone, normally yourself, that has an ability to get to the root of other people's problems – especially problems that lie deep in your subconscious.

PEN

Message from afar. A pen in a dream indicates a message from someone who will soon be returning to your life. If the pen does not work take this as a

PLEASING HUES GIVE ADDED CHARM TO FINE CRAFTSMANSHIP

'SWAN' PENS

Here are pens to please both eye and hand . . . "Swan" Pens in delightful colours and varied designs. Their matchless beauty and perfect craftsmanship make them a pleasure to use and a pride to own, and they are guaranteed, like all "Swans", to give lifetime satisfaction.

MADE IN ENGLAND

warning that you may be drawn into a situation that could harm your reputation. The colour of the ink is also significant: red can signify danger, although it is also taken to mean strength and determination; blue tends to indicate the truth and sensitivity; black can mean that you are being obstinate.

➡ *Colours, Letters*

PENCIL

Good health. Pencils in dreams represent good luck and good health. If the pencil has an eraser on the end you will be given the opportunity to rectify a mistake from the past. If you are using a pencil in the dream and find that the lead keeps breaking it signifies that stress is soon going to mount; prepare to curb your explosive temper.

PENGUIN

A message to relax. To dream of penguins may mean that you are behaving in an authoritarian manner with others. Although you may be acting with the best of intentions, others may feel that you are restricting them. To see penguins swimming suggests that you need to pay attention to the emotions of those

around you. If you see Emperor penguins swimming then leadership qualities will be conferred upon you soon.

➡ *Sea*

PEPPER

Watch your reactions. To dream of pepper indicates that you need to watch for being hot-headed. Arguments are too easy for you to get involved in. If you dream of your tongue being affected by pepper then it is a warning not to react to gossip.

PEPPERMINT

Romantic improvements. If you are eating the peppermint in your dream it suggests that you are likely to see an improvement in your love life over the next few weeks. To see someone else eating or handling peppermint signifies that a distant relative is likely to help out.

PETROL

Make sure that you have filled up. This is one of those odd dreams where your subconscious mind may have picked up that the car is low on fuel and replayed it in your mind when asleep.

PETTICOAT

Marital affairs. Changing petticoats could be an indication that you wish to change partners. Losing a petticoat means that someone else will steal your affection. The colour of the petticoat will also have an influence on the meaning: a red one will indicate a hot passionate affair, while a blue one means that you will meet someone who you feel is on the same spiritual or intellectual level as you.

PHANTOM OR SPIRIT

Message. Seeing a phantom in your dreams may mean that someone is trying to communicate a message to you. Generally this is a message of good news that you should take on board but you will have to try and work out what the message is to understand this dream fully. As you can be more psychically in tune when you are asleep it is possible that you have managed to communicate with a spirit of some sort. If the phantom is frightening then it is an indication that you need to act sooner rather than later.

➥ *Apparition*

PHEASANT

An omen of good fortune. If you see a pheasant expect some good news concerning financial matters. If you are carrying the pheasant in your dream, even better, as this indicates that you will be bestowed with honour in some way.

PHOTO ALBUM

Recollecting the past. To dream of looking into a photo album indicates that you are looking for something from the past, perhaps a happier time. If you dream that you are looking at a photo of a particular

BELOW: William Blake's Ghost of a Flea, *who urges you to act soon.*
BELOW LEFT: Dreaming of penguins means that you should relax.
BELOW FAR LEFT: Some Swan pens, whose pleasing hues give added charm.

person, it indicates that you are trying to establish a link, perhaps even a psychic link, with that person: it is a signal for you to get in touch. If you are single and dream of looking at a wedding album, this often indicates a wish to be married.

➥ *Family*

PHOTOGRAPHY

Photography represents deception in dreams. If you dream a photographer is taking a picture of you it indicates that you are about to unwittingly get yourself and others into trouble. To dream that you are taking the picture indicates that you will know about the person(s) who will cause your future prospects harm.

➥ *Camera*

PIANO

Success. To hear or play a piano signifies success and enjoyment, providing of course that the piano is played in tune. If it's out of tune then there is discordance within a relationship.

PICK

Problems from elsewhere. To have a pick or pickaxe in your dream indicates that someone is trying to put you down. However, if you persevere, you will outwit them and overcome the setbacks placed before you.

PICKLE

Love life is confused. Pickles in a dream mean that your relationship may be up in the air. However, you should not be discouraged, as there is still a lot of love and affection and your romance will soon be back on course for a very stable future.

PICKPOCKET

Violation. To dream that you have been pickpocketed indicates that you feel that someone has emotionally been sniping or prying into your affairs. If you dream that you have been pickpocketing someone else then you have been acting falsely against a friend.

PICNIC

If the weather holds out and it is a sunny day then a picnic indicates that you will feel satisfaction in

the relationships you have, with family around. If the picnic is prevented by bad weather, however, this can hint that there might be some relationship issues that need to be tackled.

PIG

Some cultures regard the pig as an unclean animal, and therefore the persons (character traits) represented are seen by yourself, or those around you, as being unclean, and/or unsavoury in some way. To see a sow suckling indicates concerns and protective instincts, often relating to the nursing of children.

PIGEON

The ultimate messenger. Pigeons were traditionally used for carrying messages of importance. Dreaming of a pigeon means that you will receive a message at high speed, maybe even faster than email, as there may be some form of telepathic or clairvoyant link to this message. On receipt of this message act upon it straightaway.

PILLOW

Pillow talk. If the pillows are dirty in your dream it suggests that you are being unfaithful to your partner. Otherwise this dream simply means that you need to spend some time discussing personal issues with your partner.

PIN

Annoyances. Pins are said to stand for family annoyances and minor problems. If you can hear a pin drop then it indicates that you are calm and content with the situation around you. Finding a pin in your dreams is a sign of good luck. If someone else is pricked in your dream then you will be called upon to help them. Likewise someone will come and help you if you managed to get pricked by a pin in your dream.

PINEAPPLE

Social happiness. Eating a pineapple indicates a social success and that you will find yourself in an elevated position. You will also be able to go on an exotic holiday with family or friends as you take advantage of this success.

PIRATE

Adventure. Dreaming of pirates is an indication that you are seeking emotional excitement. The sea represents your emotions and pirates seem to add a sense of excitement. The dream could simply mean that you are about to embark on an adventurous business manoeuvre. There is, however, need for caution because just as pirates are untrustworthy, so too can be business colleagues.

PITCHER

Help for a friend. To dream of a pitcher indicates that you will be out celebrating with friends. One of those friends will need help in recovering something from the past.

PLANETS

An indication of feelings. The planets in dreams have an archetypal astrological imagery and influence specific areas of life and the way in which you approach situations and problems. The planet you see in your dream will give an indication of the area of your life that is affected. Mercury represents travel and is an indicator of news and communications. Venus is the planet of love and brings relationships into focus and is also believed to bring luck in financial issues. Mars can herald arguments as well as action and activity. Jupiter in a dream indicates promotion and status. Saturn is an indication of time and age. Uranus indicates computers and ideas, while Neptune in a dream indicates the mystical side of life. Pluto is a look at the restrictions we place upon ourselves.
➡ *Mars, Mercury*

PLASTERING

Preparation. If you dream of plastering, it can suggest that you are preparing your thoughts into solid foundations for a future family. The ease with which the walls are plastered and the speed at which they dry reflect how quickly you can expect things to work domestically. Crumbling plaster denotes family disputes whilst plaster casting suggests repetition of an old cycle of events.

PLEASURE

Enjoyment. If you dream of pleasure it means that you are going to have the time to enjoy the rewards of all the hard effort you have put in recently. It is a sign that a relaxing and pleasurable time is on its way.

LEFT: A poster of Bluebeard, who would symbolize adventure in a dream.
ABOVE LEFT: Pineapples, signs of social happiness, on a fruit stall in Malaysia.
FAR LEFT: Cezanne's Dejeuner sur l'Herbe, *representing secure and satisfying relationships when seen in your dream.*

PLUM

Career enhancement. If you dream of eating plums, like the nursery rhyme of Jack Horner who pulled out a plum which turned out to be title deeds, plums in dreams represent property gains connected with land investments. If they are dried or tinned, however, this indicates that your collateral and finances are bound up with property problems.

PLUMBER

Bladder problems. A reference to waterworks like this in a dream is an indication that there are physical problems that should be checked out.

POCKETS

Hidden surprises. If you have dreamt that your pockets were full but when you checked them there was nothing there, this indicates that someone has let you down. However, if you find an object inside your pocket it will be the key to the dream and often represents issues that will come into your life by unexpected means.

POISON

Tension. If you dream that you have been given poison then it is an indication that you feel that a lot of people are against you; however, if you stick to your guns you will win the arguments. If you dream that you have administered the poison to someone else then it is an indication that you want to end that particular friendship.

POLICE

Security. Police in dreams represent security and assistance. If the police are coming to your rescue it means that security will be put in place to ensure that you do not run into problems. Even if you find yourself on the wrong side of the law this is still a fortunate omen and leads to assistance being given to you.

POLISHING

Working for the future. If you dream of polishing in your dream then it indicates that you will be rewarded for the efforts you have put in. The greater the depth of the shine, the greater the prestige you can expect to enjoy. To inadvertently dull the shine whilst polishing indicates that you have a tendency to shy away from success.

POLITICS OR POLITICIAN

Success and status. Dreaming of politics is an indication of future success; however, if you are dreaming of talking politics with a member of the opposite sex then it indicates that you will not fulfil your hopes in matters of the heart. Dreaming of running for a political post or working as part of a political campaign indicates that you will achieve success and status, but may also lose out on friendships as a result.

POMEGRANATE

Fertility. If you dream of eating or seeing pomegranates then it indicates that you or someone close to you is just about to fall pregnant, for pomegranates indicate fertility. If the pomegranate seeds were unripe the omen is one of fertility treatment.

POPPY

Remembrance. So ingrained on the subconscious are the memories of the two World Wars that now the red poppy in a dream is sign of remembrance. It hints that you will remember someone who has departed.

PORCELAIN

Fragile domestic life. Although your relationship looks good to others, you feel that all is not right. You need to rely on others to help you through what may be a difficult time.

PORCUPINE

A need for protection. Whether you dream of a porcupine or a hedgehog, the meaning is the same: someone is trying to protect themselves, however, if you approach them carefully and with kindness they will open their heart to you. If you are dreaming that you are the porcupine, it indicates that you are trying to hide away from others.

PORK

Property achievements. If you dream of pork it suggests that you will do well in property dealings. If you are eating pork in your dream then it is a warning to be careful in these property transactions. To serve pork indicates that you will be involved in heavy negotiations before achieving your goals.

➡ *Meat*

PORRIDGE

Guilt. Porridge in a dream is associated with prison and therefore it can represent a feeling of guilt in some way. It may not be a criminal offence, but someone feels guilty over something they did or failed to do. This shortcoming will soon be found out and revealed to all.

PORTER

Help yourself. If you see a porter in your dreams it indicates that you feel you need help with a situation. In reality, though, you should face this particular problem on your own rather than relying on others.

POT

Domestic circumstances. Pots in a home indicate your happiness with the arrangement – all is well unless you see

LEFT: Jack Horner, whose plums turned out to be title deeds.
BELOW LEFT: Poppies in a dream represent remembrance.
BELOW FAR LEFT: Victorian policemen, bringing security to your dreams.

broken pots, which indicate marital disputes and relationship breakdowns.

POTATO

Good luck all round. If you dream of potatoes it indicates that not only will you enter a state of happiness in your home but also that work will see improvements and your income will also be significantly better.

POULTRY

Extravagance. To dream that you are eating or cooking poultry it indicates that you will have to be careful in dealing with domestic financial issues. This dream is a hint that you are inclined to overspend – a fault you should watch carefully in the near future.

POWER

Achievement. Dreaming of being powerful is an indication that achievement is going to come your way. This dream is an omen not to give up now but to fight for your goals and continue the struggles. This is a time when you are harnessing your skills and talents effectively. Victory is very possible if you endure the road ahead.

PRAIRIE

The world is before you. If you dream of a prairie, tundra or rolling open plain, it indicates that you feel a little lost and uncertain which direction to take next. However, the dream is a message that whatever direction you go in will be the right one. Even if you feel lost now you are certain to succeed – you just need to set yourself a target and go for it.

PRAYER

Contemplation. If you dream that you are in prayer then it means that you need to reflect on what is happening around you. If you hear others pray then it indicates that you will get the support of others.

PREGNANCY

Fertility. To dream of pregnancy may indicate that you are actually going to have a baby. Many women dream that they are pregnant and feel pregnant before any tests can prove one way or the other. However, it may be the body's way of telling the mind that changes need to be made. On the other hand pregnancy in a dream can be a warning against infidelity.

PREJUDICE

Complaisance. If you are prejudiced against someone in your dreams it indicates that you are not taking their views into consideration and this will have a detrimental effect on your success. If someone bears prejudice against you in a dream then you will need to make more effort to explain your plans.

PRIDE

Pride comes before a fall. Showing pride in a dream about your own activities indicates that your plans may not work out and that others will undermine your work. However, if pride is shown by others then this can indicate rapid progress concerning your career over the next few months.

PRIMROSE

Passion. If you dream of a primrose then it indicates a very hot and steamy relationship. It is also a very hot-headed one and there will be plenty of arguments, and it is unlikely to stand the test of time.

PROCESSION

An occasion to rejoice. The meaning of this dream depends on the type of procession: a sombre church procession indicates the illness of someone close; however, if the procession is of a fun nature, then this implies there will be a celebration.
➡ *Carnival*

PROFANITY

Embarrassment. A man issuing profanities indicates financial problems that could cause an embarrassment with another person, while for a woman, to issue profanities in a dream suggests that an affair will come out into the open to the embarrassment of all.
➡ *Anger, Insult*

PROSTITUTE

Help at hand. If your dream involves a prostitute, it often means that you will receive help from an unlikely source in solving a problematic issue. If the prostitute is sympathetic then you are likely to gain the support of others. If she is hardened and brazen in her attitude then it means you should stay clear of unscrupulous behaviour. If you dream that you are a prostitute it signifies the outward expression of your sexuality.
➡ *Garter*

PSYCHIATRIST

Advice. If you dream about yourself as a psychiatrist, it indicates that you feel that everyone is using you as a shoulder to cry on and that there is no one left for you to turn to. You want to find someone that is willing to listen to you for a change.

PUBLIC HOUSE

Friendship. If you dream that you are in a public house with a group of friends then it indicates that

you are about to enter into social activities and exchange valuable communications in pleasant surroundings. If the pub is sparse and you are drinking alone it denotes a period of retrospection. If you speak to others, then you will have the chance to communicate these old feelings with your friends.

PUDDING

Caution with investments. To dream of puddings indicates that you might be putting more investment into a project then you can afford, or that the eventual return will warrant. If you dream of making a pudding for your lover it has a similar meaning, suggesting that what might be a very passionate start to the relationship will belie its eventual outcome.

PUDDLES

Social mistakes. If you dream of stepping in a puddle or being splashed, then consider it a warning that you could be about to embarrass yourself at a party or other social event. If you manage to avoid the puddle then you will avoid the problem.

PULPIT

Learning required. If you dream of standing at a pulpit addressing a congregation or meeting, it could mean that you are about to dispense advice to someone. However, if you are listening to someone else or you see an empty pulpit it is a warning to heed the advice of others.

PULSE

New activity. If you dream, of taking your own pulse it signifies that you will be starting a new and busy business prospect. However, if you dream that you are taking someone else's it could mean that you lose out to their initiative.

PUMP

Obstacles to which you hold the solution. Regardless of what type of pump it is – even a bicycle pump – this dream means that you hold the key to a problem yourself. If you are pumping away and there does not seem to be any progress it means that you will have to push harder in your work. Dreaming of an oil well pump will bring rich rewards in the long-term future.

BELOW: A pump in your dream symbolizes a problem which you can solve.
BOTTOM: The fourth Dynasty pyramid of Cheops at Giza, Egypt.
BELOW LEFT: A festival procession, symbolizing a celebration.

PUNCH

Selfishness. If you dream of drinking punch then it indicates that you are acting in a hedonistic and selfish way, and that you need to consider other people's requirements. To prepare the punch yourself indicates that you are contemplating selfish endeavours and intend to usurp others' energies for your own gains.

PYJAMAS

This dream means that emotional issues need to be resolved. The dream is also common for couples going through problems and indicates that they may need to communicate with each other more when they have privacy, away from children and family.

PYRAMID

Focus in life. The pyramid is said to represent the karmic past, and therefore represents our base in life and our ideals for the future. If you dream of a pyramid it means that you are laying foundations in career and family and hope that through this you will be able to go on and achieve greater goals. This can often be associated with starting a new business or beginning a family.

QUAIL

The quail is a messenger. Dreaming of quail often signifies a message from someone who is close to you, though in order to avoid hurting your feelings, they may have given you only part of the message. You may have to read between the lines to understand the full message intended for you.

QUARTET

A reunion. To hear a string quartet or even a vocal quartet means you will hear news of friends. If you are part of the quartet in your dream this indicates that you will be partly responsible for the organization of the celebrations.
➠ *Fiddle*

QUAY

Reflection. If you dream that you are at a quay then it can represent a yearning for an old love. If there are ships in the harbour then you will meet someone via a travel opportunity. If you get on board a boat at a quay it suggests that feelings of former times need to be recaptured before any new relationship can be launched.

QUESTIONING

Reasoning. If you are being questioned in a dream then this is a way of trying to get to the root of your problems. Your mind is assimilating the facts in your dream and when you awake you will have the answers before you.

QUILT

Prosperity. In a dream a quilt is considered a sign of happiness and luxury. The type of pattern and the particular colour of the quilt will further indicate the meaning, but basically you will see improvements in your relationship.
➠ *Colours*

QUIZ

Decisions to make. If you dream that you are in a quiz, you have to give yourself time to answer problems. It may be that you are unsure of yourself. It also indicates that you are about to be asked problematic questions and that you fear it. It is quite common for people to dream that they are in a quiz just before a job interview.
➠ *Reading*

QUOITS

Loss of employment. Should you dream of playing quoits you could find yourself without a job the next day. To lose in the game indicates that you will experience a period of distress due to dramatic corporate fluctuations, which are beyond your control. To win, however, modifies the meaning by making you aware of the inevitable changes that are looming and so providing you with the upper hand to take the initiative and plan accordingly.

RABBIT

Rabbits represent fertility; this sort of dream is often indicative of the prospect of children. Be prepared, as a dream of this nature may mean that a lot of expense is heading in your direction. You are certainly going to need plenty of energy to undertake new commitments. Pet rabbits in a dream indicate impending engagements and marriages.

BELOW: A Power-Tone radio, from the 1930s.
LEFT: A baby raccoon, which if seen in your dreams would signify adaptation.
BELOW FAR LEFT: The quay at Naples, from the Tavola Strozzi *panel.*

RACE

 Perseverance against time. A race indicates something that needs to be finished: you may lose out if you do not complete what you have started. If you win the race in your dream then you are likely to win and achieve your goals very soon in reality.

RACCOON

Raccoons indicate adaptation. Dreaming of a raccoon implies that you need to adapt to new circumstances; this may mean that you have to review your life, and prepare to adapt to make the necessary changes, in order to emerge into the future unscathed.

RACING SEE BETTING

RADIO

Communication issues. Radios represent difficulties communicating with loved ones. This is particularly true if the radio reception is hazy. The dream is literally speaking to your wavelength and is telling you to buck up your ideas and communicate with loved ones, especially if there has been some distance between you, either through time or geographical residence.

SUPER-OCTODE
445

SÉLECTIF : un seul bouton à tourner pour faire défiler avec une grande puissance, séparément et sans brouillages, toutes les émissions européennes.

ANTIFADING : aucun évanouissement des auditions.

MUSICALITÉ : inégalable grâce à la nouvelle lampe octode.

CADRAN A VISIBILITÉ TOTALE avec 54 noms de stations repérées et gradué en longueurs d'ondes. Réglage à la portée d'un enfant.

AUTRES PARTICULARITÉS : 5 lampes "DARIO" à rendement multiple - Puissance 9 watts - Prise pour pick-up - Fonctionnant sur 110, 130, 220, 240 volts alternatif - Ébénisterie luxueuse en noyer verni.

PRIX IMPOSÉ : 1.495 Francs
ENSEMBLE RADIO-PHONO : 2.275 Francs

POWER-TONE-RADIO
CONSTRUCTEURS
9, rue du Faubourg Poissonnière - PARIS IXe

RAFFLE

 Wishful thinking. To win a raffle or a lottery is perhaps something that we all dream of: taking off on luxury holidays and revelling in the luxury of untold wealth. Unfortunately, this dream is not a premonition of future fortunes; it is simply a case of wishful thinking.

➠ *Betting*

RAFT

 Sort yourself out. To construct a raft yourself indicates achievements through your own volition. To float on a raft suggests that your own lethargy will lead to someone else taking advantage of your efforts.

➠ *Apathy, Laziness, Water*

RAILWAY STATION SEE TRAIN

RAIN

 Money issues. Rain in dreams relates to your financial circumstances. A light pouring of rain indicates that you will have one or two minor financial issues to sort out, but if the rain in your dream is heavier, this indicates that you will be able to spend some of the money you have saved for a rainy day. To hear raindrops on the roof of your house indicates that you will be secure in your home – just as long as the roof is not leaking. To be drenched by rain indicates that you are about to receive a substantial amount of money. A thunderstorm or monsoon means that a business venture is about to take off and, although you will be working harder, you will also be rewarded for the effort.

➠ *Colours, Rainbow, Water*

RAINBOW

 A dream comes true. If you dream of a rainbow then it indicates that you will find happiness and reward soon. Rainbows signify promotions and success If your dream included your partner, it indicates the fulfilment of your desires and hopes from the relationship, and suggests that your commitments are about to bear fruit.

RAISIN

 Financial issues. If you dream of eating or seeing raisins then it is an indication that you need to tighten your belt. Money seems to be draining out faster than it comes in so it is also time to re-evaluate your expenditure.

RAM SEE SHEEP

RAMBLING

 A difficult time. If you dream of rambling it means that at the moment things are quite difficult for you and there are quite a few obstacles. However, if you persevere you will be able to reach your target and achieve your dreams.

RANSOM

Unexpected money. Whether you have paid or received ransom money in your dream it indicates that you will have received some money from an unexpected source, though you may have to work harder than expected to earn it, and you may have had to go some distance to collect your reward.

RAPE

Reputation. As a dream omen being raped or committing a rape warns you to be careful in a current relationship situation. This may not even be in a sexual situation; it is just that you could be taken advantage of and therefore need to be on your guard.
➠ *Family, Fear*

RASPBERRY

Business success. To dream of raspberries indicates that you will do well in business. This is particularly trus for those who are self-employed. It also bodes well for those who would like to stop working for a structured company and take the initiative of starting a venture of their own.

BELOW: A carved wooden raven rattle, found in Alaska.
LEFT: Constable's Landscape with a Double Rainbow, *indicating happiness.*
FAR LEFT: Being drenched by rain in a dream promises financial gain.

RAT SEE MOUSE

RAVEN

A magical message. Dreaming of ravens on land is often associated with messages from spirits and teaches us to look inwards at our soul. Because the raven at sea brings change with it, the implications of this type of dream are not so good and indicates a possible shipwreck. An Englishman dreaming of ravens, particularly if they are flying away from the home, is a warning. It is for this reason that the ravens of the Tower of London provide magical protection for the British monarch, which would die if they left the grounds of the castle.

READING

 Literary endeavours. To dream of reading a book may be the mind's way of telling us to sit down and write a book: a dream of this nature often leads to literary success in some form.

➡ *Quiz*

RELIEF

Talk to someone. If your dream includes a feeling of relief it is an indication that you are going through some problems. If you discuss your problems with someone in your dream then you will be able to sort them out.

RELIGION

Contentment. If you dream of religion in general then it indicates that you are content with your own spirituality, particularly if outside. Dreaming of being inside a church may indicate that you have problems understanding or coming to terms with your spiritual identity.

➡ *Synagogue*

RELIGIOUS ICONS

Religious upbringing will influence the religious characters and icons that you see in a dream, with the imagery tailored to your religious background. Whatever your beliefs though, religious icons in dreams seem to have a powerful influence on the dreamer. To dream of the Pope, for instance, may seem far more significant to a Catholic than a follower of any other religion, but is a universal indication of strength of purpose, and may be an indication that in a time of need you need to rely on yourself rather than those around you.

Angels are always seen as a positive omen, and indicate that your wishes will be granted. Cherubs also hint at forthcoming happiness.

The Devil symbolizes your 'inner devils' and indicates the need to take responsibility for your own actions in order for you to experience freedom. It often indicates a situation where the dreamer feels tied down, but where it is up to the dreamer to find their own solution, instead of blaming others.

God: The appearance of God in your dreams represents contentment with your present situation.

Healer: To dream of a healer signifies forthcoming emotional turmoil, but that you will have a confidant to share your worries.

Priests: The meaning of priests in a dream varies depending on their position within the religious hierarchy. If you see the local priest in your dreams then you are probably ill at ease with a recent event, whereas to dream of a Bishop or Archbishop suggests that you need to ask someone for advice, but don't know how to go about it.

Rabbi: To dream of a rabbi is a powerful omen, whatever your religion, and symbolizes a friend who will make an effort to understand your problems.

REPRIEVE

Time to act. If in your dream you have been reprieved, this is a warning for you to act now before it is too late. You will only get the time if you put in the effort to sort out the situation now.

REPTILE EGG

Fear of a future event. Eggs in dreams often represent pregnancy, and to dream of reptile eggs is a dream that suggests that you may have an unwanted pregnancy. It is therefore a warning that if you are not expecting a child to take sensible precautions. For expectant mothers, reptile eggs represent fear and foreboding about the future birth and a trip to the doctor is advised for reassurance.

RESTAURANT

According to your means. If you dream of eating at a restaurant of the type you would normally frequent then this indicates a social event will take place soon. If the restaurant is more expensive than you thought then this would indicate that you need to be careful of wasting money. If the restaurant is a café or fast-food place then it indicates that you will have some money coming to you soon.

RESURRECTION

Preparation. Dreaming of the Resurrection suggests that, although you are confused with events around you at the moment, you will find that they are soon sorted out.

REVENGE

Acceptance. If you dream that you have taken revenge against someone in your dream then it means that you cannot accept your current situation and are unable to go forward. If someone is seeking revenge against you then it indicates that you may have let someone down and so it may be time to make amends.
➡ *Killing*

RHEUMATISM

Freedom from restriction. If you dream that you have rheumatism or arthritis it means that you want to break free of restrictions that are delaying you at the moment. Don't worry, though, as the restrictions are temporary. In all, this is a positive dream that allows you to overcome stubborn obstacles.
➡ *Bones*

ABOVE: Lechers are punished by devils, the dreamer's inner demons.
LEFT: Piero della Francesca's Baptism of Christ, *symbolizing spirituality.*
FAR LEFT: Dreaming of a Pope indicates strength of purpose.

RHINOCEROS

An aphrodisiac. Rhinoceros' horns have always been thought to be a potent aphrodisiac and in dreams indicate your powers in sexual matters. However, if you see one chasing you, it means that you are scared of another person's sexual advances.

RHUBARB

Arguments at work. To dream of eating rhubarb indicates that you are going to fall out with someone at work over something they should have said or done. If you cook rhubarb in your dream it suggests that it might be advantageous if you just ignored their comments and continued to work in your efficient way.

RIBBON

Ribbons relate to relationships. If you dream of new ribbons then it means that there is a new partner on the way. It is worth noting the colour of the ribbon as this will indicate what the basis of the relationship is. Red ribbons signify passionate love, while green ribbons signify jealousy. Yellow ribbons show an emergence of independent thinking. Blue indicates a soul-to-soul kinship forming and black is a sign to let go of the old ways and habits that may have usurped your energy in the past.

➡ *Colours*

RICE

Family gain. If you dream of rice it indicates that there will soon be new additions to the family. Dreaming of rice indicates fertility and children, and that there will be a family celebration for a new arrival soon.

RIDDLES

Confusion. If you dream of riddles or undertaking crosswords it means that your are confused at the moment. This dream also indicates that confusing and mixed messages from other people, either in the work place or at home, are making it hard for you to decide where you are going in your life.

➡ *Quiz*

another person it represents a period of instability and set-backs brought about by irritating arrangements that have been cast upon you unexpectedly from someone in need.

➠ *Doctors, Health*

SCHOLARSHIP

Escape from the present. If you dream of winning a scholarship you are looking for a way to escape the difficulties surrounding a current situation. This dream warns you not to take things easy and make that escape, but instead to persevere: there is still a lesson or two to be learnt from the environment in which you find yourself.

➠ *Certificate, Graduation, Mortarboard*

SCHOOL

Looking to the past. Dreaming you are at school – particularly if it is one of the schools you attended – suggests that you are not letting go of the past. This is causing a problem as you are unable to move on fully

until you lay the past to rest. Exiting the school or looking at it from the outside denotes that a windfall of some kind is coming your way.

SCIENCE

Be more practical. This type of dream can be misleading as it can imply that you need to use and develop your mind and intellectual skills. In fact, dreaming of attending a science class, or undertaking scientific work, means that you should focus on skills using the hands more, such as art.

BELOW LEFT: A school scene from a thirteenth-century Latin manuscript.
BOTTOM: Seeing the sea in your dream refers to your emotional state.
FAR LEFT: An angel uses scales to weigh good and bad souls.

SCISSORS

Prompt action required. Scissors in a dream are a warning that you must do something fast, normally in the next few days. There are often associations with a relationship and scissors will break a relationship apart. This is normally due to a rival in love, and so to avoid the problem, you have the chance of rectifying the situation quickly.

SCRIPT

Seeking new opportunities. If you dream of seeing a script, this is an opportunity to study your life in some detail. Perhaps you feel a change of script, or a new direction, is needed. If there is something you do not like about your life, this script gives you the opportunities to change that.

➠ *Reading*

SCULPTURE SEE STATUE

SEA

Emotional issues. The sea represents emotional issues: the rougher the weather and the choppier the sea, the more problems you face. If you are able to sail through the sea in the course of your dream, then your problems will ease. Crossing the sea also indicates that your opportunities for company will increase through cross-cultural experiences.

are likely to take six months to resolve. To dream of winter when it is not winter indicates that financial issues will be resolved by then. Autumn brings new friendships, spring new relationships and the summer brings news.

SEAT

Be careful. If you dream that you are falling off a seat this is an indication that not only will you let yourself down, but another person as well. To fall from a high chair implies a fall from grace. To fall off a chair in a public place means that you are neglecting the opinions of others, which will cause you to lose credibility.

SECURITY GUARD

Look after yourself. Although a security guard normally looks after someone's property or money, in a dream it means to look after yourself. Usually this is with regard to health and emotions rather than property or finance.

➠ *Money*

SEDUCTION

Flattery. If you dream of being seduced then this should be taken as a warning that you are about to be led into something that will not be good for you in the long term. You need to check the work you are doing and whether it is the right thing for you or whether you are doing it to boost your ego.

SEED

Plans for future success. If you dream of planting seeds in the ground it indicates that new projects started now will be successful and profitable. To dream of

SEAL

Seals represent balancing acts. Just as the seal balances a ball at the zoo, our mind uses the symbol of the seal to represent issues that we are trying to weigh up. If the seal is having trouble in your dream, it could be that you are trying to take on too much at this moment in time.

SEARCH

Focus. To know and be fully aware of the purpose of the search means that you are in need of details from the object, person or information that is featured in the dream. To search aimlessly is your subconscious mind telling you to stop drifting and wasting your time in directions that bear no fruit.

SEASONS

Time frames. Seasons in a dream can represent time frames and may indicate when something is going to happen. So, if it is autumn and you dream of spring, it suggests that the issues about which you dreamt eating seeds could mean that now is the time of thinking about starting a family or having additional children.

➠ *Gardener, Grain*

BELOW: Serenading someone in your dream means that romance is blooming.
BELOW LEFT: Dreaming of winter suggests that issues may be resolved by then.
LEFT: An adult female Antarctic fur seal asleep on a log.

SERENADE

Romance. To dream of being serenaded – or if you are serenading someone – shows that a romance has started and will blossom, providing, of course, that the person does not throw a bucket of water over you.

SERMON

Warning. To hear a sermon either in a church or as a lecture indicates that there are going to be delays to plans you have been making. If you are delivering a sermon it means that you would like others to delay their activities until they have been properly thought through.

➠ *Priest*

SERPENT SEE SNAKE

SERVANT

Contentment. Dreaming that you are a servant yourself hints that you may be asked to help someone else, and you will gladly undertake that role. To dream of having servants of your own means that you need to watch your bank balance at the moment and curb expenditure on luxuries that you cannot afford.

SEWING

Preparation. If you dream someone is sewing then this dream is telling you to prepare for the future, particularly in regard to long term issues, such as pensions and investments. Leaving sewing unfinished is a sign that that you have not sorted things out properly. Mending things with thread shows that you are going to sort things out soon, particularly if you are near completion. However, if you dream of darning, then the chances are you have left it too late and you are going to have to work really hard to sort out your future retirement.

SEX

Fantasy. Dreams of a sexual nature are very common and act as an emotional release and as a reassurance of your sexual identity and prowess. Sex with a stranger is a common fantasy and could represent a whim for sexual experience or experimentation. Alternatively, it indicates an identity crisis, where your personality is searching to consummate indiscriminately in order to understand itself better through absorbing the qualities of the person represented in the dream. Sex with your boss indicates a wish to be dominated, but also means that you admire your boss and therefore would like to possess the same leadership qualities. Sex with your partner in a dream acts as a reassurance of your love – strengthening and cementing the bond, especially if there have been bouts of low performance within your relationship.

➠ *Genitals*

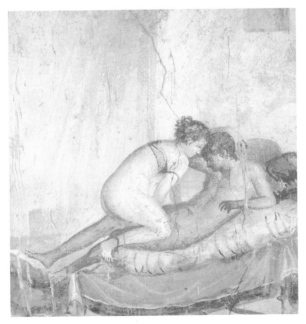

SHARPENER

Sharpen up your approach. Sharpeners in dreams are a warning to smarten up your attitude. If the point of your pencil keeps breaking, and you need to keep sharpening it, it suggests that you need to be more lucid in your explanations.

➠ *Pencil*

SHAWL

Difficulties. If you dream of wearing a shawl over your head it indicates that you have emotional difficulties at home that need to be resolved. If the shawl is over your shoulders then it indicates that financial worries need to be resolved.

SHEARS

To act miserly. If the shears are broken you will not only behave in a misery fashion, but you will also lose friends over a financial matter.

➠ *Gardener, Tailor*

SHEEP

A peaceful night's sleep. We count sheep to go to sleep, and, therefore, sheep in a dream indicate a pleasant situation. To shear sheep means a successful and profitable enterprise will show rewards soon. To hold a fleece indicates a triumphant and successful conclusion to a personal ambition. A flock of sheep means that celebrations – involving crowds of people – will gather around you soon.

SHELVES

Knowledge. To dream of shelves, particularly if they have objects and books on them indicates that you will be shortly taking up a new interest or study in a new subject. There is a wish to absorb new knowledge and the type of shelves, old, wood or new will determine the type of knowledge you will learn.

SHERIFF

Quarrels. If you dream of meeting with the sheriff then it indicates that there have been disputes affecting home and work that need to be resolved. By talking over the situation you will be able to resolve the problems that you face.

SHIP

Business prospects. Ships or journeys by ship represent business opportunities and prospects. How rough the seas are will indicate how much work will be required for success. Calm seas herald easy success and rough seas difficulties ahead, requiring a great deal of tenacity and stamina. The greater the number of ships seen the greater the success.

SHIRT

New options. A clean shirt is a good omen indicating new opportunities, while a dirty shirt implies loss of a new opportunity. To lose your shirt in a dream is an indication that business is not going well and you need to take stock of the situation.

SHOES

Opportunities. Shoes that are well-polished indicate that there is going to be an opportunity at work. This is particularly true if you dream that you are buying them, as it represents the possibility of an interview. If the shoes are neat but well-used it shows that you should be wealthy in life. If you lose your shoes it would indicate that you are wasting your efforts on something that is not going to work out.
➠ *Heels*

BELOW: An attractive selection of 1350s shoes, which represent opportunities.
LEFT: An ivory panel of shepherds and their sheep, from a twelfth-century portable altar. Dreaming of sheep will guarantee a good night's sleep.
BELOW LEFT: An erotic fresco from the House of the Centenary, Pompeii.

SHOOTING

Disputes. Shooting someone in your dream indicates that you have a dispute with them. There is a need to curb your temper and to sit down and discuss the problems if you want to resolve them. If you do not resolve the problems the situation could get worse. To be shot by someone else indicates that you will suffer at the hands of evil people and may suffer some illness.
➠ *Gun, Killing*

SHOP

Be careful with finances. To dream that you are about to go on a shopping spree indicates that money is tight and you could be heading for financial difficulties. However, to dream that you are working in a shop indicates that a financial bonus may be coming your way.

SHOULDER *SEE* ARM

your dream will tell you whether or not you can reveal yourself to those around you in the business world. To see shrouded corpses indicates a sequence of material and emotional losses.

➡ *Corpse, Veil*

SICKNESS

Dilemmas. If you dream that you are sick then it indicates that you are finding it difficult to make decisions at the moment and you are facing a bit of a quandary. If you dream that you are just beginning to fall sick then the dilemma has only just started, but if you dream you are recovering then you will have sorted the problems out.

SIGHING

Light at the end of the tunnel. To dream of sighing means that, although you have problems at the moment, they will soon be out of the way. The louder the sigh the more transformation there will be in your life.

SIGNPOST

Direction. Seeing a signpost in your dream is important as it often shows something of significance, and of which you should take note. Signposts appear when a new path is needed for fulfilment, and point the way to a new opportunity or to a different route in life.

SHOVEL *SEE* SPADE

SHROUD

A period of distress and anxiety. The problems you are worrying about can be resolved if you take control and prevent others from running your business for you. Depending on whether the shroud was lifted in

SILK

Luxury. Although this dream is one that shows a forthcoming time of luxury, it also warns that you must not rest on your laurels; otherwise things could easily go wrong for you. To dream that you or your partner are dressed in silk means that you feel happy when you are close to that person. If your dream is about old silk then you may receive a present from an elderly relative.

SILKWORM

Fortunate chances. Providing that the silkworms are alive in your dream then dreaming of them brings fortunate opportunities in business and finance. If the silk worms are dead, however, then it indicates a downturn in business, and if you have stocks or shares in the clothing industry then there could be bad news concerning those investments.

SILVER

Do not overvalue money. Although finding silver in your dream is generally a good sign for moderate financial improvements, there is also a warning that you could be depending too much on money. You are also warned against making rash and hasty decisions; you should also be putting spiritual ideas before financial matters.

SINGING

To sing by yourself is to want personal recognition. This dream indicates that you feel that you are not being appreciated by those around you. To sing in a group indicates that you are likely to be feeling very fragile after a party in a few days.

SISTER

Emotional support. If you are a woman and you dream of your sister it could mean you are heading for an argument. However, if a man dreams of his sister it means that she is there to help you with an emotional problem.
➡ *Brother*

SKY

An indication of your state of mind. If the sky is clear then it indicates you are content or even happy with your current situation. If the sky clears and brightens up in the course of your dream it suggests that any problems you have will soon disappear. If the sky darkens then this can indicate a worsening of the situation.

ABOVE: An eighteenth-century Japanese kimono made from silk and gold thread. If you dream of silk, this indicates that a time of luxury is on it way.
ABOVE LEFT: The Turin Shroud, believed by many to be the burial garment of Jesus Christ. Due to their associations with death, shrouds can be a frightening image in a dream, but the problems that they indicate are not insoluble.

SLIPPERS

Domestic issues. If you are wearing a pair of slippers that seem comfortable it indicates that you are very content at the moment. However, if someone other than your partner is looking at your slippers in your dream then it indicates an affair.

SMOKING

Attitude. If you dream that you are smoking a cigarette and you are a smoker then you may just be picturing yourself in a normal situation. However, if your body is giving off smoke then your mind is telling you to pack in the habit before it is too late. If you are a non-smoker this dream signifies that you want people's attitudes towards you to change, as you feel you are taken for granted.

➡ *Breathing*

SNAIL

Take your time. We talk about going at 'a snail's pace', and if you have dreams involving snails, then it is time to take things slowly. Snails are considered to be beneficial in dreams, as they often represent love affairs that will develop at a gentle pace. To eat snails in a dream means that you are going to have a long and peaceful domestic life ahead.

SLEEPING

Exhaustion. To dream that you are sleeping is an indication that you have been burning the candles at both ends. Psychologists think that dreaming of sleep is a wish to escape from reality, but one must also watch out for impending illness. If you dream of being asleep it is a craving to be able to totally relax and indicates that family and personal problems have been heavy: your mind is effectively trying to work double time and put you into a deeper sleep. The dream will be modified by what you sleep on in your dream and naturally who with, and this may give further insight into your fears and hopes.

SLEIGH

Love affairs. A dream sleigh ride represents an exciting new relationship and brings new happiness and a feeling of love and affection. If the journey is down a steep hill, it will be a rapid heady romance, whilst if it is a gentle rolling hill it signifies a gentle gradual relationship that will surely blossom.

SNAKE

Knowledge and temptation. Snakes have a very important meaning in dreams. In Ancient Egypt the snake was a symbol of rebirth (because it sheds its skin). A snake opened knowledge to man in the Garden of Eden; therefore, the snake also means knowledge. It also indicates the cycle of life, which is why a snake is used as a symbol in medicine.

A snake appearing with a staff (Caduceus) indicates that you are about to help someone else out.

The snake is a strong phallic or sexual symbol and in a dream can represent the dreamer's libido, showing the repression of one's sexual feelings. This is particularly true if you dream that you have a snake coiled around you. To dream of being chased by a snake may mean that you are scared of the sexual advances of someone else. To be bitten by a snake indicates that you fear a sexual liaison. However, if someone else rescues you from the snake then there is a longing for a relationship with that person.

If you dream of your children playing with snakes then it can indicate a fear that they are growing up and can mean that you are trying to be over protective of them, depending on their age.

If you dream of handling snakes then it means that you are conquering your fears. The type of snake you see will also be an indication of the type of fear you have. Generally the more dangerous or bigger the snake is, the bigger the problem appears to you. A cobra, for instance, indicates that a situation is fast approaching and that you will have to manouevre quickly to resolve it.

If the cobra was dancing to the music of a snake charmer, it indicates that your character is being criticized by malicious gossip of a sexual nature by those around you.

A grass snake, which is non-poisonous, represents a smaller fear but much depends on whether it is pursuing you or not.

An overriding fear of snakes in both sleep and waking life may indicate a hangover from a past life. Therefore, dreams of snakes bring with them a lot of emotional symbolism.

To see many snakes wriggling over each other represents many emotional issues intermingling and over-lapping. It can also indicate a feeling of not handling relationships properly.

To dream of a gorgon, such as Medusa, with her head of snakes indicates that you feel that you cannot commit to a relationship, and, just as the gaze of Medusa was said to turn men to stone, the gaze is turning your heart to stone in this relationship. To dream of walking over a pit of snakes, yet escaping without being hurt or killing the snakes, indicates that you will overcome any problems.

If you find that in your dream a snake approaches you and you chase it away, only for it to reappear in a later dream, it indicates that there is someone who is trying to pursue you. It suggests that possibly someone does not seem to want to take no for an answer.

ABOVE: La Charmeuse de Serpents by Rousseau. Snakes represent many things if seen in a dream, ranging from the dreamer's libido to a fear of commitment.
LEFT: If you see a snail in your dream, you are being advised to take your time.
ABOVE LEFT: To dream that you are sleeping means you are overdoing it.

play a part in advancing your career. If you are engaged in a snowball fight, this is a warning not get involved in disputes at the moment, as there is no need and you will only lose the argument.

SOFA

Friendship. If you dream of sitting on a sofa or even just looking at one then this is an indication that you need to have a heart-to-heart with a friend. It appears that you may be taking one or two people for granted.

SOLDIER

Reputation. For a woman to see soldiers (particularly in huge numbers) implies wanton romantic self-indulgence, which is likely to lead to her being thought of by others as a woman of ill-repute. For a man to dream that he is a good, noble soldier means that he will honour his principles and will reap the fulfilment of his ideals.

SNOW

A positive omen. If you are walking through the snow in your dream it is an indication of contentment in a relationship and bodes well for the future. If the snow is heavy you will be rewarded greatly for the efforts that you have put in. If the snow is light then it is a good time to look at business investments.

If the snow falls in winter – when expected – it means that you will succeed after perhaps some minor difficulties. If it falls in the summer – when least expected – you will find that your business plans flourish and that you have no difficulty hitting your targets.

If you are clearing snow off your drive or elsewhere, this suggests that others are about to

SOLE

Sudden changes. If you dream that you break the sole of a shoe then a long-term friendship will suddenly break up. Dreaming of repairing your own soles means financial difficulties could ensue. It can also be a fear that you will end up by yourself.

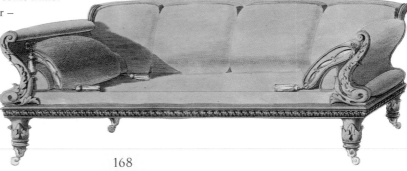

SON

Pride. If you are a father and you dream of your son then it augurs well for any business dealings. For a mother to dream of a son indicates that she is very proud of him; however, if you hear him calling then he is asking for your help and may be in some despair.

SORCERER

Change. If your dream contains a sorcerer it indicates that changes are going to take place for you and that you need to be ready to adapt. Ambitions must be looked at again and you will need to see who can help you and enlist their support.

SOUP

Good effort after bad. To hear the slurping of soup in a dream portends new and exciting liaisons through party invites. To drink cold soup suggests that a love life issue is leading to the realization that a companion is not going to listen to your needs – cut your losses and let the relationship go. To dream of drinking hot soup means that you will have to fight on with a project of worth, if your are to come out the other end with a successful resolution.

SPACE

Isolation. To dream that you are in space suggests a need for isolation. You should be warned, however, not to cut yourself off from others too much. Dreaming of space simply indicates a time of your life when you could do with some time to reflect on your own.

SPADE

Work hard. If you see a spade in your dream it means that you are about to embark on a lot of hard work. You will need strength and perseverance for the task and to be willing to take up the challenge. If you do you will get the rewards that you deserve.

SPARROW

Fleeting assistance. To dream of sparrows indicates that there are people around you who cannot be relied upon for help: you will have to do all the hard work yourself. If you are about to start a new job then don't rely too much on help from others.
➥ *Jealousy*

SPIDER

The web of life. It is thought that the spider's web represents the web of life, and the spider is something that weaves the life of people. Therefore, spiders are generally thought of as lucky. A climbing spider means success, and a spider spinning a web means it could be spinning some money for you. The one exception is if you dream of a tarantula or a black widow spider: this means that a medical check-up is in order, particularly if it bit you.

SPINNING

Perseverance. To dream that you are spinning wool indicates that you need to persevere, particularly at this time in your life. You are diligent and will get your rewards when the time comes. You will, however, have to take your time and be very patient.

SPIRITS

Warning. If in your dream you are drinking spirits and you keep to safe limits then it indicates a celebration. If you drink to excess, however, it indicates that you find yourself in an embarrassing situation and may let others down.

ABOVE: A relief of a woman spinning, from around 650 BC.
LEFT: Dreaming of a sofa serves to remind you of your friends.
ABOVE LEFT: Seeing snow in your dream can be a positive omen.

SPONGE

 Recognition. If you work with a sponge in your dream it is a recognition of all the work that you have put in. It may not be much of a reward but you feel glad for the support that others have given you.

SPOOL

 Adjustment of pace. Spools in a dream depend on the state of the spool: if it is full then, although it is going to be hectic for you over the next few months, it will be an enjoyable time. If you have just started winding on to a spool then it indicates that you need to re-adjust the way you are doing things, as you are being over-cautious and need to speed up your work rate.

SQUIRREL

Squirrels indicate saving for tomorrow. Just as a squirrel gathers a harvest of nuts to store for the winter months, this dream is warning you to prepare for what could be a lean time: a warning to save money rather than spend. If you are female, this dream can indicate that a shy person is seeking your attention.

STAGECOACH

Sexual indiscretions. To dream of being on a stagecoach indicates a romantic involvement which may not be appreciated by others. There is a need for caution as you may obtain the object of your desire but at a high cost.

STAIRS

Obstacles. If you climb up stairs you are achieving minor gains in work and finance; if you are going downstairs then it indicates that things are not going well. The fact that the stairs lead upwards to a sleeping area indicates emotional security in a committed relationship.

To descend into a basement implies a search for your roots to your identity.
➠ **Building, Magic and the Occult**

STAMMERING

 Worry. If you start to stammer in your dream it indicates that you are worried about the situations around you but are not sure how to change them. To see others stammer means that other people are worrying you unnecessarily.

STARS

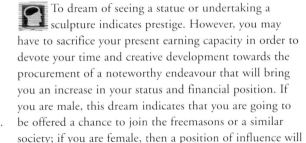 Success. Stars in a dream bring success; if you see just one star, this indicates that success will come in the form of the companionship and influence of a prospective partner. A multitude of stars in your dream indicates success through the help of others, and also means that you will be admired by others. For those with aspirations of stardom, this dream could also herald a burst of activity that might end with the realization of your goals; prepare to work to your full potential.
➠ **Sun**

STATUE

To dream of seeing a statue or undertaking a sculpture indicates prestige. However, you may have to sacrifice your present earning capacity in order to devote your time and creative development towards the procurement of a noteworthy endeavour that will bring you an increase in your status and financial position. If you are male, this dream indicates that you are going to be offered a chance to join the freemasons or a similar society; if you are female, then a position of influence will be offered to you.

STEEPLE OR SPIRE

 Challenges and achievements. If you see a steeple in your dream it indicates that you are striving for success and recognition from other people. It also suggests that you are about to gain the love of a particular person. If the steeple is in ruins, or bent, it could mean that there are some relationship issues that need to be sorted out to establish a secure footing for the future.

STEPS

Obstacles. If you climb up steps you are achieving minor gains in work and finance; if you are going down steps then it indicates that things are not going too well and that you will need to pick yourself up and climb back up the steps to succeed.

STILLBORN CHILD

Distress. To dream of a stillborn child if you are not pregnant indicates that you will receive some distressing news. If you are pregnant, this is just an anxiety dream and most probably everything is well; however, if you are worried about your pregnancy you should consult your GP for advice.
➠ *Bereavement*

STING SEE BITE

ABOVE: Things are apparently not going too well for these Burne-Jones ladies.
ABOVE LEFT: A Burmese spire, which represents challenges and achievements.
ABOVE FAR LEFT: Dante Alighieri and Beatrice survey the stars in Paradise.

ASTVPL

STOCKINGS

Changes. Putting on stockings generally means an upturn in business, whereas taking them off means that there will be changes in work for you. Getting ladders in your stockings means that you may find yourself in some short-term financial difficulty, but there will be a way out.

STOCK MARKET

Win and you lose. Many dreams have the opposite effect and if the stock market plays a part in your dream this is the case. If you dream that you win on the stock market you will lose. If you lose you are more likely to win. If you are not actually trading shares then this could be a warning to sit still.

STOMACH

Trust. If you dream that you have a pain in this region at night then as long as there is no physical cause this dream means that your health and strength will improve. However, if you dream of being bare-chested this indicates unfaithfulness.

STORM

Obstacles to overcome. To dream of a storm indicates that you may have some problem facing you but that you will be able to battle through and come out the other side. The intensity of the storm will dictate the level of difficulty you will face in the course of these problems, but the positive side of such dreams is that they show that the problems are surmountable.

➠ *Lightning, Thunder*

STRAWBERRY

Happy in love. If you dream that you are eating strawberries it indicates that you are content with the relationship you are in; this is a particularly good omen for a relationship that has just started, suggesting a strong long-term future.

SUBMARINE

Deep emotional disputes. A submarine in your dream indicates that you are struggling with your emotions and that you need to resolve some relationship difficulties. If the submarine in your dream is following a

SUFFOCATION

Time for a check-up. If you dream of suffocation it may indicate that you are having breathing difficulties in your sleep. You may simply be ill at the moment with a cold; however, this dream indicates that you need to check your health.

SUGAR

Happiness in moderation. Sugar brings sweetness to a dream and indicates a happy life, although you are shown to still want more. If you eat sugar in your dreams then you will have to attend to some unpleasant duties for a short while but all will end up well.

SUICIDE

A need for relaxation. To dream of suicide means that you could be overstressed at the moment and need to relax. It is perhaps a time to find someone that you can share your feelings with. Should this dream occur it may well be worth having a chat with a doctor or a therapist.

steady direction you will find it easier to resolve your relationship problems. The deeper the submarine dives the more entrenched is the unspoken problem. So fathom the emotional depths of your history together with your partner and clarify the seeds of discontent.

➠ *Sea, Water*

SUBWAY

Emotional depth. To dream that you are taking a subway or underground train on a journey is an indication of a painful emotional duty that must be executed. It is not something you can avoid, for it has a convoluted history and the quicker you confront and deal with it the better.

➠ *Labyrinth, Maze, Metamorphoses*

SUMMONS

Act now. If you receive a summons in your dream it means that you have left something undone. Often this dream means that you have forgotten to pay your bills and is a warning to make sure that your paperwork is up to date.

ABOVE: A dream involving strawberries indicates that you are happy in love.
ABOVE LEFT: A sailing ship tossed about in a storm at sea is protected by the Madonna and Child as a man prays from the shore.

SUN

Success. The Sun in a dream represents success. If you see the Sun rising in a dream it means you are at the beginning of a period of success. A sunset indicates success looming after a long stretch of hard work and effort. If the Sun is high in the midday sky, then your lofty ambitions will succeed.

➡ *Stars*

SURGERY

Change in lifestyle. If you dream you are having surgery, or even performing surgery on someone else, then it indicates unexpected changes of lifestyle for you. The areas of the body will have significance that will enlighten you on the meaning of the dream. You can look up the name of the body part in this book to further understand your dream.

SURROGATE

You will help out others. To dream that you are holding a surrogate baby indicates that you will soon be supporting others concerning a problem that they are facing with their children.

SWAN

A message of purity. To dream of swans symbolizes the purity of the vision and can indicate a celebration of marriage or engagement. However, be careful if the swan is singing for it foretells an accident.

SWEEPING

Sweeping out the past. If you dream that you are sweeping then it indicates that you are sweeping some aspects of your life into the past. This is a good omen for the future as you are able to leave behind in the past those bits that have caused unhappiness.

SWEETS

If you dream about giving or eating sweets then this indicates a happy time. The only exception to this is if you dream of eating sticky toffee, which hints that you need to be careful not to repeat gossip, otherwise you could find yourself falling out with some friends.

SWIMMING

Inner emotions. Swimming represents getting in touch with your deep subconscious. The surroundings in your dream will be of importance; for instance, to swim at sea indicates greater luck than swimming in a pool. To swim nude denotes success in your current endeavours, whereas swimming with clothes on means that you are not letting others get emotionally close to you.
➠ *Water*

SWORD

Protection. The sword is a symbol of strength and protection. You will be able to cut your way successfully through problems that you face at the moment if you have dreamt of the sword. However, if the sword is broken in your dream it means that you are trying to hide from current problems.

SYNAGOGUE

Social status. If you climb to the top of the synagogue in your dream then it means that you will be able to achieve status in the eyes of others. If you are inside the synagogue, however, this suggests you are experiencing difficulties with other people that need to be resolved.

SYRINGE

Bad luck. To give an injection in a dream or to receive one indicates that there is some bad luck coming your way.
➠ *Hospital*

TABLE

Hard work and effort rewarded. To dream of a table indicates that you are about to undertake hard work and effort but that it will be worth it in the end when you are rewarded for your diligence.

TAILOR

Travel. To dream of seeing a tailor brings unexpected travel arrangements. If you talk to a tailor in your dream there will be arguments in the future. If you saw a tailor measuring you up in your dream, much care and diplomacy is needed if you want to avoid giving your strength away to someone else.

TALISMAN

Good luck. Talismans are symbols of protection or good luck and the exact meaning will depend on the type of material used in its making. Generally, however, seeing a talisman in your dream indicates a need to make some decisions, but it also suggests that you will have help, support and luck in doing so.

TAMBOURINE

A rumour. Tambourines bring rumours to dreams and you have to make sure that they are acted upon. If you were playing the tambourine yourself it portends that you are the instigator of the gossip and rumours, and thereby can nip it in the bud before any real damage to another's credibility occurs. Hearing others play, however, means that your will become the target of slanderous and malicious gossip and rumours.

LEFT: The swan, a symbol of purity, is depicted here on a stained glass.
FAR LEFT: Medieval surgeons sterilize their instruments in a fire.
ABOVE LEFT: If you see the Sun in your dream, it represents success.

TANNERY

Loss of trade. To dream of working at a tannery means that there is a downturn in business and that you will have to undertake work that you would rather not. To trade with a tannery in your dream means that you will be unpopular with others.

TAPE

Remedy. Using tape on clothes means that there are areas of your life that need to be adjusted. This dream is giving you the opportunity to make those changes. Tape indicates that what you are doing at the moment is not very profitable, and even worse, is not stimulating your mind in any way. This dream is, therefore, urging you to change your circumstances.

TAPE MEASURE

Start making plans. To dream of a tape measure means that you have need to revisit plans that you may previously have made. It could also mean that you have underestimated costs on something you are about to purchase or that family members are in need of new clothes.

➡ *Tailor*

TAPESTRY

Domestic issues. If tapestry appears in your dream it can indicate that you feel uncomfortable with your domestic situation at the moment and that you feel you are destined for better things. If you are single it brings a solution to a domestic problem in the guise of a new partner.

TASSELS

Hassles. Dreaming of tassels will bring hard work but as long as you fight through the problems you will win in the end. It will not necessarily be a pleasant experience but you can persevere to the end with effort.

TASTE

Our attitude to events taking place. How you taste in dreams is an indication of how you feel things are going in your waking life. If something is sweet then it indicates your happiness, if sour then it suggests that you need to re-think things. If it is bitter then it means that you are holding a grudge about a situation.

TAXI

Sudden news. A speeding automobile means that you can expect sudden news. If this vehicle is a taxi then it indicates that other people are helping you along your path. To run out of fuel en route implies misplaced confidences that will lead to an embarrassing situation for you. Otherwise, take note of the part of the vehicle that you dreamed of, for it may be warning you about a problem requiring the attention of a mechanic.

➡ *Road*

TEA

Popularity. If you dream of drinking tea then it indicates that you will do well socially over the next few weeks. However, to dream simply of the teapot brewing, with no drinking, indicates that you will be apologetic over a liaison that has caused upset to someone else.

TEACHER

Learn and teach. The presence of a teacher in your dream is an indication that you need to pull your socks up and do better. If you are the one doing the teaching then you have some knowledge that you wish to pass on to others.

➡ *Lecture*

TEACUP

Social pleasures. Dreaming of teacups indicates a happy party, afternoon tea or morning coffee that you will be invited to, and which will result in a new friendship.

TEASING

Gatherings. If you dream of teasing someone then it indicates that there will be a social party soon that will bring enjoyment. If someone is teasing you in your dream then it indicates that there will be improvement in your life.

TEETH

Teeth in dreams are very common and are a very important indication of your emotional state. Teeth that are white and pristine indicate that things are going well. Stained or tarnished teeth suggest difficulties building up through negligence. Teeth falling out indicate a phase of growth into new spheres of activities and social circles.

Obviously, as people get older they tend to dream about retirement. Loss of teeth, in a dream such as this, means that the person does not feel ready to be put out to pasture by their work colleagues just yet. This indicates some underlying problems in the work area.

Clenched teeth in a dream are a sign of anger, and whether they are your teeth or another person's, will determine the source of the anger: is it from you or towards you? Dreams about teeth can also be a way of your subconscious telling you it is time to visit the dentist.

If you dream that your teeth are in an unhealthy state and going black then it indicates that you feel unhappy with your relationship at the moment. The blacker the teeth, then the worse the situation is likely to be. If your teeth are suddenly longer than they should be this indicates a forthcoming legal issue.

If you dream that your teeth are knocked out by someone else then this indicates financial problems brought about by that person.

If someone has prominent or buck teeth then it indicates travel opportunities are nearby. For a child of course, dreaming that they are going to lose a milk tooth is an indication of the wish to grow up. Going to the dentist is actually good news in a dream as it represents sorting things out. Having teeth removed means that major transformations and upheavals in your life are about to take place.

A set of false teeth signifies unexpected help from another person. Having fillings points to help from another source, and gold teeth or crowns indicate financial help of some sort. Having root filling work on your teeth indicates that you should dig deep into your resources and be more careful with financial speculations in the future.

Having bridge work done to your teeth indicates that you have to pay more attention to your plans rather then hoping for the best.

BELOW: Prominent teeth in a dream can indicate travel opportunities.
BELOW LEFT: A Chinese porcelain teacup, indicating social pleasures.
BELOW FAR LEFT: Two Parisian ladies take afternoon tea.

In dreams it is also thought by some that teeth represent our family and best friends. The front teeth indicate children, brothers, sisters and other close relatives. The upper teeth represent males and the female family members are represented by the lower teeth. The eye or canine top teeth represent the father and the lower canines the mother. Therefore, damage to the particular tooth could represent damage to the associated relative.

There is another school of thought, however, that suggests female teeth are on the left side and male teeth on the right, and that the whole mouth represents the house. Loss of teeth could also affect your finances, as each tooth lost represents a family debt which will be gained.

To dream of having animal teeth, such as a wolf or bat means that you may need to take on the strength of that animal. Therefore, in your dream it will show you an area of your personality that should be focused on in order to succeed.

Finally, brushing your teeth in a dream indicates that you will have obstacles to overcome. If the brush gets stuck in your dreams, or you have to use a toothpick, this indicates an obstacle which still needs to be resolved. Picking your teeth for no other reasons means that your friends will let you down.

➡ *Dentist, Vampire*

TELEVISION

Don't just watch, take action! This dream is telling you to take a chance on your dreams and hopes. Too much of the time you are acting as a spectator and are not taking control of the situation: it is time to make your own judgements and activate your ambitions.

TEMPTATION

Do not give up. Your strength of purpose is required at the moment, particularly as others may be trying to slow you down. This is a dream about perseverance and if you resisted falling for temptation then you will succeed in a worthwhile objective.

TENANCY OR RENT

Mortgages. To dream that you are only a tenant or paying rent implies that you wish to move on and buy a place of your own. This dream can be taken as a sign that you are about to make a move and finances look good for long-term investments.

TENT

Financial issues. If you are in a tent then it indicates that you will soon see an improvement in your finances, just as long as the tent does not collapse – which indicates the loss of investments and money through careless speculation. Erecting a tent or sleeping in one implies that you will soon be purchasing a new home.

TERROR

Success. Being terrified in dreams is about learning to cope with the situation. As you overcome the situation you will not be frightened any more: a successful outcome is assured. To see others terrified means that their terror will worry you and that you will help them by contributing towards bringing about a resolution.

THATCH

Gossip. Dreaming of a thatched house means that there is gossip around you. If the thatch is breaking down or the wind and rain make it through the roof an affair is implied. This is a warning to sort out a relationship before it breaks down irretrievably.

ABOVE: A thatched house in your dream can indicate gossip.
LEFT: If in your dream you are as terrified as this man from Edgar Allen Poe's The Pit and the Pendulum, *you are heading for success in real life.*
FAR LEFT: Van der Goes' Fall of Man; *a dream involving temptation urges you to persevere in pursuit of your goals.*

THEATRE

To see yourself acting is a wish fulfilment dream, unless of course you are an actor, in which case this could simply be your internal way of rehearsing and acting out the scenes before the performance. On a negative note this dream can mean that you are trying to achieve status by upholding false pretensions. So, stop acting and face your truth before you get yourself in too deep.

➨ *Ballet, Comedy, Drama*

THERMOS

Preservation. If you dream of a thermos flask it indicates that there is a friend who needs to be contacted before you lose their companionship altogether. You do not want a minor disagreement to spoil a long-term friendship.

THIMBLE

Marriage. Regardless of your gender, dreaming of a thimble brings domestic contentment and a happy married life. If the thimble collection grows in your dream, so shall the contentment in your life. To lose a thimble, however, indicates marital strife.

THIRST

Obstacles. If you are not actually thirsty, this dream can suggest that you have an obstacle to face in dealing with others. If you are able to quench your thirst you will be able to overcome the obstacle, and enjoy success beyond your expectations.

THORN

Obstacles. You will need to be careful if you dream of thorns as these represent underhanded traits from other people which will pose great obstacles in the path of your ambitions. These people might hold you back but if you persevere and not succumb to their allure you will be able to find a way to continue untarnished by their unruliness.

➨ *Brambles*

THREAD

Gossip. Finding loose thread on your or someone else's clothing indicates that you will be involved in idle gossip over the next few days. Long pieces of thread indicate that you are not taking the best path with regard to your work: a re-structure of your long-term goals and aspirations would help.

THRONE

Change of position. To sit on a throne indicates that your situation and place in society may be about to change. If you are not in a position of authority you will soon see a rise in status, and will be placed in a position of trust. However, if you already hold such a position you may find yourself the victim of a cabinet shuffle and thrown out of your exalted position.

➨ *Royalty*

THUNDER

Obstacles to overcome. If you hear thunder in your dreams then it means you need to face up to certain problems. If the thunder is of the low rumbling type then it indicates that friends have let you down. If it is loud and noisy then it indicates that the problems you face are temporary and will not be with you for much longer.

➨ *Storm*

TICKET

News. Dreaming of tickets is an indication of news: the tickets will indicate what is expected and if it is travel then it indicates that your travel plans may be delayed, but news of the re-arrangement will come soon.

TIE

Restriction. If you dream of ties, you are feeling restricted by your job or your personal circumstances at the moment. If the tie was loosened in your dream it means that the restrictions will ease and you will feel that you are able to regain control of your life.

TIGER

A struggle, but you win. The tiger has a strong mind and is powerful; it is able to take advantage of the opportunities that surround it. Effectively you need

to be like the tiger in your dreams and then you will succeed. If you are able to subdue or kill the tiger then you will succeed. However, if the tiger is attacking you, then you will be the loser.

➠ *Hide, Hunting, Killing*

TIGER'S EYE

Work with groups. Tiger's or cat's eye gems in a dream indicate that this is a time when you should be working with others. You need to demonstrate an ability to work as part of a team and share the responsibilities. By behaving as part of the group mechanism and its intrinsic thought processes you will enjoy both camaraderie and success in your quest.

TIME

Time for action. If you dream about time in a very obvious or significant way – looking at a watch, for example – then this is your subconscious telling you to get on with things straightaway rather than putting them off. The dream is telling you to stop simply waiting for things to happen and activate your plans now.

ABOVE: Time, represented here by a late fourteenth-century astronomical clock, urges you to act sooner rather than later.
TOP: Tigers in dreams represent the power of the dreamer.
LEFT: A thirsty man sits with his beer in a pub in Birmingham.

TOAD

Toads indicate success. Toads have a similar meaning to frogs in dreams. In a dream it might be difficult to tell the two apart: if it is a toad that you see in your dream then you can expect success and luck in the future; this is good news financially. The toad could represent a trusted friend.

➤ *Frog*

TOILET

Flush away the past. Seeing a toilet in your dreams can occasionally be the mind's way of giving you a wake-up call to answer the call of nature. If this is not the case then this dream indicates that you have problems concerning your finances, i.e. you are literally flushing money down the toilet. If you see someone else using the toilet then you may be asked for a loan.

➤ *Excrement*

TOMATO

Fertility and love. Tomatoes in a dream represent love and fertility. In a dream this could be informing you that a relationship is about to start. For a woman in particular it means that you could be thinking of having children and you are in a very fertile period of your life.

TOOLS

Perseverance. Dreaming of gardening tools is a clue to the sort of skills that you need in order to ensure success in your projects. A hoe means that you have to tread carefully and adapt to other people's needs. A rake indicates that you will need to evaluate something you did in the past to go forward. A spade suggests that you will need to really push and commit yourself to your ideas and a scythe means that to go forward you have got to leave the past behind.

TOPAZ

Personal power. Topaz in a dream brings with it the opportunities of leadership. This dream indicates that you need to take responsibility, not just for yourself but also others, by delegating and getting the others to help you. Losing topaz in a dream means that you are being autocratic in your dealings.

TORTOISE

The tortoise is slow but sure. Just like the fable about 'the hare and the tortoise' a tortoise in a dream will indicate a slow but steady progress towards a chosen goal. Your dream may indicate that you have to slow down and avoid rushing a project, or you will lose it. There is a need to let things work at their own pace.

➤ *Turtle*

TORTURE

Disappointment. To experience torture in your dream indicates that you will be let down by a friend. If, however, you are torturing someone else then this means that you are being unhelpful in a situation with someone close to you: the relationship will break down unless you mend your ways.

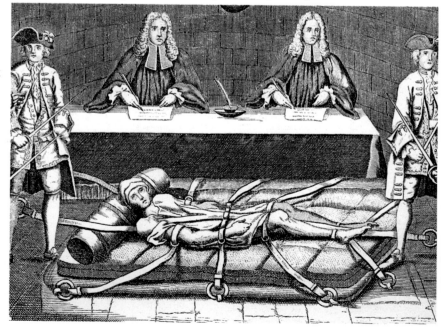

TOURIST

Relaxation. To dream of being a tourist simply reflects a wish to be one, and probably suggests that now is as good a time as any for making holiday arrangements.

TOWER

Destruction and rebuilding. If you have a dream of a tower then you are about to face a fairly difficult time. The signs are that you will find your life turns around and what was once important to you seems quite insignificant. Your priorities will change over the course of the coming months.

TOWN

Commerce and opportunities. Dreaming of a new town could indicate a search for new work opportunities. If it is a town close to your own place

BELOW: Building the Tower of Babel – an indication of changing priorities.
BOTTOM: Picasso's Girls With Toy Boat; toys symbolize a revisited childhood.
BOTTOM LEFT: This man certainly seems disappointed at his torture.

of residence then it indicates that you have got to get yourself out and about to take advantage of the commercial opportunities that are awaiting you on your own doorstep.

➠ *City*

TOYS

Reliving your childhood. If you are older in years, then this dream indicates a desire to regain your younger years. If you are single, and would like to have children, then the toys are a way of recapturing those innocent carefree days.

TRADE

Negotiations. To dream of trading indicates that you need to embark on some careful negotiation. The outcome in the dream can predict the outcome in real life, so if all goes well in the dream, you can expect a similar outome in your negotiations.

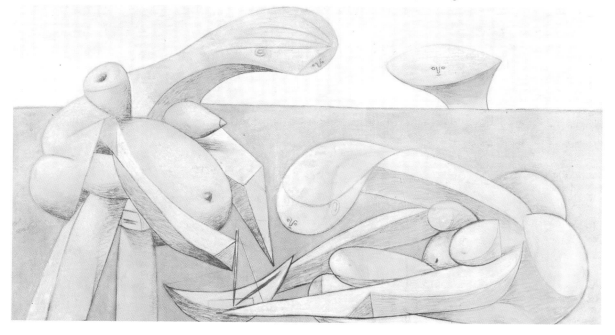

TRAGEDY

 Sorrow. It is possible that your dream of a tragedy may be a premonition of a distressing event to unfold. The tragedy is likely to affect others and not yourself, and therefore, this dream is a warning that you may have to help others with their sorrow.

➠ *Celebration*

TRAIN

Progress in your career. If you dream of railways or travelling on trains then your career is moving swiftly on. It bodes well for support from others as well. The only concern is that if you dream that you are at a railway station and miss the train, then it is an indication that you are going to miss the opportunity unless you make a move for it now.

TRAM *SEE* BUS

TRAPPED

A warning. If you dream about trapping an animal then it means success in business and work endeavours. However, if you dream of being trapped or trapping another person it relates to relationships that are fruitless to pursue. If you dream about feeling claustrophobic then it is important that you look to other people around you. For instance, if you feel claustro-phobic in your dream and you have a partner then it indicates that perhaps you feel that you need a little time apart from each other.

➠ *Breathing*

TRAVELLING

To travel in your dream is to achieve your results. If you dream of travelling you are on your way to reaching your goals. Take note of the journey and the type of conditions, as these will give clues as to how fast and easy it will be for you to attain your desires.

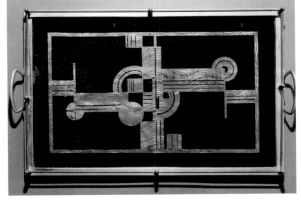

TRAY

Good luck. Dreaming of carrying a tray means that you will come into some good fortune shortly, ushered in by your quick-wittedness and charisma, but do not drop the tray as that indicates social embarrassment through a bad talk or presentation of significance that highlights the wrong points.

TREASURE

Profitable work. To dream of finding treasure means that the effort you have been putting into work recently will result in success. This may not simply be about money, but can also be success in anything you are putting effort into at the moment.

➡ *Gold*

TREE

Lucky in love but not in work. To dream of planting and growing trees is an indication of a new love in your life and relationships will go well. However, to dream of climbing trees indicates that finances will be severely tested as the amount of effort you are putting into work at this moment does not seem to give a particularly good return.

➡ *Nut*

TRIPE

Danger from others. To dream of tripe indicates that you are going to be let down badly by others around you. You have to trust your own instincts and not rely on anyone else at the moment, otherwise you may end up getting hurt.

TRUMPET

Surprise. Playing or hearing a trumpet means that you are about to get an unexpected but welcome surprise, which usually reflects a significant and long awaited achievement. Trumpet fanfares indicate a personal achievement that will make your heart glow with joy. Well done, you owe this success to your own uniqueness.

TUNNEL

Deep feelings. Tunnels in dreams can represent the subconscious. If you make a journey by tunnel then it means that you have to face some difficult emotional situation needing to be crossed and resolved before you can go on. Relationships need to be evaluated; if you can see a light at the end of the tunnel then you can solve the relationship issues.

ABOVE: An elegant woman in a large hat walks through a park among trees, which can be a symbol of good fortune in love.
LEFT: Viking coins and jewellery from 830–850 AD, found at Birka, Sweden. Dreaming of finding this hoard would mean that your hard work will pay off.
ABOVE LEFT: An American 1930s tray made from wood, metal and coloured foil – a symbol of good luck if seen in a dream.

TURKEY

A good harvest. The meaning of turkeys in dreams has changed over the years. Whereas it was once thought of as an ill omen, now, with its association with Christmas and Thanksgiving, it indicates a good harvest in a dream, representing the fruition of projects.

➡ *Christmas*

TURNIP

Rewards gained. If you have dreamt of turnips then it indicates that you have worked hard and will reap the rewards for the efforts you have put in lately. If you dream of planting turnip seeds then you could come into some property soon.

TURQUOISE

Be alert. To see turquoise is a warning that you need to be on your guard and to pay close attention to what is going on around you. As long as you remain alert then you will be able to take advantage of the situation. If you do not then someone will take advantage of you.

TURTLE

The turtle is slow but sure. Much that can be said about the tortoise is also true for the turtle, and both signify success if time is taken to achieve the results. The only difference between the tortoise and the turtle is that the turtle represents emotional projects with an aquatic link and may also suggest an event abroad, involving the nurturing of a young enterprise.

➡ *Tortoise, Water*

TWINS

Double meanings. Dreaming of twins means that we have to be aware of the negative and positive aspects of the dream. If the twins are happy then your work will be doubly rewarded. If they are shown as unhealthy then you are in for double the trouble.

➡ *Adoption*

TYPIST

Progress. As long as the typewriter or computer that you are working on in your dream is working then you are able to make progress in your life. A jammed or broken typewriter suggests there are obstacles in your way. To dream that the keyboard on the computer keeps jamming and you have to re-boot the computer indicates that something you have started is not finished and you will not be able to move on until that is complete.

➡ *Learning, Machinery, Trade*

UGLINESS

Look into the heart. If you dream of seeing an ugly person it means that help will come from an unexpected source. If you dream that you are ugly it means that you are trying to project a false image and someone will see through you.

➡ *Beauty*

UMBRELLA

Something to fall back on. If you dream of an umbrella it means that you are protected from the problems with which you are faced at that time. If the umbrella blows inside out then you will still get through the problems, but only when you have dealt with some minor difficulties.

UNCLE

Arguments and support. These may seem contradictory interpretations, but often the nature of your relationship with your uncle will change what the dream means. To dream that your uncle is dead means that you have strong hostile opposition. To dream of arguing with an uncle indicates an unpleasant bout of illness that will befall a family member.

UNDERGROUND

Subconscious. Being underground in your dream can represent deep emotional issues that seem to be coming to the surface. You need to resolve them before you can go on. It is a time for opening your heart and unveiling your true feelings towards the other person.

UNDRESSING

Secrets to hide. Avoid sharing secrets with new friends if you dream of someone of the opposite sex undressing, as they may take advantage of the knowledge they have of you, whereas someone of the same sex undressing will share a secret with you. If you see yourself undressing it indicates that you would benefit by withdrawing from a relationship you are in. If the undressing is done in a provocative or erotic way in your dream then it indicates a wish for sexual adventure.

UNICORN

True romantic prospects. The appearance of a unicorn in a dream is a good omen, symbolizing new prospects for true romance entering your life. A unicorn is often dreamt of at the start of a very significant and long-term relationship and indicates your happiness with the situation.

BELOW: Dreaming of a unicorn means that romance is just around the corner.
BELOW LEFT: An umbrella in a dream symbolizes protection.
TOP LEFT: The typewriter in your dream must work for progress to be made.

UNIFORM

Status. A man dreaming of a uniform can indicate a rise in status. For females this type of dream traditionally meant that a new relationship opportunity would arise; however, nowadays it also represents a promotional opportunity. Dreaming of a member of the opposite sex in a uniform could be a secret fantasy wish.

UNIVERSITY

Learning. If you dream that you are at university it is often a reflection of a waking fear that you did not make the most of educational opportunities offered in the past. It can be taken as a signal to return to your studies in some way. For those involved in higher education, this dream heralds a time that requires focus and attention to detail. You need to correlate these details with other aspects of the dream to assess what you need to do in order to succeed.

➡ *Certificate, Graduation, Lecture, Mortarboard*

UNKNOWN PLACES

Isolation. To dream that you are in an unknown area or a place that is unfamiliar to you indicates that you are feeling alone and isolated. This is a time to reflect on the moves you need to make to change this situation, and to realize that there are people out there who are willing to help you out of this isolation.

URINE

Release from tension. Dreaming of urinating is quite often a signal that you need to visit the toilet. It is also, however, a sign that any tension that has been aggravating you is now released. This dream is telling you to concentrate on the future and not the past.

➡ *Relief, Bladder*

VALENTINE

Romantic problems. If you dream of receiving a valentine it suggests that you are experiencing problems in your relationship. If you are sending a card in your dream it indicates that you are not taking advantage of the opportunities that surround you.

VALLEY

Emotional conflict. Although a dream such as this reflects some difficulties with emotional issues, it also shows that the foundation to the relationship is strong and stable. You may need to work hard and a couple may be advised to seek some help in reconciling their differences.

VAMPIRE

Conflict with others. If you dream of meeting a vampire it is a warning that there could be an individual who is becoming an emotional drain on you. The person who resembles the vampire may give you a clue as to who this might be. To dream that you are a vampire indicates a wish to have control of others and can also be read as a warning that you may be abusing a position of trust.

➡ *Bat*

VARNISH

Work brings success. If you are doing the varnishing then the dream indicates that you are putting effort in and will be rewarded. However, if you are getting someone else to varnish then you will lose opportunities to that person.

VASE

Emotional issues. A vase in a dream represents tedious emotional issues that need to be dealt with. This dream indicates that the problems may have been put aside but not forgotten, lest they begin to fester and grow with the passage of time.

VATICAN

 Influential meetings. If you dream of being at the Vatican it suggests that you will meet someone who will be able to influence on your career progression. However, you will need to show them respect first as they can be quite demanding.

VEGETABLE

To dream that you are eating a variety of vegetables hints that, although you seem to have hit the jackpot with a project, the passage of time will reveal that you have actually been exploited for your talents. To grow a variety of vegetables in a dream signifies that your possessiveness in a relationship may lead to its demise.

VEIL

Secrets. If you dream of a veil then you are trying to keep something secret (and often in some clandestine way) that you are scared of others finding out about. If you see a wedding veil it brings new. A funeral veil indicates disappointment and sorrow. A torn veil, whether on you or someone else, is interesting because it means that you will find out about a secret that will help you understand yourself.

VELVET

Luxury. Velvet in dreams represents luxury; the exact area of your life that it may affect will depend on the colour. Purple, for instance, represents royalty or the church. Red represents matters of the heart, blue is for commerce, while green is for luck.

ABOVE: An early nineteenth-century engraving of a papal benediction at St Peters, Vatican. A dream of this nature represents influential meetings.
LEFT: A Roman pavement mosaic of a vase from the first century AD.
ABOVE LEFT: Munch's Vampire, *which in a dream would symbolize conflict.*

VERANDA

Long-term goals. Dreaming of a veranda indicates setting long-term objectives. Now is the time to look at pension issues or retirement locations. It is a time for thought on the things that will give you a long-range sense of security and comfort for yourself and for those around you.

VERTIGO

Exploitation. Vertigo in a dream indicates that you need to be careful about a relationship in which you are being sexually exploited. You need to take control of the situation before you get hurt.

VICTIM

Self-pity. If you feel that you are a victim in a dream then it may indicate that you need to think about other people's positions, not just your own. Family problems are highlighted and indicate that it is no use just ignoring the issues but that you need to sit down with all the parties involved and sort them out.

VICTORY

Decisions have been reached. Battles of any type in dreams represent decisions that we have to make about current issues. To win a battle signifies solving a problem, but make sure that you listen to the point of view of the person that you are fighting with or you will leave yourself open to attack through lack of information about the issues. Winning a battle in dreams means that you have overcome the problem, whilst losing a battle indicates that you may need help from friends who can help you with decisions.

VILLAGE

Stability. A village in a dream is a bit like an extended family: it shows that there is support from others around you for whatever problems that you feel that you are going through. Neighbours and friends will help you out in your hour of need.

VINE

Success. If the vines look healthy then it indicates that any business or other projects that you start now will bring more success than your wildest dreams. If the vines are withered and dying on the ground, then it means business will have problems and you should think about cutting your losses now.

VIOLENCE *SEE* FIGHT

VIOLET

New affection. If you dream of violets then there is someone nearby who has not shown an interest in you up to now, but whose affections begin to awaken.

You could find they start to make approaches to you over the course of the next few weeks.

VIOLIN

Harmony. If you hear a violin in your dreams it denotes a peaceful time. However, if the strings break or the sound is unbearable, then you have quarrels at hand to deal with.

➠ *Quartet*

VIRGINITY

New beginnings. If you are not a virgin and you dream of virginity then this can reflect a wish to start something over again. Virginity also represents new

BELOW: A dream involving Fra Angelico's virgin represents new beginnings.
LEFT: An eighteenth-century Swedish textile carpet showing a violin player.
FAR LEFT: Violets and butterflies from a fifteenth-century Flemish manuscript.

projects and so this dream can indicate that you are planning to start a new career just as much as a start of a new relationship.

VISION

Foresight. If you dream that you have a vision it could well be prophetic, indicating events to come. It is therefore important that you take a note of what you saw in the dream vision. If the dream is a revelation, it suggests something that will happen if you follow your current course of action. If the vision shows something you are not happy about then the dream is giving you an opportunity to view the scenario before it comes about and therefore you are in a commanding position to change direction if you wish to.

VOID

Isolation. To dream that you are in a void indicates that you feel alone and isolated. This is a time to reflect on the steps you need to take to rectify this situation and to realize that there are people who are willing to help and support you in endeavours and to help you on the path to a new direction.

➠ *Space*

191

VOLCANO

Dangerous situation. If your dream includes a volcano, this is a major warning of situations that could get out of control. If the volcano is extinct or inactive then it is a warning to delay decisions. A smoking volcano indicates a relationship that is underhand and needs to be looked at carefully. An erupting volcano indicates that disputes and arguments that will be difficult to resolve are about to erupt and may mean drastic changes are made to your life.

VOMIT

Money issues. If you dream of being sick in your dreams then this normally relates to financial issues. If you are financially secure this dream may mean that you will lose some money, where, if you are struggling financially you could find yourself a little better off.
➡ *Guts, Leeches*

VOUCHERS

Effort required. If you dream that you will win vouchers this indicates that you need to put more effort into something. If you are giving vouchers away then you have the backing of others. If you lose one, however, then there will be arguments over an inheritance with relatives.

VOYAGE

Emotional success. A rapid and significant increase in your stature or financial standing is heralded in a dream featuring a voyage. The type of voyage and the destination need to be correlated for a full interpretation. To see yourself going on a sea voyage suggests the love and affection of those around you, and the satisfaction you have in your personal relationship. Voyaging by air suggests a business increase.
➡ *Aeroplane, Foreign Lands, Ship, Travelling*

VULTURE

End of a cycle and regeneration. A vulture, particularly one which is circling, indicates the end of a phase of life. The meaning of a dream involving vultures implies enemies and competitors are waiting for

you to make a mistake so complete whatever you are currently involved in and correct any mistakes as you go along, and soon a new era and lifestyle will dawn.

WAIST

Tighten your belt. If you dream your waist is thinning then it can be an indication of financial problems. To be aware of someone else's waist in your dream means that they are about to ask you for support by asking you to carry some of their load and share the responsibility.

WAITER

 News from relatives. If you dream of a waiter or waitress then this indicates that you are about to receive some news where you will have to go and support a family member or close friend that is ill.

➠ *Restaurant*

WALKING

Paths to tread. If you are walking in a dream it indicates that you have a particular direction in which to go; the type of terrain and the ease with which you tread the path in your dream reflect the ease with which you will accomplish the results.

WALL

Structure of your domestic life. The walls on buildings in dreams indicate how you feel about the current situation. If the walls are fine then you are secure, but if they are crumbling your home life may be unsettled. If you are whitewashing the walls then it indicates that your efforts to repair the relationship are not getting to the root of the problem, only papering over the cracks.

WALNUT

Obstacle in love. Dreaming of a walnut indicates there is a communication issue in a relationship. If you are able to crack the walnut in your dream then it indicates that you will be able to resolve the problem. If you are unable to crack the walnut then your partner is likely to meet someone else.

WANDERING

Find a direction. If you have a dream in which you are wandering around, it means that you are confused and need help in deciding which direction to take. It is perhaps a time for reflection and sitting down and thinking about what you would like to do next rather then just accepting things as they happen.

WAR SEE BATTLE

WARDROBE

Bank balance. Your wardrobe represents your bank balance in a dream and therefore an empty wardrobe means financial woes, though a full one will mean financial contentment. Finding a door in the back of the wardrobe indicates a wish to escape from your current situation and spend some of your bank balance on exotic excursions.

WARRANT

Duty. If you dream of receiving a warrant then it indicates that you have to undertake a task that you may not want to do but needs to be done. The quicker you perform the task, the quicker you will be able to go on to something more rewarding for you.

ABOVE: Giacometti's Walking Man, *who in dreams symbolizes paths to tread.*
ABOVE LEFT: Walnuts represent romantic obstacles.
FAR LEFT: Seeing a vulture in your dreams indicates new beginnings.

WATER

 Emotional feelings. Water in your dreams is a representation of your emotions and also how you are reacting to relationships at the moment. The calmer the water, the less you will feel any emotional problems at the moment. Murky or rough water indicates that you have deep emotional issues to deal with.

Spilling water while you are carrying it indicates that you are taking a careless attitude with your partner and you also need to be able to curb your temper. If you feel that you are in hot water then this indicates financial and career issues that are affecting your relationship.

Dreaming of drinking water means that you wish to involve yourself in a relationship. However, drinking dirty water warns against contagions that could be contracted from a partner, leading you to seeking medical assistance soon.

A waterfall indicates that you will do well with others and could see new opportunities in relationships.
➠ *Sea*

WEAVING

Contentment if all goes well. If you are contentedly weaving in your dreams then life is going to go smoothly for you. However, if you get knots or tangles when weaving in your dream you will encounter problems that you will need to overcome.

WASP

Money disruptions. Wasps in a dream represent financial issues that need to be sorted out. For women in particular, it can often mean jealousy in other females who are envious of you, not just financially, but also socially. It is time to selectively remove ties that are retarding your progress.
➠ *Annoyance*

WEDDING CELEBRATION

Dreaming of an engagement often heralds news of a celebration, frequently weddings or babies. If you are single and you dream of a wedding then it indicates that your are about to be introduced to a prospective suitor.
➠ *Ring*

YACHTING SEE SAILING

YARN

Romance. To dream of making a ball out of yarn indicates new friendships and is often the precursor to a romance and eventual marriage. It is important to look at the colours of the wool or yarn as this may tell you a little more about the situation. Generally a red yarn indicates a passionate and sexy relationship, whereas a yellow one represents a shy person who will need to be wooed slowly. A blue yarn represents someone that is very philosophical, and a green one represents a business person.

YEW

Disappointment in relationships. To dream of a yew tree indicates that there could be disappointment in love. If you see your partner under a yew tree then it indicates that he/she is about to move out of your life.

ZEBRA

Take care and you will be rewarded. If you dream of the zebra then take care (just as you would at a zebra crossing when crossing the road); as long as you are cautious in your ventures they will be fruitful.

ZEPHYR

Conflicts between heart and head. If you dream of the warm zephyr then it indicates that you are not thinking straight and that you are taking too much of an

emotional attitude towards things. You need to sit back and analyze the situation properly. This dream also warns against lots of talk and no action. Prepare to back your words by thinking the situation through and then with a clear head engage in communications to resolve the bones of contention.

ZOMBIE

Out of control. If you dream of zombies or dream that you are a zombie yourself, it is an indication that your life is out of control. You need to be careful as

you could be suffering from exhaustion. You are doing too much for others and not enough for yourself.

ZOO

An enjoyable time. To visit the zoo in your dream is a pleasurable experience, which indicates that the mind is trying to recollect that feeling from the past. Often, dreams of zoos indicate a new relationship and mean that a meeting with a prospective suitor is on the cards. However, if you are trapped inside the zoo, the meaning is very different: it is time for you to break free if you are tied down in a relationship.

➡ *Cage*

ABOVE: Dreaming of zombies is a sign that you have lost control over your life.
LEFT: Botticelli's zephyr (top right) symbolizes inner conflicts.
FAR LEFT: Zebras in dreams warn you to be careful.

CASE STUDIES

A HELPFUL TELEPATHIC DREAM:
A CATTY AFFAIR

Kaaren is 30 years old and works as a receptionist in the city of London. The company deals with recruitment and human resources. Kaaren is married with two sons aged 5 and 7 years respectively, and she has been training as a psychotherapist for the last three years. Her close friend Sally works in the same company and confides in Kaaren completely.

The Conversation Preceding the Dream

The phone rang – It was Kaarens close friend Sally. She started to tell Kaaren that she suspected that her husband was having an affair. On hearing this, Kaaren replied that it felt like De ja Vu, that she recalled having experienced this very moment about two weeks ago in a dream, and began to tell Sally about it. Sally listened quietly at first and then angrily blurted out "I knew it... he's having an affair... I saw a woman outside my window about a month ago and then I saw him kissing that same woman just before he got on his train to go to work."

Kaaren's Dream

"In this dream I saw a sly cat hiding behind the curtains, which I perceived as being a threat and I felt afraid. I remembered how in the dream it had bedroom eyes and was looking at a wedding photograph of Sally and her husband John, although the photograph was in my house. The cat emerged from behind the curtains, kissed the photograph and viciously clawed it in half, and then I scared it away. Once I knew it had gone I felt the fear go away then I picked up the pieces of the photograph and stuck them together again."

Kaaren's dream seems to highlight Sally's situation. But can we surmise from this that there is a connection between Kaarens dream and Sally's real life predicament? Was the cat in the dream the other woman lurking outside, just behind the curtain?

How to Interpret the Dream

To make a full interpretation, it is important firstly to analyse the dream symbols in the light of Kaaren's experience of the dream, making sure that we include the general theme, the feelings that are aroused by the dream content and any features that stood out in the dream, such as where the action took place – in this case Kaaren's house. As I read through the dream description the following feelings came forward: jealousy, and fear, whilst in terms of the elements and the theme the main features seemed to be the cat and the photograph. In this instance, the cat does not represent a real life cat but is instead a metaphor what is lurking (hiding) behind the curtains.

If there is another woman, then she has appeared in the dream symbolically as a cat. The woman herself does not feature or show in the dream as a person. Biases have been removed by the dreaming sub-conscious leaving behind only the essential quality that is under review; that being a lurking, feminine, opposition that viciously clawed the photograph of Sally and her husband in half. The implication is that the rival would separate Sally from her husband and would secretly take him away, hence the hiding behind the curtains in Kaaren's dream.

Unravelling the Dream

As we begin to unravel the dream and break it down into its component parts we have a number of clues that we can use as guides.

Feelings: fear.
The Elements: cat, curtain, photograph (of Sally and her husband).
Theme: the theme is about hiding (the cat being behind the curtain), and clawing the photograph in half.

How to Use the Entries in This Book

There may well be other elements that have not been recalled but on the basis of the information available the following is a possible interpretation: Fear means that the dreamer will be able to conquer the problem. She is playing out the scenario in order to work out a resolution so that when the situation appears in real life she will be able to face it. The cat represents feminine treachery, in this case towards Sally, by way of clawing the photograph of Sally and John, and what that infers for their relationship. As the dreamed cat was hiding behind the curtain (which protects the inside world) it suggests that the personal and private world of the dreamer is under threat. In the dream it is the wedding photograph that is clawed as though to "claw" John away from Sally. When we look up the entry for photograph it tells us that because we are seeing a photo of a particular person it means that we are trying to make a psychic link with that person. This is exactly what Kaaren's conversation on the telephone in real life did. It produced a timely link that brought Kaaren's dream to the recipient's (Sally's) attention.

Correlation Between Dream and Reality

Kaaren's dream seems to have captured the sentiments of Sally's situation, (seeing a rival kissing her husband) through the metaphorical enactment of the other woman's (cats) activities. This, as a dream would strongly implicate a case for foul play. In some way Kaaren was already aware, through her peripheral vision and thoughts, that Sally's husband may have been involved with another woman, which until this conversation had no outlet but to produce a dream.

SELF AWARENESS AND CREATIVE POWER: SEX WITH THE BOSS, AND SNAKES

Dreamer's Profile

Alexis is an attractive 27 year old who always aspires to do her best. She is an outgoing, gregarious, single woman, though was inwardly shy with men. At work, she was a popular member throughout the department. Working alongside her senior manager Stacy, whom she admired a lot. The whole department had celebrated the completion of a major publication and there were organisational plans

to reshuffle and streamline the work force, and although apprehensive, Alexis remained focused on her goals. Her steady, determined attitude gave rise to Alexis experiencing the following revealing dream.

Alexis's Dream

"I'm at home relaxing and my boss Stacy is at the door. I'm really surprised and excited to see her. As I go to hug her, she kisses me, and though I feel shocked I don't pull away. Instead I kiss her back. Very quickly, we are both naked. I notice her breasts and she says to me that I can feed from them if I like and reassures me it's natural. I can hear a dog barking and I look away. Three snakes coil around us and tighten their grip forcing us to become physically close. The snakes then start to melt as though they were made of plastic. She gets dressed and walks to the door and then blows me a kiss saying 'I knew you had it in you. You're just like me.' A few moments after she'd gone, the dog appeared at the window wagging its tail and I felt really invigorated and powerful."

Unravelling the Dream

Start by looking at the main theme of intimacy and then start to look for the qualities that Stacy, the stand-in character, represents. In this case Stacy is the boss and so represents authority and power. By using Stacy as a recognisable symbol, similarities between Stacy (the stand-in character) and Alexis have been accepted by Alexis's Sub-conscious, in readiness for Alexis becoming the boss figure herself at a later date.

Alexis has used Stacy as a role model from whom she can absorb the qualities necessary to be a boss, hence the binding together by the coiling snakes – which represent sexuality and creative power. These act to reinforce Alexis's confidence both as an attractive woman, helping her to overcome her shyness with men and by recognising that she too has the powers and presence of Stacy, and that Alexis admires.

This dream awakens Alexis and makes her inwardly aware and confident

of her own qualities and potential, via the act of absorbing and emulating Stacey's character traits. The essence of the dream is that of a consumption of equals, hence the binding of the two women as one.

There is then a further indication of togetherness and camaraderie. The dog wagging its tail in joy at the window after Stacy has left seems to heighten and re-emphasise that there is a strong bond of loyalty between them in the outside world, which is represented by the window.

Once the core part of the dream is impressed on your conscious mind, the additional details allow you to unravel the minature pictures, or sub-plots within the dream, allowing you to fine-tune the meaning.

The Dream Details

Theme: Intimacy with the boss, nakedness.
Characters: boss, dog, snakes.
Feelings: relaxation, surprise, excitement, shock.
The Elements and Action: home environment, hugging, kissing, barking, window, breasts.
Special Details: message from Stacy 'I knew you had it in you You're just like me'.

Incorporating the Dream Details

Having established a sense of the overall objective of the dream (that being to make Alexis aware of her own power and charisma as a real candidate for a position in authority) we can start to look at the peripheral details and see what they are trying to tell us. The general theme is about the intimacy of the two women. Both become naked, aided by Stacey's encouragement. Alexis' initial response to Stacey's advances is surprise, then excitement, and finally shock. In the dream Alexis reciprocates Stacey's kisses. She feels at 'home' with Stacy being so close in her personal space. Stacy offers to nourish Alexis from her own breast showing Alexis that she will protect and feed her as if she were her own. After the consummation of equals qualities is completed (and indeed enforced by the libido representatives, the snakes) Stacy caps off her role in the dream by her statement "I knew you had it in you. You're just like me". And then right at the finish of the dream, (just as an added reinforcement of the bond of friendship and loyalty), we hear the joyous barking of a dog wagging its tail.

How to Use the Entries in This Book
Body: see naked and breasts.
Animals: See snakes and dog (remember to keep in mind that the dog was friendly, because it was barking and wagging its tail).
Feelings: see relaxation, suprise, excitment, shock.
Home: see also window and buildings
Kissing: see also relationships

Correlation Between Dream and Reality
Some time after this dream Alexis was assigned to a senior post in the reshuffle of the organisation, implying that her dream had confirmed her abilities and was worthy of the leadership role embodied by her boss Stacey.

REHEARSAL: EXAMINATION PREPARATION AND THE CLOWN

Dreamer's Profile
Ray is 30 years old and had been researching a pioneering therapy for his masters' degree based on the old traditions of Ayurvedic medicines. Ray was convinced that he had a unique, innovative, service he could offer. He had been trying to launch his service to the general market for three years but found that he just could not make his target audience understand his service and embrace it fully. An opportunity arose to work with a German Doctor who had an established health clinic in Hamburg. He had made initial enquiries and made a visit to Germany to investigate both the potential of working alongside the doctor and the expansion of his research into a viable business proposition.

Ray's Dream

"In this dream I am working very hard to revise my medical notes. But I just do not understand the exam questions and as I look around at my friends I notice that they also look troubled. In this dream we have a week to go before the real exams. So I go to the secretary and asked her to make an appointment for me to see the professor, but she informs me that he is not available. I begin to panic and got outside to try and figure out who I could talk to about these exam papers. The McDonalds clown approaches me and is singing and dancing I don't find it amusing, but the clown keeps going on and on. I get annoyed with him and tell him to get lost. He takes off the wig and wipes away the make-up. And says 'You'll find it in the strangest places. Look for the big picture first.' 'Who do you think you are... telling me what to do?' I say to him. He wipes away more of the make up and I feel embarrassed. It is the professor."

The Dream Details

Theme: exams, revision.
Characters: professor.
Feelings: panic, annoyance embarrassment.
The elements and action: a clown singing and dancing, wig, make-up.
Special Details: professor and the message 'You'll find it in the strangest places. Look for the big picture first.'

Unravelling the Dream

The theme of this dream is the revision for exams and the dreamer's pursuit of the professor. When a stand-in character such as the professor appears in a dream we must also bear in mind the relevance, significance or role that the person may have played in real life for the dreamer. This could make a connection from the personal experiences of the dreamer that only he would be able to relate to. The dreamer seemed to mistrust the secretary and the clown but readily accepted him as a role model, when the clown wiped away the make-up to reveal the professor.

Incorporating the Dream Details

The initial focus of the dream seems to be on the clown giving the advice but the dreamer refusing to take him seriously. The dreamer is in a panic and bothered by the clown's tomfoolery. For a while it seems that the dreamer will not relate to any lesser person than the professor. But the professor has shown himself to the dreamer as a clown. This leads us to believe that the professor is trying to draw the dreamer's attention to the more light-hearted elements of life, as well as perhaps making the dreamer aware that lessons can be learned from the not-so-serious as well as the serious. Before revealing his full identity the professor says 'You'll find it in the strangest places. Look for the big picture first.' The dreamer does not seem to take the clown seriously and retorts 'Who do you think you are, telling me what to do?' The dreamer will only tolerate the professor's advice and so the professor having made his point reveals his true identity, and the dreamer experiences embarrassment because it is the professor.

How to Use the Entries in This Book

Where an entry is not given, it is likely to be under a word that has a similar meaning e.g. panic is similar to anxiety, so we would look up the entry for anxiety. This also has a cross-reference to breathing, which may be a relevant detail in the dream, so we may need to look look this word up as well.

Exams: revision (*education*)
Professor: (*education*)
Panic: see anxiety annoyance (*feelings*)
Embarrassment: see humiliation(*Fears*)
Clown: see jester (*people*) singing and dancing (*leisure*)
Wig: see hair, make-up, beauty(*body*)

Correlation Between Dream and Reality

The service that Ray was trying to launch was innovative and required high levels of knowledge, which he evidently had acquired (M.A In Ayurvedic Medicines). Ray's problem was that he was too close to the minute details of the problem, and had failed to see the big picture. This was about identifying his target audience for marketing purposes, hence the appearance of the McDonald's clown – a globally recognised marketing icon – to give Ray an insight into the marketing strategies of large companies. The professor is a part of Ray's psyche reminding him that the exams were not academic but more in line with the mass consciousness. The dream indicated that he would succeed, once he rid himself of the annoyances. So the lesson for Ray was to learn to relax and start to view things from a bigger perspective. The clown appeared so that Ray would have the ability to see things with fresh innovative ideas.

A RECURRING THEME: ONION RINGS BIND A RELATIONSHIP

Dreamer's Profile
Pauline is 23 and has been married to Jack for six months. She gave up working as a secretary and took on the domestic chores. Jack was promoted in his job, which involved new training and longer hours at work, in order to adjust to the new working methods. Pauline became increasingly depressed and isolated, and repeatedly accused Jack of not spending time with her but he always told her that he loved her and that she was worrying unnecessarily.

Pauline's Dream
"I have had several dreams like this, and every time I lose my engagement ring. Only in this dream I'm in the kitchen cutting the onions and I notice that I have lost

both the engagement ring and my wedding ring. I start to cry and my husband says to me that onions have that effect on him too. As he says this I get annoyed with him because he doesn't notice my fear of losing him. So I grab the onions and throw them at him. He puts his hands out to defend himself and one of the rings hoops onto his wrist. He raises his hand and says 'what's this sweetheart?' 'I don't know' I reply. He then says 'It's a ring of confidence that binds us for ever.' He comes over and places my wedding ring back onto my finger and I recline into his comfortable embrace. He shows me the engagement ring and then and throws it out of the window, but I'm not bothered as I feel secure with my husband."

The Dream Details
Theme: security
Characters: husband
Feelings: annoyance, fear
The Elements and Action: crying, engagement and wedding rings, onion rings, wrist
Special Details: husband's message 'It's a ring of confidence that binds us for life'.

Unravelling the Dream
The theme is essentially about the insecurity following the demise of the honeymoon phase of the relationship, which gives way to the more mundane aspects of familiarity and domestic issues. The dreamer is annoyed and fears losing of her husband.

Incorporating the Dream Details
Looking at the details we see that Pauline is crying and feels annoyed that her husband does not seem to notice her fear. The entry crying tells us that it portends good news and that things will get better. Her annoyance should be interpreted as more symbolic than literal, and indicates that there will be speedy fulfilment of her desires. As she is annoyed with her husband she is likely to find that by the next day her annoyance will have gone and in fact bodes well for a pleasant day. Pauline's feelings appear in the dream as contrary omens, which later on in the dream give way to confirmations of unity between her and her husband.

As we assess the elements and action, we get a sense that the rings have served their purpose. The rings are not required because this relationship is united by the love that the couple have for one another. We see this in the husband's statement to Pauline when the onion ring loops around his wrist. 'It's a ring of confidence that binds us for life'.

How to Use the Entries in This Book
Husband: engagement and wedding rings (*family*)
Annoyance: fear (*feelings*) crying (*birth*)
Onion Rings: (*vegetables*), wrist (*body*)

Correlation Between Dream and Reality
Pauline has since acclimatised to her husband's schedule, and feels secure and happy. They have a son. And are thinking about having another child quite soon.

PROBLEM SOLVING: JOURNEY TO A NEW LIFE

Dreamer's Profile
Andrea is a young Australian nurse working in a large hospital. She is married to Matt, a street trader and had spoken to him constantly about starting a new life in Australia together. At the point of having the following dream, they had not made any plans to move, largely held back by the infirmity of Matt's mother. A diplomatic decision had to be made very soon as to whether to put her in a home, or take her with them if they decided to make a new life in Australia. All this angst gave rise to the symbolic resolution in Andrea's dream.

Andrea's Dream
"I got on a boat and was about to go down a canal. The water was very polluted and there were rats all around me. I didn't want to continue down the canal because it was narrow and there were rats coming out of the sewer pipes. I saw a footpath that led to a bridge, so I got out of the boat and headed for the bridge. An old lady was standing there and she said 'oh no lovey this bridge isn't for you. You have to fly over.' And then for no apparent reason she started to laugh at me. Within seconds I felt the bridge break under me and then catapult me into

the air like a springboard. I landed on the other side of the canal into a pile of of fish. I found myself in an open market. Every one was buying and bartering for goods. Most of the stalls were selling fresh meat or vegetable products.
I climbed off the fish and went over to a meat seller and asked him for a pound of beef. 'Certainly' he said and grinned sneakily. I thought he was trying to sell me old meat. 'What!' he said 'Do you want it or not? Others are waiting to be served you know.' I didn't know whether to trust him or not? And then out of a van he brought out another carcass. 'Freshly shot this morning' he said. 'Too many Kangaroos around. Its as good as any meat you'll ever taste.' I wasn't sure whether or not I should eat it though."

The Dream Details
Theme: travelling to the other side.
Characters: old lady, market trader.
Feelings: panic, mistrust.
The Elements and Action: rats, lots of fish, canal, footpath, boat, bridge, beef kangaroo, meat.
Special Details: the old lady's message 'oh no lovey this bridge isn't for you. You have to fly over.' And the market trader's messages 'Do you want it or not? Others are waiting to be served you know' and 'Freshly shot this morning .... Too many Kangaroos around. Its as good as any meat you'll ever taste.'

Unravelling the Dream
The theme is about travelling. Andrea's decision is coded as action in her dream, action which takes place on two sides of the canal. The journey is hindered by rats, which prevent the downstream route of travel, so the bridge seems to be the best option. Our dreamer is told the bridge is not for her by the old lady (the real life mother-in-law?) and she is catapulted across into a market where the atmosphere is very different. There is bustling trade, and they sell 'Kangaroo meat that's as good as any she'll taste', or at least this is the view of the market trader who is selling her the meat.

Incorporating the Dream Details

The travelling is highlighted by the crossing-over element in many different forms, indicating that her psyche is very much attuned to the move overseas. The kangaroo, is native to Australia, and in the dream shows itself to be fresh meat, as tasty as any other. Andrea's partner was the trader who was selling the Kangaroo meat, implying that he too has his vision focused on Australia. His statement 'it's as good as any' indicates that he would not miss his home country if they did emigrate to start a new life in Australia.

Throughout the dream there is mistrust. For example, Andrea is not sure whether or not to eat the meat. The old lady seems to be giving her blessing, even encouraging them, saying that the bridge is too slow and that Andrea needs to fly over.

Andrea lands in lots of fish, which symbolize prosperity and rewards. And finally the market trader asks Andrea 'Do you want it or not? Others are waiting to be served you know.' In the dream she has already crossed to the other side of the canal, and now she must make a decision... Could this be a reference to the future new life in Australia?

How to Use the Entries in This Book

Travelling: (*travel*)
Old lady: see age (*body*), market trader (*commerce*)
Panic: mistrust. (*Feelings*)
Rats: lots of fish, kangaroo, beef (*animals*)
Meat: (*food*) canal, footpath bridge (*travel*), boat (*transport*)

Correlation Between Dream and Reality

Andrea felt besieged by problems at work and in the dream this symbolically gave rise to the rats blocking her natural travel down the canal. But she decided there were more rats coming out of the pipes and that she would change route. This translated in her handing in her notice in real life, because no matter how hard she worked there were more and more problems coming at her 'out of the pipes'.

The mother in law was happy for them all to move away, and she resided in their home with a day care nurse attending to her needs. As for eating Kangaroo meat – I'm still waiting for a postcard saying that it tastes great!

STAND-INS FOR QUALITIES: ROYALTY

Dreamer's Profile

Jamie is a successful entrepreneur and was in the property business at the height of the Eighties boom. He is a shrewd strategist who employs many people on different projects simultaneously, and always makes sure that his workers are well looked after, even to the point of holding regular parties and barbecues for his friends, family and workers.

He has always treated everyone with open arms and equality. Handsome and debonair, he saw himself as a ladies man. Preceding this dream, he was puzzled by the rejection from a beautiful young woman at his gym club. It made no sense to him that she preferred the attention of an inexperienced younger man. He persisted in trying to win her over and that night Jamie experienced the following metaphorical dream.

Jamie's Dream

"I was searching for something in the dream but had to cross a lock in order to get it. I had no idea in the dream what it was that I was going to find. A beautiful, young lady was jogging by. She was followed by lots of

photographers, one of whom told me to move over, before thrusting a microphone towards the woman, and asking her 'Are you ready to be the Queen of England?'. she replied 'no comment' and continued to jog. She looked over at me and smiled. I couldn't believe it, this was a real Princess and she smiled at me. She called my name and then told the photographers that I was the true heir to the throne. Suddenly, they were all flashing their cameras at me. I was confused by all the attention. The woman turned to me and said, 'look after the people for me.' Then she glided away in angel form."

The Dream Details

Theme: searching.

Characters: princess, photographers.

Feelings: confusion.

The Elements and Action: flashing photographers, jogging, meeting a princess.

Special Details: photographer asking 'Are you ready to be the Queen of England?'
And the message 'look after the people for me.'

Unravelling the Dream

The theme is about searching Jamie's attracting prowess and his ability to gain the princess' trust, leading the princess to say, 'look after the people for me.'

Very quickly the attention of the photographers shifts from the Princess onto Jamie, who feels confused by it all. The key element is the Princess who represents a move away from the humdrum, to the pursuit of the ideal woman, that being the eternally young and flirtatious girl within the woman. The other face of the princess relates to the young attractive woman, whose femme fatale qualities could lead Jamie astray.

In the dream Jamie seems confused. This would indicate that he has sensed her allure and woken up to the possible dangers of pursuing such a temptation. She does

not intend to harm him but in fact acts as the courier of his salvation, indicating where he should focus his attention, and making him aware that he should not be taken in by the external attention of the photographers.

Incorporating the Dream Details

The action of the dream revolves around meeting a princess and also the intense attention of the photographers. When we look up the entry for photographer we see that it indicates unwitting deceptions and trouble brought upon the dreamer by himself. The Princess is acting as a reference point for those of Jamie's personality traits that are similar to the Princess: debonair attractive, charismatic and so on, and perhaps drawing Jamie's attention to his tendency to display snobbery in some way.

The photographers ask the princess 'Are you ready to be the Queen of England?' but instead of answering the question, she indicates that Jamie will take on the role and she makes the request 'look after the people for me.' Is she a stand-in for the beautiful lady at the gym? And is she trying to remind him that he has responsibility to his family and workers? I would say so, because he is, in effect, the figure-head of a small community.

How to Use the Entries in This Book

Searching: (*travel*)

Princess: (*people- royalty*),

Photographers: (*commerce*)

Cameras: (*leisure*)

Confusion: (*feelings*)

Correlation Between Dream and Reality

The flashing cameras were a clear sign of falseness and a clear warning of deceptions, especially since there were so many cameras. So Jamie may well have been spared through this dream from experiencing his own social demise.

In real life Jamie's approach and expectations towards the woman in the gym would have caused him problems. It was later discovered by Jamie that she had a habit of kiss and tell to the Newspapers, and often employed emotional blackmail tactics to extract monies from the victim. Had Jamie allowed his ego and sense of grandeur to get the better of him the consequences could have been dire.

NIGHTMARE: THE COLLAPSING HOUSE

Dreamer's Profile

Jenna was in a period of transition. She liked to take on challenges and had already accumulated many successes in her artistic field. For some time she felt that her work was growing, then because of financial hardship she started to produce textile print designs for swimwear and fashion. These were for the main design houses in Europe. She enjoyed and understood the design side of her work but felt shaky about the payment schedule from the agent because it was done on a sale or returns basis. She did ask the agent for an advance to help her with her rent arrears. But the agent refused, saying that she was very confident that her collection would sell and that she would enjoy the reputation that she would develop in the European Markets. Even so, Jenna still felt ill at ease and uncertain about her future. The result of her anxiety led to Jenna having the following dream.

Jenna's Dream

"The house is collapsing and I am very frightened. I feel that there is nowhere for me to go. The stairs are on fire, but somehow a unicorn appeared and I manage to get on its back. It said that I had earned the ultimate prize. I asked it 'what is the prize?' The unicorn replied 'your truth and now its time to use your truth. Prepare yourself.' The stairwell was on blazing and was falling apart. But the unicorn leapt effortlessly upwards, and gently landed in the attic. There was no roof. I also remember that the sky was very bright and clear and that I could feel a gentle breeze. I didn't realise it at the time but the unicorn had leapt away and seemed to run through the air. I was alone but somehow I felt it was alright even though I could see the rest of the house burning below me.

Then the scene changed and I was in a field picking blackberries but they were red and sour. The devil appeared and said that if you eat them you'll be free. So I ate them. They were bitter at first and them I got used to them. By the third one I quite like the tangy zest they sparked in me."

The Dream Details

Theme: house collapsing
Characters: unicorn, devil
Feelings: panic, frightened, alone
The Elements and Action: fire, stairs, breeze, attic, sky, eating blackberries
Special Details: The unicorn reveals the message that I had earned the ultimate prize I asked it 'what is the prize?' The unicorn replied 'your truth and now it's time to use your truth. Prepare yourself'. Also the detail that there was no roof and message given by the devil 'if you eat them you'll be free'.

Unravelling the Dream

This dream seems to be about two different issues: the house collapsing and the devil enticing her to eat unripe blackberries.

The main theme infers the collapse of the identity of the soul or psyche symbollically, through the collapse of the house. The house represents each room of the dreamer's and it would seem that every room has collapsed, except the attic where our dreamer finds both safety (with the assistance of the unicorn) and a place of solace as she awaits her ultimate prize...her truth, for which she must prepare. As she waits she is propelled into another scene where she eats unripe blackberries.

Incorporating the Dream Details

The house below is burning away, yet the dreamer feels alright about it, suggesting that it is under control. As a dream omen this tells us that her determination combined with her strength of purpose will see her through and that she will deal with the problems that are facing her.

The unicorn indicates that the prospect of true romance lies ahead. When we look up the entry Unicorn we are told that it signifies '...the start of a very significant and very long-term relationship, and indicates happiness with the situation.' As Jenna is developing a bond with her agent it would suggest a long-term friendship and relationship with her. Alternatively it could refer to a romantic connection that has long-term prospects in the near future that Jenna must consider very carefully.

Eating blackberries tells us that she senses her immediate future and that it is likely to cause her some illness, perhaps in the form of stress or bodily anxiety. But the devil says that, 'if you eat them you'll be free', suggesting that once the stress is alleviated the tensions will give way to a burst of freedom..

This is reinforced through the conversation with the Unicorn, in which the dreamer asks 'what is the prize?' The unicorn replied 'your truth and now its time to use your truth. Prepare yourself.' In the dream Jenna is contemplating the future as she gazes at a clear sky, implying the sky is the limit if she can prepare herself.

How to Use the Entries in This Book

House Attic: stairs (*home*) fire, collapsing see ruin (*destruction*)
Unicorn: (*magic*) devil (*worship*)
Panic: frightened alone. (*Feelings*),
Breeze: sky (*weather*) eating blackberries. (*Food*)
Fire: (*elements*)

Correlation Between Dream and Reality

Jenna did not fall ill at all, but she did experience much anxiety and stress during the lean period between doing the collections and getting paid for them.

Both Jenna and her agent have become close friends and socialise together. Her collections were introduced to the European market in 2001 and her designs were hotly tipped to enter the New York scene in the spring of 2002.

EMOTIONAL: WATER, DROWNING AND THE 'CROCODILE'

Dreamer's Profile

Lucielle was a 24 year old student who had recently graduated from university. She was a very sensitive Piscean who wanted people to support her. Her general outlook on life was positive and progressive, and her nature veered towards being highly conscientious and industrious. After graduating she had been trying to reach a decision as to whether to continue her studies further and send in her M.A proposals, or to do a teacher training course.

Her boyfriend Bradley was a good natured, easy-going, young man who had always encouraged and supported her in all her endeavours. Their relationship though, was under a lot of strain because of Lucielle's decisions. This was compounded by several outbreaks of violence in their neighbourhood, which raised the issue of moving from the area altogether. Consequently Lucielle had the following dream.

Lucielle's Dream

"I was standing by the riverside and I saw this crocodile on the other bank. It was motionless. A Tide came crashing towards me and caught me off guard. I was in the river swimming. But the undercurrents were so strong that I kept on going under. I felt scared knowing that the crocodile was on the other side. I couldn't see anyone around me and I thought 'that's it' and that I was either going to either drown or be savaged by the crocodile. Then the tide suddenly died away and the water was still. The crocodile was in the water and I started to panic. I could see Bradley in a balloon overhead and he shouted 'its raining, we'll be fine soon', and threw me a rope ladder. I grabbed it but was very weak and exhausted by this stage. As he pulled me up I lost my grip and fell back in. I was terrified because the crocodile was next to me in the water. I started to swim as hard as I could to get away but it just kept floating nearer and nearer to me. 'Kick it' Shouted Bradley. So I did. I felt so relieved when I realised that it wasn't a crocodile but a large piece of bark."

The Dream Details
Theme: swimming and crocodile.
Characters: the dreamer and Bradley.
Feelings: panic, scared.
The Elements and Action: crocodile, tide, balloon.
Special Details: Bradley's message 'its raining, we'll be fine soon' and 'kick it'.

Unravelling the Dream
The essential feature of this dream is what it is assumed to be a crocodile, and the general theme emphasises this as a twist, revealing the crocodile to be only a log. Bradley's message 'it's raining, we'll be fine soon' and 'kick it' indicate that Bradley can see more clearly than the dreamer, and is able to confidently advise her that it is OK to kick the crocodile, something that few people would even contemplate.

Incorporating the Dream Details
The elements and action involve the crocodile, tide, and balloon. For Lucielle, the feelings of being scared and in a panic seem to take over her rational side, and so from above comes the clear-thinking Bradley who provides the not-so-needed rescue, but a clear picture of the emotional problems surrounding Lucille and the dangers that the perceived crocodile had conjured up for her.

How to Use the Entries in This Book
Drowning (*fears*) See also water tide (*elements*), crocodile. (*animals*)
Panic see anxiety, scared see frightened. (*fears*)

Correlation Between Dream and Reality
As there was no crocodile in the dream, Lucielle was able to confront the potential dangers that the crocodile represented and which vanished when it was realised that the crocodile was actually a log – indicating that externally there is no threat at all.

FEAR: JUMPING OVER THE CLIFF

Dreamer's Profile

At the time that Twain had this dream he was 35 years old and had been working as a branch manager with a leading computer outlet for six months. He felt that he was making progress in his career and sensed that he would reach his goals soon.

Twain was an independent, self-motivated, high flyer, who always took risks. This particular week a discussion with the senior manager revealed that there was a vacancy for an Area Manager. Twain saw this as an opportunity for promotion and it was soon after this discussion that Twain had the following dream.

Twain's Dream

"I'm putting my best suit on and then I find a pair of gold cufflinks that I'd lost some years ago. I want to wear them but I don't feel ready to yet. I look in the mirror and I see a jester.

I'm not sure whether I am the jester or the man in the suit anymore. I go downstairs and open the garage doors and I'm mildly shocked to find that my car has gone but there in the corner is my old bicycle that I used to ride as a child. Realising that I'm late I ride the bicycle. The road is badly damaged and there are riots on every turning that I take, so I try to escape the danger by taking a short cut. I'm panicking that I will be late. As I get further down this narrow cobbled road I lose my bearings, so I stop to find out which way to go. I look ahead of me and I can see the ocean on the horizon. The sun is just beginning

to rise and I have the impression that it is the escape route. It feels like the right direction so I ride on ahead. Amidst the explosions I can hear Big Ben striking the hour. Now I know I'm late, so I stop to wipe the sweat from my brow. I reach into my pocket for a handkerchief only to draw out a jester's hat. Just as I wipe my brow with it the road below is becoming transparent and falling away. I feel as though I'm on the edge of a cliff. I can see a steep precipice below me and I feel very scared. Everything around is breaking and collapsing so I jump over the edge."

The Dream Details

Theme: being late and violence.
Characters: the dreamer as himself and as the jester.
Feelings: panic, mild shock, fear.
The Elements and Action: suit, mirror, gold. cufflinks, bicycle, riots ocean, sun, explosions, jester's hat, dreamer jumping over the cliff edge.
Special Details: the road below becoming transparent and falling away, and everything around breaking and collapsing

Incorporating the Dream Details

The basic theme is about both being late and violence. We see in this dream an unusual feature of the multifaceted self. The dreamer appears as himself and as the jester, which means that the dreamer is very aware of his inner nature.

The action forces the dreamer to slow down, by removing his car, and leaving him no choice but to travel on a slower form of transport that requires quite a lot of his own effort to move. His journey is bumpy and there are constant reminders of time.

All this culminates in the dreamer reaching the end of the road, which becomes transparent below. He is left at the end of this dream jumping over the edge because everything around him is breaking and collapsing.

How to Use the Entries in This Book
Violence: riots explosion.(*destruction*)
Jester: (*people*)
Road: (*travel*) bicycle (*transport*)
Panic: mild shock, scared, see frightened (*fears*)
Suit: gold cufflinks (*clothes*), ocean, see sea (*elements*), sun (*space,*) jesters hat

Correlation Between Dream and Reality

Although a difficult journey in the dream it heralded the end of a phase and a rapid promotion. Twain recognised his capabilities hence the jester, who is no fool. The sun inspired success in his endeavours whilst the symbol of the ocean provides an endless amount of emotional fulfilment.

TRANSFORMATION AND PREMONITION: YOUR OWN DEATH

Dreamer's Profile

Gupta is a 27year old, mature, overseas, student from India completing his industrial placement with an airline company. His field of study is engineering systems and this is his last month of training. He is a single man who looks after his family financially. His father (A reputable man with strong, traditional values) died when he was fifteen. Gupta's aim was to become an engineer and provide for his immediate family. On qualifying he intended to get married, before his mother's health declined too much.

Gupta's Dream

"I was reading the newspaper and a voice said that I must look up the dead. So I turned the pages until I found the obituary columns where I saw my name and the date 01/01/2000.

I look at the calendar in the dream and a year had elapsed; yet I still haven't died. My father approaches me and I feel anxious that he is about to die. He is very old and fragile in the dream like a wise monk. I try to warn him that he is about to die, but he doesn't hear or acknowledge me at all. The scene changes in the dream and I'm piloting an aeroplane but we have no fuel and my father says that we can use sugar cane instead and it will fly us back home."

Details of the Dream

Characters: Son, father, and wise monk.
Feelings: anxious
The Elements: aeroplane, fuel
Theme: Gupta's own death.
Other Details: date 01/01/2000, obituary (*newspaper*) Also the detail about realising that he is piloting an aeroplane '... but we have no fuel and my father says that we can use sugar cane instead and it will fly us back home.'